"Morris Eagle strikes us once again. Relentlessly, and brilliantly, he examines across these two books every aspect of the major psychoanalytic concepts. And differently from most authors, he does not remain at the theoretical level, but always relates theory to clinical evidence and empirical research, in the best academic tradition. These works will be a classic, an unavoidable reference for our field, and will be used by training programs worldwide."

– **Paolo Migone, MD**, *editor of the journal* Psicoterapia e Scienze Umane *(www.psicoterapiaescienzeumane.it)*

"These two works, both 'Classical' and 'Contemporary', should be in the library of every serious student of psychoanalysis and the psychoanalytic therapies. Applying his wide-ranging critical intelligence to decades of empirical research and cross-disciplinary scholarship, Morris Eagle evaluates seminal psychoanalytic ideas with verve and incisiveness. His comprehensive integration is easy to read, persuasive, and – rare in the professional literature – fascinating."

– **Nancy McWilliams, PhD, ABPP**, *Visiting Full Professor, Rutgers Graduate School of Applied & Professional Psychology*

"In order to prosper it is important for any complex theory in psychology to undergo evaluation of its core constructs to ascertain which aspects have received support, clarify areas in need of modification and also, if we are to be honest and fair, identify those elements that need to be jettisoned. In both 'Classical' and 'Contemporary', Eagle undertakes such an examination of psychoanalytic theory in a thoughtful, clear and incisive review of research evidence, clinical material and conceptual issues. Be forewarned, this is no rubber-stamp of or love letter to psychoanalytic theory. To the contrary, it is a balanced and often critical review of psychoanalytic constructs discussed in an experience-near descriptive manner, eschewing meta-psychological jargon, delivered with a good deal of wit and skillfulness that is typical of Eagle's previous work. Agree or disagree with his conclusions, any serious psychoanalytic scholar or student will benefit a great deal from the discussion contained in these volumes and be much better situated to help psychoanalytic theory evolve and thrive in the contemporary mental health landscape."

– **Mark J. Hilsenroth, PhD,** *Professor, Derner School of Psychology, Adelphi University*

"Morris Eagle's thoughtful, probing, and insightful writings have long stood out as examples of the finest thinking the psychoanalytic tradition has to offer. Bringing a remarkable clarity and rigor of thought to reexamining some of our most fundamental concepts and assumptions, Eagle offers fresh insights that both affirm and challenge analysts of all stripes. These two books, 'Classical' and 'Contemporary', the capstone of a long and brilliant career, are virtually a blueprint for how psychoanalysis can survive in the coming decades."

– **Paul L. Wachtel, PhD**, *CUNY Distinguished Professor, Doctoral Program in Clinical Psychology, City College of CUNY*

"The clarity and richness, the thoughtful analysis and overall assessment of where psychoanalysis stands in these two books by Morris Eagle makes them indispensable for all psychoanalysts and psychoanalytic therapists who are concerned for the future of our field."

– **Otto F. Kernberg**, *Professor of Psychiatry, Weill Medical College of Cornell University; Director of the Personality Disorders Institute of the New York Presbyterian Hospital (Westchester Division), Training Analyst at Columbia University Center for Psychoanalytic Training and Research of New York and Past-President of the International Psychoanalytic Association (IPA)*

"Eagle's integrative work just goes on improving! This is the best, most comprehensive and visionary work so far. He is the best commentator on theoretical and clinical psychoanalysis bar none. A highly recommended book."

– **Peter Fonagy**, *Professor of Contemporary Psychoanalysis and Developmental Science, University College London*

Core Concepts in Contemporary Psychoanalysis

In *Core Concepts in Contemporary Psychoanalysis*, alongside its companion piece *Core Concepts in Classical Psychoanalysis*, Morris N. Eagle asks: of the core concepts and formulations of psychoanalytic theory, which ones should be retained, which should be modified and in what ways, and which should be discarded?

The key concepts and issues explored in this book include:

- Are transference interpretations necessary for positive therapeutic outcome?
- Are the analyst's countertransference reactions a reliable guide to the patient's unconscious mental states?
- Is projective identification a coherent concept?
- Psychoanalytic styles of thinking and writing.

Unlike other previous discussions of such concepts, this book systematically evaluates them in the light of conceptual critique as well as recent research-based evidence and empirical data.

Written with Eagle's piercing clarity of voice, *Core Concepts in Contemporary Psychoanalysis* challenges previously unquestioned psychoanalytic assumptions and will appeal to psychoanalysts, psychoanalytic psychotherapists, and anyone interested in integrating core psychoanalytic concepts, research, and theory with other disciplines including psychiatry, psychology, and social work.

Morris N. Eagle, PhD, is Distinguished Educator-in-Residence at California Lutheran University, Professor Emeritus at the Derner Institute for Advanced Psychological Studies, Adelphi University, and is in part-time private practice. He is the author of *From Classical to Contemporary Psychoanalysis: A Critique and Integratio*n and many journal articles. He is former President of the Division of Psychoanalysis of the American Psychological Association and recipient of the Sigourney Award, 2009.

PSYCHOLOGICAL ISSUES BOOK SERIES

DAVID WOLITZKY
Series Editor

The basic mission of *Psychological Issues* is to contribute to the further development of psychoanalysis as a science, as a respected scholarly enterprise, as a theory of human behavior, and as a therapeutic method.

Over the past 50 years, the series has focused on fundamental aspects and foundations of psychoanalytic theory and clinical practice, as well as on work in related disciplines relevant to psychoanalysis. *Psychological Issues* does not aim to represent or promote a particular point of view. The contributions cover broad and integrative topics of vital interest to all psychoanalysts as well as to colleagues in related disciplines. They cut across particular schools of thought and tackle key issues, such as the philosophical underpinnings of psychoanalysis, psychoanalytic theories of motivation, conceptions of therapeutic action, the nature of unconscious mental functioning, psychoanalysis and social issues, and reports of original empirical research relevant to psychoanalysis. The authors often take a critical stance toward theories and offer a careful theoretical analysis and conceptual clarification of the complexities of theories and their clinical implications, drawing upon relevant empirical findings from psychoanalytic research as well as from research in related fields.

The Editorial Board continues to invite contributions from social/behavioral sciences such as anthropology and sociology, from biological sciences such as physiology and the various brain sciences, and from scholarly humanistic disciplines such as philosophy, law, and ethics. Volumes 1–64 in this series were published by International Universities Press. Volumes 65–69 were published by Jason Aronson.

Routledge titles in this series:

Vol. 75 Psychoanalytic Perspectives on Conflict
Edited by Christopher Christian, Morris N. Eagle, & David L. Wolitzky

Vol. 76 Death and Fallibility in the Psychoanalytic Encounter
Mortal Gifts
Ellen Pinsky

Vol. 77 Core Concepts in Classical Psychoanalysis
Clinical, Research Evidence and Conceptual Critiques
Morris N. Eagle

Vol. 78 Core Concepts in Contemporary Psychoanalysis
Clinical, Research Evidence and Conceptual Critiques
Morris N. Eagle

Core Concepts in Contemporary Psychoanalysis

Clinical, Research Evidence and Conceptual Critiques

Morris N. Eagle

Routledge
Taylor & Francis Group
LONDON AND NEW YORK

First published 2018
by Routledge
2 Park Square, Milton Park, Abingdon, Oxon OX14 4RN

and by Routledge
605 Third Avenue, New York, NY 10017

Routledge is an imprint of the Taylor & Francis Group, an informa business

British Library Cataloguing-in-Publication Data
A catalogue record for this book is available from the British Library

Library of Congress Cataloging-in-Publication Data
Names: Eagle, Morris N., author.
Title: Core concepts in contemporary psychoanalysis : clinical, research evidence and conceptual critiques / Morris N. Eagle.
Description: Abingdon, Oxon ; New York, NY : Routledge, 2018. |
Includes bibliographical references and index.
Identifiers: LCCN 2017028249 (print) | LCCN 2017039744 (ebook) |
ISBN 9781315142111 (Master) | ISBN 9781351392655 (Web PDF) |
ISBN 9781351392648 (ePub) | ISBN 9781351392631 (Mobipocket/Kindle) |
ISBN 9781138306912 (hbk : alk. paper) | ISBN 9781138306929 (pbk. : alk. paper)
Subjects: LCSH: Psychoanalysis.
Classification: LCC BF173 (ebook) | LCC BF173 .E154 2018 (print) |
DDC 150.19/5—dc23
LC record available at https://lccn.loc.gov/2017028249

ISBN: 978-1-138-30691-2 (hbk)
ISBN: 978-1-138-30692-9 (pbk)
ISBN: 978-1-315-14211-1 (ebk)

Typeset in Times New Roman
by Florence Production Ltd, Stoodleigh, Devon, UK

Contents

Acknowledgements

I want to express my appreciation to my wife Rita who provided her usual invaluable help with the substance and organization of each chapter; to Robert Holt who commented on selected chapters with his usual care and precision; and to Lauren Jensen for her impressive ability to track down references and most remarkable, her ability to read my handwriting. My appreciation to Kate Hawes for her confidence and flexibility in the simultaneous publication of this book and the companion book. I also want to express my appreciation to Victoria Kelly for her care, competence, and patience in the copy-editing.

Introduction

As stated in the Introduction to the companion book on *Core Concepts in Classical Psychoanalysis*, the main purpose of both books is to address one large question: Of the core concepts and formulations of psychoanalytic theory, which ones should be discarded; which ones should be modified and in what ways; and which ones should be retained, all in the light of research findings, clinical evidence, and conceptual critiques?

The companion book deals with concepts and formulations more closely related to classical psychoanalysis, and includes chapters on unconscious processes, inner conflict, defense, the Oedipus complex, and a concluding chapter. The concepts and formulations dealt with in this book, although also linked to classical theory, are especially prominent in contemporary psychoanalytic theories. This book includes chapters on transference, countertransference, projection and projective identification, psychoanalytic styles of writing, thinking, and habits of mind, and a concluding chapter.

The links to contemporary psychoanalytic theories are apparent with regard to the chapters on countertransference and projective identification and less apparent with regard to the chapter on transference. However, I include a discussion of transference in this volume because it has undergone substantial revisions in contemporary theoretical developments. Although the chapter on psychoanalytic styles of writing and thinking deals with problems that are characteristic of much psychoanalytic theorizing, classical and contemporary, they are especially severe in contemporary theories. Hence, that is included in this volume.

Chapter 1

Transference

Along with unconscious processes and defense, transference and countertransference were cited most frequently as core psychoanalytic concepts. Further, both transference and countertransference have been referred to as the "common ground" of psychoanalysis that cuts across different psychoanalytic "schools" (Gabbard, 1995; Wallerstein, 1992). Also, along with unconscious processes and defense, a good deal of empirical research has been carried out on the concept of transference.

The organization of the chapter is as follows: the first section will present different conceptions of transference from Freudian to contemporary psychoanalytic theories. The second section deals with different aspects of transference, including transference as resistance, analysis of the transference, resolution of the transference, transference and gratification, and analytic love. The third section will discuss certain conceptual issues attending the assumption that transference involves distortion. The fourth section covers selected research on transference. The fifth section discusses the clinical implications of research findings on transference. And finally, the last section presents a summary and set of conclusions.

Different conceptions of transference

I begin with a sampling of brief definitions of transference and then move on to a more detailed discussion of transference from different theoretical perspectives:

> transference refers to the patient's transfer of feelings, wishes, and reactions experienced toward an important figure from his or her childhood

> (usually a parental figure) onto the analyst . . . transference is a universal phenomenon that occurs in many spheres of life in which one's reactions to a current person (e.g., boss, spouse) are reminiscent of early patterns.
>
> (Eagle, 2006, p. 462)

> transference is the experience of feelings, drives, attitudes, fantasies, and defenses toward a person in the present which do not befit that person but are repetitions of reactions originating in regard to significant persons in early childhood, unconsciously displaced onto figures in the present.
>
> (Greenson, 1967, p. 171)

> the displacement of patterns of feelings, thoughts, and behavior in relation to significant figures during childhood onto a person involved in a current interpersonal relationship.
>
> (Moore & Fine, 1990)

> the distortion of a realistic patient–analyst relationship by additions from past unconscious and repressed object-relations.
>
> (Freud, 1968, pp. 95–96)

Freud's conception of transference

Let me turn now to spell out in some detail Freud's conception of transference.

In a relatively early paper, Freud (1905[1901]) defined transference in the following way:

> They are new editions or facsimiles of the impulses and phantasies which are roused and made conscious during the progress of analysis; but they have this peculiarity, which is characteristic for their species, that they replace some earlier person by the person of the physician. To put it another way: a whole series of psychological experiences are revived, not as belonging to the past, but as applying to the person of the physician at the present moment. Some of these transferences have a content which differs from that of their model in no respect whatever except for the substitution. These then—to keep to the same

> metaphor —are merely new impressions or reprints. Others are more ingeniously constructed; their content has been subjected to a moderating influence—to sublimation, as I call it—and they may even become conscious, by cleverly taking advantage of some real peculiarity in the physician's person or circumstances and attaching themselves to that. These, then, will no longer be new impressions, but revised editions. (p. 116)

Thus, according to Freud, even when the patient reacts to some actual characteristic of the analyst, it is recruited into the transference.

In a later paper on "The dynamics of transference," Freud (1912a) writes that the ultimate nature and source of transference is erotic. On the very first page of the paper, he notes "that each individual . . . has acquired a specific method of his own in his conduct of his erotic life—that is, in the preconditions to falling in love" (p. 99). It is this "specific method" or what Freud refers to as "prototype" or "stereotype plates" (p. 100) that are transferred on to the therapist. Freud further writes that "if someone's need for love is not entirely satisfied by reality, he is bound to approach every new person whom he meets with libidinal anticipatory ideas" (p. 100).

One can see from the above citations that, according to Freud, the essence of transference is the tendency to experience the analyst (as well as contemporary figures outside the analytic situation) in terms of early significant figures from one's past. This includes, among other things, the attribution to the current figure of various characteristics, intentions, and motives of early figures as represented in one's mind; expectations that the current figure will behave in a way that is similar to the behavior of early figures; and the transfer of early feelings, fantasies, attitudes, and defenses on to the current figure. The feelings and attitudes noted by Freud that one transfers on to the current figure include, importantly, the assignment of a parental role such that one looks to the current figure to satisfy early needs and wishes. This aspect of transference is highlighted by Freud's (1905[1901]) comment that "if someone's need for love is not entirely satisfied by reality, he is bound to approach every new person whom he meets with libidinal anticipatory needs" (p. 100).

The clear implications here are: first, that transference of a parental role is more likely or perhaps more intense for individuals whose need for love has not been met; and second, that the mode of relating, that is, the "stereotype plate" that defines the transference entails actively seeking to have one's libidinal needs met by the transference figure. As far as I know, individual differences in the threshold for transference reactions as well as intensity of transference as a function of early deprivation of libidinal needs have not been subject to clinical or empirical research. (However, see Parish & Eagle, 2003, for a study on individual differences in intensity of attachment to therapist as a function of different attachment patterns.)

Different patterns of transference

Freud (1912a) identified three patterns of transference all of which may coexist: (1) positive transference, which need not be analyzed and "which is admissible to consciousness . . . persists and is the vehicle of success in psychoanalysis exactly as it is in other methods of treatment" (p. 105),[1] (2) "a positive transference of repressed erotic impulses" (p. 105); and (3) a negative transference. As we know, there has been much debate regarding the "unobjectionable" positive transference, particularly the implication that it need not be analyzed (e.g., Brenner, 1979, 1982). The criticism of that concept is given weight by Freud's (1912a) own comment that "positive transference is then further divisible into transference of friendly or affectionate feelings, which are admissible to consciousness and transference of prolongations of those feelings into unconsciousness. As regards the latter, analysis shows that they invariably go back to erotic sources." He then writes, "we are thus led to the discovery that all the emotional relations of sympathy, friendship, trust, and the like . . . are genetically linked with sexuality and have developed from purely sexual desires through a softening of their sexual aim, however pure and unsensual they may appear to our conscious self-perception" (p. 105).

In one of his last papers, Freud (1940[1938]) describes transference in the following way: "the patient sees in him [i.e., the analyst] the return, the reincarnation, of some important figure out of his childhood or past, and consequently transfers on to him feelings and reactions which are undoubtedly applied to this stereotype" (p. 175). He then describes transference as "ambivalent," which "comprises positive (affectionate) as well as negative (hostile) attitudes toward the analyst, who as a rule is put in the place of one or other of the patient's parents, his father or mother" (p. 175).

If the origin of transference lies in the patient's erotic life, why does hostile negative transference arise? As expressed in the following passage,

Freud's answer is that negative transference develops in response to the frustration of the patient's erotic wishes:

> His obedience to his father (if it is his father that is in question), his courting of his father's favor, had its roots in an erotic wish directed towards him. Some time or other that demand will press its way forward in the transference as well as insist on being satisfied. In the analytic situation it can only meet with frustration. Real sexual relations between patients and analysts are out of the question, and even subtler methods of satisfaction, such as the giving of preference, intimacy and so on, are only sparingly granted by the analyst. A rejection of this kind is taken as the occasion for the change-over; probably things happened in the same way in the patient's childhood.
>
> (p. 176)

In Freud's view of transference, it is of critical importance that the analyst reveals as little of himself or herself to the patient. As he puts it, "The doctor should be opaque to his patients, and like a mirror, should show them nothing but what is shown to him" (Freud, 1912a, p. 118). The analyst can thereby serve as a "blank screen" on to which the patient can project his or her feelings, thoughts, perceptions, patterns of relating, fantasies, and so on. According to this perspective, deviations from a "blank screen" stance muddy the water with regard to being able to comprehend the patient's versus the analyst's contributions to the former's pattern of responses in the analytic situation.

Transference as both resistance and invaluable aid

Freud (1912a) viewed transference as both an invaluable aid to the analysis as well as "the most powerful resistance to the treatment" (p. 101). With regard to the former, the transference represents an invaluable aid in a number of ways. First, positive transference, entails the patient's "aim of pleasing the analyst and winning his applause and love" and serves as the "true motive force of the patient's collaboration" (Freud, 1940[1938], p. 175). What Freud referred to as the "unobjectionable positive transference" has been essentially transformed, originally in the psychoanalytic literature (e.g., Greenson, 1967) and later in the general psychotherapy literature, for example, into the concept of "therapeutic alliance." (As we will see, there is a large research literature on the relationship between therapeutic alliance and therapeutic process and outcome.)

Second, insofar as the transference presumably repeats the past, it lays out for the analyst in vivo the patient's neurosis (thus, the "transference neurosis"). Third, to the extent that "the patient puts the analyst in the place of his father (or mother), he is also giving him the power which his superego exercises over his ego, since his parents were, as we know, the origin of his superego. The new superego now has an opportunity for a sort of *after-education* of the neurotic" (p. 175). And fourth, the here-and-now immediacy of transference experiences is more likely to produce a greater sense of emotional conviction (and a counter against intellectualization) than material having to do with accounts of figures from the past. As Freud (1940[1938]) puts it, "a patient never forgets again what he has experienced in the form of transference; it carries a greater force of conviction than anything he can acquire in other ways" (p. 177). One can see from the above why analysis of the transference is given a critical role in the theory of psychoanalytic treatment (see also Strachey, 1934).

Transference constitutes a form of resistance in a number of ways. First, the transference is a quintessential example of repeating rather than remembering. Second, both negative and erotic transferences constitute resistance, the former in an obvious way. As for the latter, according to Freud (1915 [1914]), the patient's falling in love with the analyst and wanting him or her to satisfy that love are based on infantile object choice.[2] Further, the patient continues the futile pursuit of the gratification of infantile wishes, this time in relation to the analyst. In this sense, one can think of the erotic transference as an expression of repeating rather than remembering, that is, as an attempt to gratify infantile wishes rather than subject them to analytic understanding.

Transference in self psychology

The traditional concept of transference has been altered in a number of ways, which reflect broader theoretical changes in contemporary psychoanalytic theories. Thus, associated with the rejection of Freudian drive theory is a corresponding rejection of the Freudian claim that the nature and ultimate source of transference is the patient's erotic life. It appears that whatever component a particular theory posits as a fundamental factor in psychological life finds its place as the primary motivational source of transference. Or, to put it another way, whatever it is that a particular theory proposes as our fundamental longings is, according to that theory, the motive force for transference.

Thus, from a self-psychology perspective, a primary motivation underlying the development of transference is the longing to have one's unmet needs for empathic mirroring met. This motivation is reflected in a mirroring transference. Other motivations are reflected in twinship, idealizing, and merger transferences. In all cases, transference consists of a self–selfobject relationship, the latter defined as relating to another in terms of the other's function in contributing to one's self-cohesiveness. As the term "selfobject" suggests, in a self–selfobject relationship, the other is neither a fully separate object nor fully a part of oneself, but is located somewhere between the two.

Although, as noted earlier, in his 1912 discussion of the sources of transference, Freud (1912a) refers to the individual's "need for love" (p. 100), his primary emphasis is on infantile *wishes* rather than needs. In this regard, Freud's conception of transference can be contrasted with Kohut's (1984) view that the patient attempts to meet unmet developmental *needs* in the transference—primarily the need for empathic understanding—rather than to gratify infantile instinctual *wishes*. The contrast between the two perspectives is further highlighted by the difference between the Freudian idea that infantile wishes need to be either sublimated or repudiated and the Kohutian stance that unmet developmental needs should be met in the treatment (see Eagle, 1990, for a discussion of wishes versus needs in self psychology).

The contrast between Freud and Kohut, however, may not be as thoroughgoing as it appears. There is some similarity between Freud's insistence that infantile wishes need to be renounced or repudiated and Kohut's (1984) recognition that archaic selfobject needs for perfect mirroring cannot be met in reality. Both converge on the position that certain archaic wishes and needs cannot be realistically met in this world and to pursue them is not only chimerical, but also prolongs pathology and distress.

The degree of convergence is even greater. For insofar as, as Kohut acknowledges, the presumed need for perfect mirroring cannot possibly be met, it is best thought of as a fantasy or wish (Eagle, 1990). Thus, both Freud and Kohut appear to agree that certain wishes cannot realistically be met. They diverge in regard to what follows from the recognition of that sobering reality. For Freud, what follows is the need for either sublimation or repudiation of the impossible to gratify infantile wishes. For Kohut (1984) what follows is that, as a consequence of "repair" of self-defects (through the process of "transmuting internalization," p. 4), the patient no longer needs perfect mirroring and can now avail himself or herself of and benefit from the less than perfect empathic mirroring that is realistically available in this world.

Fairbairn on transference

Fairbairn has relatively little to say directly about transference. In his 300-page 1952 book, there are fewer than nine pages devoted to transference, most of which are passing comments rather than focused and extensive discussions. However, it is possible to characterize his conception of transference from these comments. Fairbairn (1952) refers to the transference neurosis in terms of the patient's fear of the "release of bad objects from the unconscious" consequent upon lifting repression (p. 69). He also writes that "the deepest source of resistance is the fear of the release of bad objects from the unconscious, for when such bad objects are released, the world around the patient becomes peopled with devils which are too terrifying for him to face (Fairbairn, 1952, p. 69). And yet, as Fairbairn (1952) notes, "there is now little doubt in my mind that the release of bad objects from the unconscious is one of the chief aims which the psychotherapist should set himself out to achieve, even at the expense of a severe 'transference neurosis'" (p. 69).

He goes on to say that "the patient is not slow to sense that the therapeutic endeavor threatens to reproduce the situation against which his defenses are mobilized" (p. 166). Hence, it would seem inevitable that the therapist would be experienced as a bad object (i.e., the patient would form a negative transference, which Fairbairn seems to equate with the transference neurosis). However, Fairbairn (1952) also tells us that "the bad objects can only be safely released . . . if the analyst has become established as a sufficiently good object for the patient" (p. 70).

This state of affairs confronts the patient with a dilemma. On the one hand, she or he needs the safety provided by the therapist as a good object to safely release bad objects. And on the other hand, insofar as the therapist is someone whose aim is to achieve the release of bad objects, she or he will be experienced as a bad object. A critical question, one that Fairbairn does not adequately address, is how the therapist comes to be transformed in the eyes of the patient from a bad to a good object (or at least, a more or less realistic object). What are the necessary therapeutic interactions, interventions, and processes that make possible and facilitate this transformation?

In classical theory, the predominant answer to this question is: analysis of the transference. However, it is not clear that this is Fairbairn's answer, with regard to both this question and, more broadly, the question of what is curative in psychoanalysis. Indeed, with regard to the latter, Fairbairn's emphasis appears to be, not on interpretation or analysis of the transference, but rather on the re-experience of the original bad object situation in the context of the safety and security provided by a good object. He writes that "therapeutic results are closely related to the phenomenon of transference, i.e., to the establishment of an object relationship of a special kind with the analyst on the part of the patient" (p. 87).

Fairbairn, however, does not elaborate, first, on the nature of that special kind of object relationship (it seems generally equivalent to what in Freudian theory is referred to the "unobjectionable positive transference"); and second, how the patient comes to be experienced by the patient as a good object. He does not comment on the particular qualities and interventions that constitute being a good object in the context of the therapeutic relationship.[3] He does state that "it is only by means of a working through of the analytic transference situation in the setting of an actual 'good object' relationship with the analyst that the return of repressed bad objects can be made to service a therapeutic aim" (p. 166). But he does not adequately address the nature of the good object relationship and how that is achieved. Further, his statement is somewhat circular insofar as what needs to be worked through is precisely how the patient experiences the relationship.

There are other aspects of Fairbairn's discussion of transference that are somewhat puzzling and that, I believe, require further elaboration. For example, Fairbairn (1952) refers to the "spontaneous return of repressed bad objects . . . [as] a phenomenon of transference" (p. 166). Given Fairbairn's observations of the patient's resistance to the return of repressed bad objects and his identification of one of the therapist's "chief aims" as the achievement of the release of bad objects from the unconscious, it is not clear, first, under what circumstances there would be a spontaneous return of repressed bad objects; and second, in what way such a spontaneous return is a "phenomenon of transference." In general, Fairbairn's writings focus much on the endopsychic structure of the personality and relatively little on the nature of therapeutic processes.

When Fairbairn (1952) discusses transference in general terms outside the analytic situation, his conceptualization of it is much closer to the usual understanding of it as the transferring of early modes of relating with parental figures to current figures. Thus, he writes that the soldier suffering from war neurosis is best able to sustain relationships that "conform most to the pattern of his early relationship with his mother" (p. 277). Fairbairn goes on to observe that such an individual can only sustain relationships characterized by his "infantile dependence" and therefore approaches all relationships this way. Note that Fairbairn's observation that the overly dependent individual attempts to indiscriminately establish a relationship of "infantile dependence" parallels Freud's (1912a) comment that "if someone's need for love is not entirely satisfied by reality, he is bound to approach every new person whom he meets with libidinal anticipatory ideas" (p. 100).[4]

Fairbairn's general formulations regarding the relationship between internalized objects and actual objects in external reality provide further insight into his understanding of transference, whether or not he employs that term. According to Fairbairn (1952), from one perspective, at the core of psychopathology is the tendency to relate to the actual other as a stand-in for an internalized object. Thus, when this tendency is extreme, the individual is engaged in an internalized object relation in which he or she is largely relating not to a real separate other, that is, to the other in terms of his or her characteristics, interests, needs, attitudes, and so on, but rather to an internalized object. Further, insofar as, according to Fairbairn, internalized objects are structures of the personality, in relating to an internalized object, one is, in an important sense, relating to *an aspect of oneself.* Thus, in Fairbairn's view, while transference may be an inevitable component of all our reactions to others, at its extreme it is a solipsistic and schizoid phenomenon in which one is turned totally inward and relates to projections of one's own inner structures (i.e., one's internalized object) rather than to objects in the world.[5]

Implicit in Fairbairn's formulation of transference is the central idea that in experiencing and responding to another as a stand-in for an internalized object, the individual is projecting an aspect of himself onto the other. Consider a concrete example: let us say that a patient projects a critical internalized object onto the analyst. Thus far, this involves nothing more than an extension of the meaning of projection to include not only unacceptable wishes and impulses, but also other aspects of oneself (i.e., internalized objects)—an extension that is the result of Fairbairn's rejection of "impulse psychology" and substituting for it a psychology of "endopsychic structure."

What does it mean to project one's internalized object onto another? In ordinary language, it means that the individual attributes to the other attitudes he himself has toward certain of his own feelings and needs (e.g., his contempt for his need for love), which, according to Fairbairn, is the product of internalized parental attitudes. The individual may project onto the analyst his own unconscious critical and contemptuous attitudes toward his needs and then experience the analyst as critical and contemptuous. Whether one hypothesizes that the patient is projecting an unconscious hostile wish or an internalized object, the end result of experiencing the analyst as hostile is the same. However, there are subtle differences between the two accounts.

In the former case, I project my own disowned wish onto another and then experience the other as entertaining that wish toward me. Thus, instead of experiencing my hostility toward X, I experience X as hostile toward me. Although I project my hostile wish or impulse onto the other because the wish or impulse is unacceptable to me, I do not necessarily project that attitude of finding the wish unacceptable onto the other. In the latter case of projecting an internalized object onto the other, I do, indeed, project not a wish or impulse (recall that Fairbairn rejects an "impulse psychology"), but rather my attitude of contempt for my wishes and needs. That is, I experience the other as having a critical and derogating attitude toward my experiencing and expressing my needs. Employing the language of classical theory, one can say that according to Fairbairn, in transference one projects onto the other is not an id impulse, but superego attitudes. Indeed, Fairbairn is quite explicit in acknowledging that his concept of internalized object is closely modeled after Freud's concept of the superego, in particular, the central idea of taking into one's personality structure, attitudes of early objects.

As for clinical implications of this distinction, whereas from a Freudian perspective, an analysis of the transference would be more likely to focus on interpreting and uncovering the patient's repressed wishes toward the analyst and the defense erected against them, from a Fairbairnian perspective, one would be more likely to focus on the ways in which the patient's transference patterns and behavior reflect an externalization of the conflict between different aspects of himself or herself (i.e., libidinal ego versus anti-libidinal ego in an internal object relationship with the internalized exciting and alluring object versus rejecting object). Another difference is that while for Freud, transference entails the patient's attempts to have the analyst gratify infantile wishes, for Fairbairn, there is little or no talk about attempted gratification or wishes. However, both Freud and Fairbairn conceptualize the transference as the arena for playing out of inner conflict among different structures of the personality.

Fairbairn proposes a set of criteria that differentiate psychopathology from healthy functioning. These include infantile dependence versus mature dependence, and, most relevant in the present context, relating to another as a stand-in for an internalized object versus relating to another in terms of who the other actually is. In short, for Fairbairn, the healthy individual is capable of engaging in an object relationship with a real other rather than a fantasy-ridden relationship with internalized object.

One can think of the aim of the analysis transference precisely in the same terms as Fairbairn's conception of healthy functioning. That is, at the end of treatment, the patient should be able to experience the analyst less as a version of an internalized early parental figure and more in terms of who the analyst actually is. Further, and critically important, in successful treatment this outcome should not be limited to the patient's experience of the analyst—that is not a successful outcome—but should extend to the former's experience of significant figures in his or her current life. To the extent that the patient's experience of significant others becomes more realistic, to that extent, one might say that his relational and affective reality testing has been strengthened.[6] There is a convergence between Freud and Fairbairn with regard to this aim.

Transference in Control–Mastery theory

As Bush (2005) observes, according to Control–Mastery theory, guilt is frequently implicated in the patient's transference. From that perspective, patients often come to treatment with the unconscious pathogenic belief, based on parental communications, that some of their strivings and goals (e.g., for independence and success) will harm their parents (e.g., parents will feel abandoned or envious) and therefore experience conflict and guilt when pursuing or even intending to pursue these goals. Although, according to Control–Mastery theory, patients hope to disconfirm their pathogenic beliefs in treatment, they nevertheless transfer the expectations that are part of their pathogenic beliefs onto the therapist. That is, they unconsciously expect that, like their parents, the therapist too will disapprove of and/or be harmed by their pursuits of certain strivings.

According to Control–Mastery theory, in an attempt to master unconscious guilt and disconfirm pathogenic beliefs, the patient will present tests to the therapist to determine whether he or she will show evidence of feeling harmed, abandoned, etc., in response to expressions of certain strivings. The therapist's understanding of and response to these tests are hypothesized to play a critical role in the disconfirmation of unconscious guilt and the unconscious pathogenic beliefs that are the source of the guilt.

Thus, one can see that in Control–Mastery theory, transference is understood as including both the projection onto the therapist of characteristics, attitudes, and behaviors of parental figures as well as the hope that the therapist will behave differently from one's parental figures. Thus, transference as resistance is understood in a very different way in Control–Mastery theory than it is understood in Freudian theory or self psychology. According to the former perspective, the patient is not demanding that the therapist gratify infantile wishes or, as in self psychology, the impossible demand to provide perfect mirroring. Rather, through presenting tests to the therapist, the patient is seeking assurance that he or she will not be *retraumatized* at the hands of the therapist, that is, that the therapist will behave differently from parental figures. In an important sense, one can say that the patient is seeking to undo or disconfirm his or her transference expectations and attributions.

Transference in attachment theory

According to Bowlby (1980), based on early interactions with caregivers, we develop internal working models (IWMs) that include representations of the caregiver (i.e., attachment figure), self-representations, and representations of prototypical interactions between infant and caregiver. It is these

IWMs that are assumed to underlie different attachment patterns. For example, an avoidant-dismissive attachment pattern is assumed to be underlain by a representation of the attachment figure as rejecting, a representation of the self as unworthy, and a representation of prototypical interactions characterized by expectations of rejection. Once formed, attachment patterns are relatively resistant to change, particularly when the environment remains stable.

To the extent that early representations and expectations influence subsequent relationships later in life with significant others, IWMs and their corresponding attachment patterns can be viewed as expressions of transference. Consider the above example of an avoidant attachment pattern, which includes the expectation that, like the early attachment figure, a current significant figure will reject overtures to have one's attachment needs met. Thus, the current figure is assimilated into representations and schemas of the early attachment figure. This means that the avoidant individual projects onto his or her current attachment figure expectations regarding how she will behave similar to the expectations acquired in the early interactions with caregiver and then reacts to current figure (including defensive operations) in a way that is similar to how he or she reacted to mother. In short, in certain respects, the individual is reacting to current figure as if she were someone else, namely, his mother. In doing so, he is substituting one external figure—or more accurately, his representation of an external figure—for another. This is also true in the therapeutic situation. Thus, there is evidence that differences in attachment patterns are associated with different patterns of patients' relationship to their therapist (Mallinckrodt et al., 2005; Parish & Eagle, 2003).

A Piagetian perspective on transference

In an excellent paper, Wachtel (1980) suggests that "Piaget's concept of schemas, characterized by the two basic functions of assimilation and accommodation, seems particularly useful for understanding the diverse phenomena and other more or less closely related relationship phenomena" (p. 62). Wachtel's paper is rich and it is virtually criminal to summarize it. However, I want to extract its basic ideas because I think it brings much clarity to a discussion of the nature of transference. Wachtel suggests that "Transference reactions, in Piagetian terms, may be seen simply as reflecting schemas which are characterized by a strong predominance of assimilation over accommodation. The experience with the analyst is assimilated to schemas shaped by earlier experiences, and there is very little accommodation to actualities of the present situation which makes it different from the former experience" (p. 63). As Wachtel goes on to observe, hardly any schema is either "pure" assimilation or "pure" accommodation. When assimilation is strongly predominant, it can more readily be activated by a wide range of external stimuli. However, as Wachtel cautions, this does not mean that the individual has not found an external stimulus "hook" on which to hang his or her schema. In view of the fact that all schemas that influence our experience are the product of assimilation and accommodation processes, it becomes clear that transference is not a unique phenomenon.

As Wachtel also observes, Piaget did not address affective, motivational, and interpersonal processes, which certainly influence the nature and role of schemas in interpersonal interactions. In these interactions, the stimuli to which we are reacting are influenced by our own behavior. That is, through our behavior we elicit certain responses in others, which then constitute the stimuli to which we react and which are subject to assimilation and accommodation processes. Or, to put it another way, the schemas we form of others are partly a function of the behavior we have elicited in others through our own behavior (see Wachtel, 2014). It is the mutual examination of these interactional processes that for many contemporary psychoanalytic theorists constitute the analysis of the transference. This, of course, raises the question of the value and usefulness of invoking a special concept that we refer to as transference—a question that will be taken up again later.

Some issues related to transference

Transference as resistance

I have already discussed Freudian and Control–Mastery theory views of transference as resistance. There have been other important discussions of transference as resistance. Gill (1982, 1994) has distinguished between resistance to the awareness of the transference (see also Lipton, 1977) and resistance to the resolution of the transference. And Kernberg (2000) has referred to resistance against development of a transference, in particular, resistance against "development of an authentic dependency on the analyst, and with it, against all transferential developments" (Kernberg, 2000, p. 255), which, according to him, particularly characterizes narcissistic personality disorders.

Given that transference itself is defined as a major expression of resistance, the above forms of resistance lead to some odd formulations. Thus, "resistance to the awareness of the transference" can be translated as resistance to the awareness of one form of resistance; "resistance to resolution of the transference" as resistance against resolving one form of resistance; and resistance "against all transferential developments" as resistance against developing a form of resistance. These odd implications of viewing transference as a form of resistance suggest that conceptualizing transference as resistance against remembering and instead repeating is perhaps not the best way to understand it.

In my view, there are many problems with the concept of resistance that need to be discussed in their own right. However, the point I want to make in the present context is that not much light is shed on the concept of transference by viewing it as a form of resistance, a concept that itself is problematic.

Distortions versus plausible construals

Although, as noted, transference has been referred to as the "common ground" that cuts across different psychoanalytic "schools" (Wallerstein, 1992), the fact is that how the concept is understood has changed considerably over the years. In contrast to classical theory, in contemporary psychoanalytic theories, transference is no longer understood in terms of the patient's projections onto a blank screen analyst. Rather, there is now general recognition that there is no such thing as a blank screen analyst who emits no cues. For example, as Gill (1994) repeatedly observed, silence—the hallmark instance of the blank screen analyst—is itself a powerful cue. In view of these considerations, transference has come to include the patient's construals of cues emitted by the analyst.

Gill (1982, 1994), one of the leading figures in the reconceptualization of transference, eschewed the assumption, implicit in its traditional meaning, that transference necessarily involves distortion, and argued instead that, for the most part, the patient's construals of cues from the analyst are plausible and reflect his or her attempts to make sense of the analytic situation and the analyst's behavior. Further, Gill's objection to the assumption of distortion is that it sets up the analyst as the arbiter of objective reality, that is, of what constitutes distortion and what constitutes reality.

Wolitzky (2000) cites two letters from Gill to Evelyn Schwaber, which articulate the reasons for his objection to the commonly held view that transference necessarily entails distortion and his general conception of the nature of transference. In the first letter dated July 16, 1992, Gill writes: "Perhaps I should add that I am not only convinced, but messianic in my zeal, to combat what I believe is rife in our field, namely, the analyst's imposition of his views on the patient either wittingly or unwittingly" (p. 270).

In the second later dated August 6, 1992, Gill writes: "It is with due care not to superimpose our views on the patient, that we acquaint the patient with our view as something for his consideration that we may be enlightening him [about] . . . I consider neither the patient's nor the analyst's view to be the correct one, but both of them to be selective, plausible, and important views which lead to a kind of 'negotiation' between the two participants in an effort to enlarge the understanding of both. . . . Some views are better than others because they are more comprehensive, consistent, and illuminating of reality insofar as it is given to us to see reality" (pp. 271–272).

If what is referred to as the patient's transference reactions are nothing more than plausible construals of the analyst's cues, why the need for the concept of transference? In what ways does this reconceptualization of transference retain its links to the original concept, including its embeddedness in a set of theoretical formulations regarding the nature of psychological functioning and of psychoanalytic treatment. At one point, Gill (1982) states that if the term transference were not so embedded in our psychoanalytic language, he would favor relinquishing it and substituting the term "experience of the therapeutic relationship." However, even if one substituted the latter term, the question would nevertheless remain as to what degree and in what ways the patient's experience of the therapist and the therapeutic relationship is influenced by early experiences with parental figures.

I think that Gill overly polarizes the issue. A core element of the concept of transference is that one experiences and reacts to a current person in terms of characteristics of early significant figures (most frequently, parental figures). This often entails attributing these characteristics to a current person. If one assumes that the current person B is a blank screen, that is, entirely opaque, then one can conclude that person A's experience of B are necessarily projections—similar to responses to a Rorschach card or better yet, the blank screen card on the Thematic Apperception Test (TAT). In a certain sense, when the stimulus is opaque or highly ambiguous, the issue of distortion arises only when the individual's experience or attribution bears no recognizable relationship to the external stimulus (whether the external stimulus is the analyst, a Rorschach card, or a TAT card). When that occurs, the individual is, indeed, distorting. And to say that calling it a distortion is tantamount to taking on the role of arbiter of reality is unconvincing.

I think there is an excessive emphasis on distortions in discussions of transference (although, as we will see, there is experimental evidence that subtle distortions occur in transference-like processes). Transference may also be expressed largely through selectivity, that is, through selective attention to certain cues (as well as failure to attend to other cues) and idiosyncratic (even if plausible) meanings given to these cues. As Freud (1912) observes, the patient may selectively focus on "some real peculiarity in the physician's person or circumstance" (p. 116). There is a fuzzy boundary between extreme selectivity and distortion. When selective focus is sufficiently narrow and rigid, it shades into distortion. Also, even if there is little evidence of distortion, the influence of transference may be seen in the intensity of the patient's reactions to cues or events that would not normally warrant such intensity.

When I have referred to relating to another in terms of who that person actually is, one frequent response I have encountered—in effect, a claim about epistemological limits—is that because transference is ubiquitous, one can never fully experience another in terms of who that other actually is. Another frequent response, this one more explicitly philosophical, is that the very notion of responding to someone in terms of who that other actually is is misguided and reflects a hopelessly naïve pre-Kantian realism, as if such talk is equivalent to the claim that one can directly experience the *Ding an sich*.

These criticisms are associated with the view that all of our perceptions and experiences are not "mirrors of nature" (Rorty, 1979), but constructions that vary in their usefulness, that is, in the degree to which they serve us poorly or well in helping us carry out particular projects. Furthermore, according to this perspective, our constructions of the world, including other persons as well as oneself are irrevocably limited, or perhaps one should say, necessarily shaped, by the evolved instruments, that is, our perceptual, cognitive, and affective systems, through which we experience the world.

Of course, we experience the world through the categories generated by the species-specific apparatuses that have evolved in the course of evolution, what Lorenz (1973) variously refers to as our "perceiving apparatus" (p. 8) and "preexisting structures" (p. 9). We also know that the categories generated by the apparatuses of other species—the seams along which they divide nature (Goodman, 1960)—are quite different from our own (see Nagel's, 1974, "What it is like to be a bat"). However, although quite different from each other, if the categories of our own and that of other species did not have a systematic and lawful relationship to the facts of the world, the way things are, we, as well as other species, could not do the things we do, and ultimately could not survive (see Campbell, 1990, on evolutionary epistemology).

Similar considerations apply to the individual differences within a species with regard to the categories through which individuals experience the world. That is, in a broad sense, we define certain core aspects of psychopathology in terms of maladaptive categories through which the individual experiences the world, which includes others as well as oneself. One meaning of "maladaptive" is that the categories through which the individual experiences the world do not adequately correspond to certain facts of the world and therefore put the individual at risk in some way. From this perspective, a central aspect of transference is experiencing the other in terms of categories that belong to someone else; and one central aim of the analysis of transference consists in the attempt to help the patient experience the other in terms of categories that are appropriate to the current person with whom he or she is interacting—that is, as much as possible, in terms of who that other actually is. As I stated earlier, this can be understood as an attempt to enhance cognitive and affective reality testing. Of course, this does not preclude experiencing the current person with affects one experiences toward early figures nor does it preclude experiencing the current figure as similar in certain respects to early figures.

This way of understanding transference has elicited on the part of Gill (1982, 1994) and other theorists who espouse a constructivist point of view the fear that the analyst will assume an authoritarian role as the arbiter of reality and the more deeply philosophical objection that all we have is our constructions and that any effort to assess the correspondence of our categories or constructions to an independent reality is futile and misguided. However, it seems to me that a thoroughgoing constructivist position essentially does away with the concept of transference altogether. Thus, if as Gill argues, what has been thought of as transference is essentially plausible constructions based on cues emitted by the analyst, what is being transferred? Why not, as Gill suggests at one point, drop talk about transference and limit one's discussion to the patient's experience of the analyst? That could, of course, be done. However, it is not clear that this move would bypass the question of whether and to what degree the patient is distorting the meaning of the analyst's behavior.

I think the problems inherent in thinking of transference simply as plausible constructions are further highlighted by trying to apply that point of view to transference phenomena outside the clinical situation. Consider the situation described by Freud (1912b) of the patient reporting "psychical impotence," which, according to Freud, is largely because of the patient unconsciously experiencing his wife as if she were, in certain respects, his mother. Is one to say that the patient has simply produced a plausible construction based on cues emitted by his wife? Of course, given what we know about object choice and the accommodations that couples make, there may be some limited truth to this formulation. However, the facts are, first, that the patient's wife is not his mother; second, that reacting to his wife as if she were, in certain respects, his mother is an expression of a subtle failure in cognitive-affective reality testing; and third, that this failure of reality testing plays an important role in the patient's "psychical impotence."

One need not limit the content of one's example to "psychical impotence." Consider a scenario with a different content, but with a similar structure. Let us say that the patient reacts to his wife's ordinary criticisms as if they were emanating from a chronically critical mother. Or, as another example, let us say that the patient is chronically angry at and disappointed with his wife because she is not as indulgent or perhaps as overprotective as his mother was—or at least, as he remembers his mother was. The point here is that although the patient's representations of his wife are constructions—what else could they be?—they are inaccurate and therefore maladaptive constructions, ones that, paraphrasing Freud's (1917 [1916–1917], p. 452) comment regarding interpretations, do not tally with what is real regarding his wife. Furthermore, the maladaptive nature of the patient's representations or constructions is precisely linked to their inaccuracy, that is, to the fact that he is reacting to his wife as if she were his mother. One also needs to add that experiencing his wife in this way is very likely to trigger negative responses from her, an important factor that is relevant to fully understanding the vicious cycle nature of the patient's representations or constructions (see Wachtel, 2014).

There is little doubt that in one degree or another, the influence of transference on our experience of others is inevitable, which is one way of saying that there are limits to how fully one can experience someone in terms of who he or she actually is. But like many important things, it is a matter of degree. Equally important, it is also a matter of one's capacity to reflect on one's transference tendencies and thereby temper their influence (see Nagel, 1986). Isn't that the essence of analysis of the transference? The critical point here is that analysis of the transference makes no sense unless one believes that, to greater or lesser degree, it is possible to at least aim to experience someone in terms of who he or she actually is or at least to minimize the degree to which one imposes on one particular person the attributes of someone else or one's own projections. From a philosophical perspective, that aim is motivated by the belief that there is a reality independent of one's interests, needs, desires, etc., and that our constructions can be assessed with regard to the degree to which they tally with that reality (Searle, 1998).

One can take the Rortyan position that all we have is our more or less useful constructions and any talk about their correspondence to a reality independent of these constructions is not especially meaningful or useful. One may or may not be comfortable with that position with regard to the inanimate external world. But the question I want to put is what this position looks like in the context of human interaction. Let us say that in the context of relating to another person, one takes the position that all one needs to concern oneself with is the utility of one's constructions in carrying out one's projects, and that any concern with whether these constructions tally with a reality independent of one's constructions (i.e., the other person) is misguided and futile. Whatever one thinks of this position with regard to the inanimate external world, in the world of interpersonal relations, one's philosophical position has a strong potential impact on the nature of these relations. The belief that it does not matter whether these constructions correspond to who the person is or that one cannot know that person in terms of who he or she actually is has an important impact on the nature of one's relationship with that person, including the impact of one's belief on how that person will be likely to react to oneself. Also, what would loving another person mean in the context of believing that all one can have are more of less useful constructions? Would love—and I am not referring simply to infatuation here—be reduced to loving one's constructions?

These issues are pertinent with regard to not only one's relationship with another, but also one's relationship with oneself. Without assuming a reality independent of one's constructions, what would it mean to really know oneself? Would "construct thyself" replace "know thyself"? What would the search for self-knowledge mean if one did not assume that there are aspects of oneself (e.g., one's motives, intentions, wishes, desires, and fantasies, and defenses against becoming aware of and acknowledging these mental contents) that exist independently of one's current (conscious) construction of oneself and that one can come to know about oneself? What remains of the psychoanalytic project without this assumption?

It is important to note that these questions are critically important even if one questions the therapeutic value of learning about oneself. They also remain germane even while one recognizes the perils, as Gill and others have, of psychoanalytic authoritarianism inherent in the stance that it is the analyst who has special access to those independently existing aspects of the patient that the latter does not yet know about. The critical point here is that the assumption that there are aspects of oneself that exist independently of one's self-constructions is an *ontological* one, to be distinguished from the *epistemological* question of the routes through which one gains knowledge of these independently existing aspects of oneself.

Transference and treatment

Analysis of the transference

The claim that agreement regarding the primacy of analysis of the transference constitutes the "common ground" of psychoanalysis (Wallerstein, 1992) despite other theoretical differences implies one, that different analytic "schools" all mean the same thing when they refer both to transference and analysis of the transference. Neither assumption is, in fact, a valid one. Although the two assumptions are interrelated, I want to focus here on the latter one. Compared to theoretical discussions of transference, there are relatively few discussions of techniques, that is, how one goes about analyzing the transference. Let me describe some of the material available in the literature.

A Freudian perspective

Freud (1916/1917) writes that "we overcome the transference by pointing out to the patient that his feelings do not arise from the present situation and do not apply to the person of the doctor, but that they are repeating something that has happened to him earlier" (pp. 443–444). This approach to analysis of the transference seems didactic and educative, as if simply "pointing out" the presumed genetic origin of the patient's behavior will do the trick.

I recall one patient, E.S., with whom I worked many years ago became enraged whenever I made a genetic transference interpretation. She made clear that she experienced such interpretations as evasions of responsibility for my behavior. In one session in which highly troubling material emerged, E.S. began to cry, reached for a tissue only to find the tissue box empty. She reacted by saying to me angrily: "Why don't you put a sign on your door: Dr. Eagle—no crying here" and accused me of being thoughtless and uncaring. Partly influenced by Kohut's (1984) concept of "optimal failure," I responded: "I am sorry. Perhaps if I had been more thoughtful, I would have noticed that the box was empty." Her rage almost immediately subsided and after a while, entirely on her own, without any interpretation on my part, she herself related her reaction to her early experiences with her parents—thus, on her own, going from the here-and-now to early experiences rather than directly to early experiences.

A self-psychology approach

In Kohut's (1984) discussion of "optimal failure," he suggests that in response to the patient's rage and despair, the analyst acknowledge his or her empathic failure and link the patient's feelings and thoughts to his or her experience of the analyst's failure. In this description of analysis of the transference, Kohut focuses not on genetic links, but on here-and-now interactions between patient and analyst. As for resolution of transference, from a self-psychology perspective, there is no talk of renunciation or sublimation of infantile wishes. Rather, as the patient's self-cohesiveness is strengthened (through the "transmuting internalization" of repeated experiences of "optimal failure" and incremental increases in psychic structure), he or she is able to benefit from the empathic understanding that is realistically available from the analyst and from others outside the clinical situation. As Basch (1986) puts it, the demand for perfect mirroring was never a matter of gratification of infantile wishes, but rather of an individual with self-defects experiencing perfect mirroring as a vital need. Once the self is strengthened, the experienced need for perfect empathic mirroring, rather than being clung to and therefore requiring renunciation and/or sublimation, simply disappears (see Eagle, 1990, for a discussion of the issue of wishes versus needs in self psychology.[7]

In my own clinical experience, I have found that approaching analysis of the transference through calling attention to the links between the patient's feelings and thoughts in relation to the therapist and earlier figures is often experienced by the patient as my being defensive and not owning or taking responsibility for my actions—as if I were communicating something like "It's not me you are reacting to; it's your mother (or father). I didn't do or say anything that warrants your reaction."

Transference in Control–Mastery theory

According to Control–Mastery theory (Silberschatz, 2005; Weiss & Sampson, 1986), a main element of the transference is the patient's fear that he or she will be retraumatized by virtue of the therapist behaving in a manner similar to parental figures, thus serving to reinforce or confirm the patient's pathogenic beliefs. However, also stressed in Control–Mastery theory is the patient's hope that these fears will not be realized in his or her interactions with the therapist, that conditions of safety will obtain, and that experiences with the therapist will serve to disconfirm his or her pathogenic beliefs. Indeed, according to Control–Mastery theory, patients come to treatment with an unconscious plan to present tests to the therapist that, if failed, will serve to realize the patient's "worst fears" and that, if passed, will serve to disconfirm the patient's pathogenic beliefs.

In the context of Control–Mastery theory, the analysis of the transference consists mainly in addressing the patient's experience of the degree to which the therapist has succeeded or failed in recognizing and disconfirming the patient's pathogenic beliefs. Further, confirmation or disconfirmation of the patient's pathogenic beliefs is not limited to interpretation, but includes a wide range of the therapist's behaviors (Eagle, 1993). Implicit in this perspective is the idea that resolution of the transference is facilitated by the patient's experience of the therapist as disconfirming his or her pathogenic belief. In effect and perhaps simplistically, with repeated instances of test-passing, the patient comes to experience the therapist as different from his or her parental figures, particularly with regard to his or her vital strivings.

Transference and gratification

As we know, for many years, analysts have been enjoined from gratifying the patient's wishes. Aside from ethical and other considerations, one main reason for the prohibition again gratification was the argument that abstinence, deprivation, and frustration of the patient's wishes make them more available for analytic work. From Freud on, many analysts were wary of the possible criticism that they are gratifying rather than analyzing the patient's wishes. For example, although departing radically in many ways from Freudian theory, Kohut (1984) goes out of his way to say that, like classical treatment, his treatment approach does not entail gratification. He asks: "Am I not merely describing 'cure through love,' 'cure through being kind,' and the like?" (p. 102). His answer is "no." He also writes that the analyst's communication to the patient of his or her more or less correct understanding "is frustrating, because despite the analyst's understanding of what the patient feels . . . the analyst still does not act in accordance with the patient's need" (pp. 102–103). Kohut's description of the "three-step sequence" of "the nature of the psychoanalytic cure" includes:

(1) need—activation and optimal frustration[8] via (2) *nonfulfillment* (my emphasis) of the need ("abstinence") and (3) substitution of direct need fulfillment with the establishment of a bond of empathy between self and selfobject (pp. 103–104). And then Kohut goes on to assure the reader that "self psychology does not differ from traditional psychoanalysis in its characterization of what is going on between patient and analyst that eventuates in a cure" (p. 104).

It is clear from the above that Kohut is quite concerned that self psychology not be viewed as a heretical-revisionist departure from traditional psychoanalysis, one, to boot, that entails gratification rather than analysis of the transference—surely, a primal sin (I cannot resist the pun) from a traditional perspective. Given the nature of what is presumably gratified in a self-psychology framework, Kohut's concern with the bugaboo of gratification would seem to be unwarranted. From a traditional perspective, what is at issue is the gratification of infantile (sexual and aggressive) wishes, the futile and conflictual pursuit of which are at the core of the patient's neurosis. From this perspective, given its futility and psychic costs, pursuit of gratification needs to be replaced by renunciation and/or sublimation.

However, from a self-psychology perspective, the patient *needs* (rather than wishes), empathic understanding, which, in itself, is not infantile, but rather a lifelong need. Nor is this need either inherently ungratifiable in reality or antithetical to societal demands (as are, e.g., incestuous wishes). Further, the linchpin of a self-psychology theory of treatment is the analyst's provision of empathic understanding and the consequent "establishment of a bond of empathy between self and selfobject" (Kohut, 1984, p. 104). But if the patient *needs* empathic understanding, and if the analyst provides such understanding, then the analyst is surely gratifying that need. I say this, not as a criticism of self psychology, but in the service of noting that it need not be concerned with the issue of gratification. Indeed, self psychology should embrace the fact that the therapeutic approach entails gratification of the patient's need for empathic understanding. For, from a self-psychology perspective, such gratification is a key element in psychoanalytic cure. Further, self psychology can be more assertive insofar as it claims that in a classical as well as a self-psychology analysis, a key element in positive therapeutic outcome is the patient's experience of being empathically understood.

Thus, from a self-psychology perspective, the primary therapeutic consequence of a generally accurate interpretation is not cognitive expansion (insight and awareness), but rather the experience of being empathically understood. This is the truly "heretical" conclusion, not the question of whether gratification of the patient's needs is at the core of the self-psychology conception of treatment. Indeed, it is. But there is nothing to be defensive about in this acknowledgement. It is not as if self psychologists are suggesting the gratification of the infantile sexual and aggressive wishes with which traditional psychoanalysis is concerned. They are proposing the gratification (although, given history and connotation, they deny that this is so) of what is from a self-psychology perspective the vital and legitimate need for empathic understanding, which the patient has every right to expect will be gratified in the treatment. Kohut's (1984) response to the possible criticism that the self-psychology analysts offer a corrective emotional experience was: "so be it." It seems to me that that is also an appropriate response to the criticism that the self-psychology analyst offers gratification of the patient's need for empathic understanding.

Transference and needs versus wishes

In a previous paper, I tried to show that although self psychology places great emphasis on the patient's needs, it also implicitly deals with the patient's wishes even when that is not made explicit, and even when using the language of needs (Eagle, 1990). Recall that in Kohut's account, the patient suffering from self-defects demands perfect mirroring from the selfobject (e.g., the analyst) as a central component of his or her mirroring transference. Similarly, the patient with self-defects presumably experiences the need for merger with an idealized figure in an idealizing transference. Basch (1986, p. 411) describes the self-psychology approach to these transferences in the following way:

> Through interpretation, first of the *need* (i.e., to be perfectly mirrored and/or to merge with an idealized figure) and then of the origin of the need, the analyst offers and empathic bond rather than one based on fulfilling the patient's wish to have the past replayed under more auspicious circumstances.

However, wanting to be perfectly mirrored and/or to merge with an idealized figure are essentially wishes to have the past replaced under more auspicious circumstances. Were being perfectly mirrored and the demand for merging actual needs, one would have to conclude that they are needs that cannot be met, not in this world. Were perfect mirroring an actual need, "good enough" empathic understanding or what Kohut refers to as "optimal frustration" would not especially be therapeutic. Further, if being perfectly mirrored were an actual need, why would interpretation of that need be therapeutically useful, unless, similar to a Freudian perspective in regard to infantile wishes, the aim of the interpretation is to facilitate the renunciation and/or sublimation of the need? However, unlike fantasies and wishes, actual needs are the sort of thing one seeks to meet, not subject them to renunciation and/or sublimation. In short, what Basch refers to as a need is more usefully understood as the patient's wish and fantasy regarding what he or she needs. From this perspective, Kohut's account of "optimal frustration" can be understood in the following way: over time and repeated therapeutic experiences, the patient incrementally learns that he or she can benefit from less than perfect mirroring which enables him or her to give up the fantasy that he or she needs perfect mirroring. What the patient truly needs is the kind of less than perfect understanding that is available in this world. And it is that need that is, indeed, gratified through the analyst's provision of ordinary, "good enough" empathic understanding.

The patient's conviction that he or she requires perfect mirroring is not an actual need, but rather a fantasy that loses some of its force as a consequence of, one, working through the patient's rage and despair in reaction to receiving less than perfect mirroring; and second, the repeated experiences of being able to benefit from "good enough" empathic understanding. Although Kohut may describe this sequence in the language of "optimal frustration" and accretions in psychic structure due to "transmuting internalization," the above description in the language of ordinary discourse is essentially what is taking place. In short, a *wishful fantasy* (i.e., that one needs perfect mirroring) is replaced by a realistic and life-long *need* for "good enough" empathic understanding from people who are significant in one's life.[9]

A few final comments regarding the question of perfect mirroring: There is little or no evidence that the infant or child needs perfect mirroring (or that anyone needs perfect mirroring at any time in one's life). As Winnicott (1960) tells us, "good enough" mothering is likely to represent an adequate facilitating environment for normal development growth. Indeed, there is some evidence that compared to a moderate level of early maternal attunement to the infant, both an excessively low and excessively high level of maternal attunement is associated with insecure attachment rather than secure attachment (Beebe et al., 2010).

It is not uncommon to find that deprived individuals make unrealistic and poignantly futile demands in the very area in which they have been deprived. It is as if, as a function of severe deprivation, these individuals are more prone to developing an unrealistic fantasy of what they need, one that cannot be met in reality. So, I think that Kohut and Basch may be right in linking the demand for perfect mirroring with early deprivation and consequent self-defects. However, it is very likely that such self-defects are not because of the failure to be perfectly mirrored during infancy and childhood, but rather because of the failure to be mirrored in a "good enough" way. Further, such self-defects appear to be associated, not with the actual need for perfect mirroring, but rather with the fantasy that only perfect mirroring will make up for early deprivation and will enable "the past to be replaced under more auspicious circumstances."

Kohut's (1984) own account of "optimal frustration" can be understood in this way. In what is essentially a description of a transference interpretation, Kohut (1984) writes that when the patient reacts with rage and despair to his or her experience of the analyst's less than perfect mirroring ("optimal failure"), the analyst acknowledges his or her contribution and links the patient's rage and despair to the experience of not being perfectly understood. This interpretation is, at one and the same time, both an interpretation of the patient's fantasy regarding what he or she needs from others as well as gratification of the patient's actual need to be understood in ways that are humanly possible. The resolution of the transference takes place in the context of the patient's increasing experience of being able to benefit from ordinary understanding. Because this is something the therapist (as well as others outside treatment) can realistically provide, he or she comes to be experienced more in terms of who he or she actually is and what he or she can actually provide; and less and less as a depriving figure who can provide perfect mirroring, but is unwilling to do so. The irony here is that in demanding perfect mirroring from the analyst, the patient virtually guarantees that the analyst will be experienced by the patient as a depriving figure similar to his or her depriving parental figures. Breaking into the vicious circle would seem to be at the core of the resolution of the transference.

Corrective emotional experience

The concept of corrective emotional experiences and the idea that they can contribute to the resolution of the transference without explicit analysis of the transference has been lurking not too far in the background. Soon after Alexander and French (1946) introduced the concept of corrective emotional experience, it fell into disrepute for a long period of time, largely because it appeared to suggest manipulation of the transference.[10] However, the pariah status of the concept began to change markedly, and over time it has received surprisingly wide acceptance, largely as a function of an increasing emphasis on the therapeutic relationship itself as a core ingredient of therapeutic action. We find Kohut (1984) saying in response to the anticipated criticism that his theory of therapeutic action is essentially a theory of corrective emotional experience: "If an ill-disposed critic now gleefully told me that I have finally shown my true colors and . . . demonstrated that I both believe in the curative effect of the 'corrective emotional experience' and equate such experience with analysis, I could only reply: so be it" (p. 78).

We also find Control–Mastery theorists writing about modification of unconscious pathogenic beliefs as a function of the analyst passing tests set by the patient, *with or without interpretation*. Experiencing the analyst as passing a vital test is a quintessential example of a corrective emotional experience; and the positive therapeutic effects of test-passing, particularly without interpretation, is a quintessential example of the link between corrective emotional experiences and positive therapeutic outcome.

And as a final example of the respectability and implicit acceptance of the concept of corrective emotional experience, one can point to the comfort many analysts experience in accepting Fairbairn's (1952) emphasis on the importance of the analyst as a "good" object as an essential ingredient in psychoanalytic treatment. However, one understands the idea of what is entailed in the patient experiencing the analyst as a "good" object, it will surely include, directly or indirectly, corrective emotional experiences.

An implication of Alexander and French's (1946) concept of corrective emotional experience is that explicit analysis of the transference may or may not be present, but is not a necessary component of psychoanalytic treatment. The essence of therapeutic action for Alexander and French (1946) lies primarily in the fact that because the therapist does not behave in accord with the patient's maladaptive expectations (which are based on early experiences with parents), these expectations are subject to *extinction* over time. I intentionally employ the conditioning term "extinction" to make it clear that Alexander and French's (1946) account of the therapeutic effects of corrective emotional experiences does not require transference interpretations. In some respects, it is an account of conditioned responses and experiences that do not reinforce these expectations.[11]

As for *resolution* of the transference, there is the clear implication in Alexander and French's (1946) formulation that such resolution is a natural by-product of corrective emotional experience, that is, the automatic consequence of the extinction of maladaptive expectations in relation to the therapist. If transference consists mainly in expecting the therapist to behave like one's parents, then it surely follows that the extinction of those expectations is equivalent to resolution of the transference.

A similar logic also applies to Control–Mastery theory and self psychology. With regard to the former, resolution of the transference is a by-product of the therapist's test-passing and disconfirmation of the patient's unconscious pathogenic beliefs. As for self psychology, with the repeated experiences of "optimal failure" and consequent strengthening of self-cohesiveness, the patient's transference-based demand for perfect mirroring abates and he or she learns to avail himself or herself of what one might refer to as the "good enough" empathic understanding that is realistically available in this world. As Basch (1986) argues, the demands for perfect mirroring are the product of the patient's "faulty structures;" and once these structures are "repaired," these demands no longer play a prominent role in the patient's needs and motivations.

In this sense, whatever other similarities there may be between the Freudian idea that the patient seeks the gratification of infantile wishes which, at some level, is experienced as pleasurable and the Kohutian concept of archaic demands for perfect mirroring from the therapist, an important difference between them lies in Basch's (1986) claim that the archaic demand for perfect mirroring is not a matter of the patient seeking pleasurable gratification, that he or she does not want to give up, but rather is a product of a patient with self-defects who experiences perfect mirroring as a vital need. Further, once self-defects are "repaired," there is no pleasurable gratification the patient needs to give up; perfect mirroring from the therapist or anyone else is no longer experienced as a vital need (see Eagle, 1991, for a further discussion of this issue). In short, as with Control–Mastery theory, for self psychology too, resolution of the transference is a by-product of other processes, in the latter case, of strengthening of self-cohesiveness.

The issue of "transference cure"

Positive therapeutic outcomes judged to be based primarily on the therapeutic relationship or corrective emotional experiences were often dismissively referred to as merely "transference cures" (e.g., Oremland, 1972). That is, in contrast to "cures" based on lifting of defenses, insight, interpretation, awareness, resolution of conflict, and so on, "transference cures" based on corrective emotional experiences in the therapeutic relationship were deemed to be superficial, less long lasting, and essentially nonpsychoanalytic, primarily because they were based not on analysis and resolution of the transference, but rather on a continued maintenance of the transference. Indeed, the assumption was made that because the therapeutic improvement seen in transference cures was dependent on maintaining the relationship with the therapist, there was great risk that it would disappear once the relationship with the therapist was terminated. Such an assumption, however, was based on theoretical supposition rather than actual data.

From the above perspective of transference cures, it would follow that therapeutic improvement following the therapist's test-passing without interpretation and disconfirmation of the patient's pathogenic beliefs reported by Control–Mastery theorists, as well as therapeutic improvement following the therapist's empathic understanding reported by Kohut would be viewed as transference cures and essentially nonpsychoanalytic.

Some years ago, I published a paper in which I reported the dramatic disappearance of a patient's troubling and chronic symptom following an interaction in the treatment that I understood partly as my test-passing and the consequent disconfirmation of a pathogenic belief (Eagle, 1993). This took place without my interpretation of the nature of our interaction. One of the discussants of my paper, Gill (1993), took me to task for not analyzing the transference. I intuitively felt then and continue to feel that it made therapeutic sense to allow my interaction with the patient to remain implicit and let it speak for itself; and that making an explicit interpretation of the nature of our interaction would detract from its therapeutic impact.

When I presented this case at a psychoanalytic meeting, the general reaction was that the dramatic disappearance of the patient's symptom was the result of a transference cure, with the implication that the symptom would therefore return or be replaced by a substitute symptom. I received annual Christmas letters from the patient over many years and therefore had information on how her life was going. Not only had her symptom not returned, but her life in general had improved markedly following the disappearance of her symptom.

I think that, based on our theoretical assumptions, such as the inevitability of symptom substitution, we tend to overlook those instances in which symptom amelioration is followed, not by symptom substitution, but by improved ego functioning and more gratifying object relations. In short, the concept of transference cure as a means of accounting for positive therapeutic outcome in the relative absence of analysis of the transference needs reexamination. As far as I know, there is little or no empirical evidence supporting that account.

Empirical research on transference

Introduction

There are two main bodies of research on transference. One is the experimental investigation of transference and transference-like processes outside the therapeutic situation, which is associated with the work of social and personality psychologists such as Andersen and her colleagues, and Baldwin and his colleagues; and the other deals with transference processes in the clinical situation. The experimental laboratory studies largely investigate the following issues:

1. The effects of representations of significant others on one's experience of a new person, an area of research that is most directly related to the concept of transference.

2. The effects of activating different representations of significant others (e.g., approving versus disapproving) on self-evaluations.
3. The effects of self-evaluations (e.g., high versus low self-esteem) on one's expectations with regard to significant others.
4. The effects of presumably stable relational or interactional schemas (e.g., attachment patterns) on one's expectations with regard to significant others.

The second body of research consists largely of two types of investigations. One deals with the relationship between transference interpretations and therapeutic process and outcome; and the other with the question of the degree of overlap of relationship themes related to the therapist and to significant others outside the treatment situation—a question central to a basic assumption underlying the psychoanalytic conception of transference. There is also some early research on the resolution of transference. In addition to discussing these areas of research, I will also discuss the very few personal accounts available on different transference patterns established by the same individual with two different analysts.

Experimental studies of transference: effects of representations of significant others on experience of a new person

Baum and Andersen (1999) define transference "in terms of the activation and application of a significant-other representation to a new person" (p. 161). A main thrust of the work of Andersen and her colleagues is to demonstrate the existence, indeed, the ubiquitousness, of transference in ordinary social perception and interactions. According to their model, we store representations of significant others, which can be activated and applied to a new person, with the result that the new person is perceived and remembered "as having qualities that he or she does not possess because these qualities describe the significant other" (Andersen et al., 1995, p. 41). In a number of studies by Andersen and her colleagues, the experimental measure of transference was operationally defined as participants falsely remembering as belonging to a target person a description they had given of a significant other. This reflects the inference that the individual has attributed to a new person some characteristics of his or her representations of significant others. It should be noted that transference is defined in these studies in terms of false memory rather than direct attributions in an interactional encounter.

Andersen and her colleagues have not only demonstrated the role of transference—as they define it—in social perception and interaction, but have also reported a series of findings that shed light on some factors that influence transference. In one study, Andersen and Cole (1990) demonstrated that compared to a control group, individuals who are given information about a target person that resembles their own significant other, show more false-positive memory responses to the target person that are consistent with their representation of their significant other.

In another study, Andersen et al. (1995) not only replicated the above results, but also found that compared to a no-prime condition, priming the representation of the participant's significant other (through a subliminal stimulus) led to greater false-positive memory in relation to the target person. Another important finding reported was that although priming and similarity between significant other representation and target person additively increase false memory, neither is necessary to produce it.

Based on these findings, Andersen et al. (1995) conclude that transference responses are influenced by two factors that operate additively: first, the chronic accessibility of significant-other representations that are applied to a new person; and second, the degree of resemblance between characteristics of the significant other and the new person. With regard to the former, Andersen et al. (1995) write that "the significant-other representation does indeed appear to be applied to virtually any new other even when the new other does not completely resemble the significant other" (p. 53). This latter finding is especially important in the therapeutic situation where there may be little actual similarity between the target person (i.e., the therapist) and representations of significant others.

And indeed, there is some research suggesting that the individual's chronically accessible representations and expectations of significant others, which presumably underlie different attachment patterns, are transferred onto the therapist (e.g., Mallinckrodt et al., 2005; Parish & Eagle, 2003). For example, the representation of the attachment figure as rejecting and unavailable characteristic of an avoidant individual is likely to be reflected in the individual's perceptions and expectations in relation to the therapist as well as other significant others (e.g., spouse) in his or her life.

Research on the effects of representations of significant others on self-evaluation

In the above studies, the focus is on the effects of representations of significant others on one's experience of a new person. In the studies to be discussed below, the effects of the representations of significant others on self-evaluations is investigated. In one study, Baldwin et al. (1990) reported that graduate students were more critical of their research performance following subliminal exposure to a picture of their departmental chair scowling in disapproval.

In a similar study, Kumashiro and Sedikides (2005) found that activating (through visualization) a close positive, a close negative, or neutral relationship had differential effects on respondents' willingness to receive negative feedback on their performance. The authors conclude that activating "close positive relationships function[s] as a psychological resource that bolsters the self against feedback about a newly discovered liability" (p. 370). Using a similar design, Miranda et al. (2013) reported that implicit activation of a representation of a loved-but-rejecting significant other through interaction with a new person resembling that significant other resulted in increases in depressed mood and self-descriptions characterized by a sense of rejection, but only for individuals who showed preexisting symptoms for depression.

There have been a number of studies on what has been referred to as "relational selves" (Andersen & Chen, 2002). That is, there is evidence that our sense of who we are, including our self-esteem, our self-evaluations, and our self-attributes, is associated with different specific significant others and therefore can vary as a function of the activation of different significant others. Thus, in contrast to other activations, activation of representations of, say, a friend may result in a different set of self-evaluations. Further, other variables may also influence this relationship. As we have seen, the attitude of the significant other (e.g., approving versus disapproving) as well as how important the particular significant other is to us will also influence the effects of activations of representations of significant others on self-evaluations.

In a much discussed study, Baldwin et al. (1990) presented a subliminal image of a disapproving Pope John Paul II to practicing Catholic female undergraduate students who immediately afterward were asked to read a sexually provocative passage. Compared to Catholic women who received a subliminal image of a disapproving stranger or no subliminal image at all, those women who had the subliminal exposure of a disapproving Pope John Paul II reported significantly lower self-evaluations. However, the effect of the Pope prime on self-evaluations was entirely accounted for by those Catholic women who viewed themselves as highly involved in their religion, that is, for these women "for whom the Pope presumably would be a highly significant evaluative authority" (p. 446).

One of the questions that arises is the relative roles of the subliminal prime and reading the sexually provocative passages. It is possible that the same results would have been obtained even if the participants did not read the sexually provocative passage. That is, would the subliminal prime of the image of the disapproving Pope *in itself* have led to lower self-evaluations compared to the two control groups? It is also possible that for practicing Catholic women, reading sexually provocative passages would, in itself, through say, the activation of guilt and shame, result in lower self-evaluation without any prime. Because we have no information of base rate level of self-evaluation, we do not know whether simply reading the sexually provocative passage led to lower self-evaluation for all participants, but to a greater degree for those participants who were primed with the disapproving Pope. In other words, the design of the study does not allow one to assess the separate effects on self-evaluation of reading the sexually provocative passage and the subliminal prime.

According to Baldwin et al. (1990), the subliminal exposure of the disapproving Pope stimulus "served to activate an ingrained relational schema of disapproval by an authority figure . . . for their improper act of reading sexually-charged passages" (p. 55), which, in turn, resulted in lower self-evaluation. In other words, a subliminal stimulus of a disapproving significant other (e.g., the Pope), through the presumed activation of the ingrained relational schema or interpersonal script of disapproval by an authority figure, can lower self-evaluation, but only for those individuals for whom the subliminal stimulus is a significant figure.

It has been proposed that individuals' feelings of self-worth will be especially influenced by their performance in the domain in which a valued significant other wants them to excel. And, indeed, there is evidence that this is so. Horberg and Chen (2010) carried out a series of studies on feelings of self-worth as a function of a number of factors. In one study, they assessed the domain in which the participants staked their self-worth.

Several weeks later, they were subliminally primed with FATHER or, as a control, POSTMAN. They also rated the extent to which father cared about their success in 14 domains, 6 of which were the domains in which participants staked their self-worth. Participants also rated how close they want to be with their father. The results showed that when participants desired closeness with father, subliminal priming of father led to greater staking of self-worth in the domain that father deemed important.

In Study 2, in a design similar to Study 1, participants were given success versus failure feedback in a Competition domain. The results showed that in contrast to the control POSTMAN condition, in the FATHER primed condition, those participants who desired closeness to father and received success feedback reported higher self-worth. Surprisingly, failure feedback did not lead to lower self-worth.

Study 3 repeated Study 2 in a different domain—Appearance—and primed the name of a significant other who cared about their appearance. They were also subjected to a failure induction in the Appearance domain. Participants also rated their feelings of closeness as well as how accepted they felt in relation to the significant other they named. A number of findings emerged. However, the ones most relevant in the present context include: first, the finding that desired closeness to the significant other negatively predicted self-worth in the prime condition, but not in the control condition; and second, the finding that participants who strongly desire closeness to the significant other show not only decreases in feelings of self-worth following failure in a domain important to that significant other, but also decreases in feelings of closeness and acceptance in these relationships.

Effects of self and relational schemas on representations of others

Baldwin and Keelan (1999) reported that whereas individuals high in self-esteem endorsed expectations of being able to elicit friendly and accepting reactions in others, individuals low in self-esteem were pessimistic regarding their ability to generate positive reactions in others. It is very likely that these different sets of expectations will carry over to interactions with significant others, including the therapist. Furthermore, as Sakellarapoulo and Baldwin (2006) point out, these different sets of expectations individuals may have generate different behavioral cues that are likely to elicit in others the very reactions that they expect. In contrast to individuals with high self-esteem, where one can speak of a "benevolent cycle," this situation is likely to generate the kind of vicious and self-defeating cycle noted by Sakellarapoulo and Baldwin (2006) and described by Wachtel (2014).

One is reminded here of the poignant findings reported by Jacobsen and Wille (1984). They found that although insecurely attached toddlers make as many social overtures to potential playmates as securely attached toddlers, they are rejected significantly more frequently. Although not measured, there must be some behavioral cues emitted by the insecurely attached children that account for the fact that they are more frequently rejected. This is a fertile area for future research. The point to be emphasized here is that the repeated experience of rejection is likely to elicit cues in others that serve to reinforce the very set of expectations (i.e., of being rejected) that the insecurely attached children had already formed.

One is also reminded of the Dodge et al. (1994) findings of an interaction effect between early physical punishment and the development of a hostile attributional style in predicting aggressive behavior in adolescence. What these findings suggest is that if one enters a situation expecting hostility from others, one will be more likely to emit behavioral cues that will elicit from others the very hostility that is expected—another instance in which a maladaptive interpersonal script generates a self-fulfilling vicious cycle.

The significance of these findings for psychoanalysis lies not only in their relevance to the issue of transference (i.e., the individual transfers onto the therapist and other significant figures expectations based on early interactions), but also to the interaction between transference and countertransference. The nature of a vicious cycle is that it not only reinforces a maladaptive self-schema (e.g., low self-esteem), but also does so through eliciting in others the very reactions that one fears will occur. Although the issue of vicious cycles is much discussed in the research on interpersonal scripts and relational schemas, as far as I know, there is very little research on actual interactions between individuals, including how the other reacts when certain characteristics and expectations are attributed to him or her. Thus, although vicious cycles are inferred, there is little research demonstrating the specifics of how they develop and operate. As Sakellaroupolo and Baldwin (2006) note with regard to research in this area, "a dialogical component to interpersonal cognition is essentially lacking" (p. 63).

There is a good deal of empirical research dealing with representations of self–other interactions referred to as "relational schemas" and "interpersonal scripts" rather than simply representations of significant others or self-evaluations. Although the former work is carried out and discussed in the context of "interpersonal cognition" and with little reference to transference, it is, nevertheless, quite relevant to transference issues. As Baldwin (1992), one of the leading researchers in this area, notes, interpersonal scripts are comprised of self-schemas and other schemas connected to each other and include learned if–then contingency expectations that generate specific sets of feelings. For example, according to attachment theory and research, the IWM underlying anxious attachment (or, on AAI classification, enmeshed/preoccupied) includes a representation or schema of the other as inconsistent and unavailable, a representation or schema of the self as unworthy and at constant risk of abandonment, and associated effects of fear and, not infrequently, rage.

It will be noted that concepts such as the internal working models (Bowlby, 1973), representations of interactions generalized (RIGs) (Stern, 1985), interactional patterns (Beebe & Lachmann, 2002), relational configurations (Mitchell, 1988), pathogenic beliefs (Weiss & Sampson, 1986), and habitual relationship patterns (Schachter, 2001) can all be viewed as instances of relational schemas and interpersonal scripts. They all include self, other, and interactional schemas, if–then contingency expectations, and accompanying strong affects. Furthermore, they can all be understood as transference phenomena in the important sense that they entail the transfer of early patterns to contemporary others. More specifically, they all involve the attributions of characteristics and expectations associated with early significant others to contemporary significant others (e.g., therapist, spouse, boss). In one illustrative study, Baldwin et al. (1993) found that individuals' attachment patterns predicted their endorsement of different interpersonal scripts. For example, avoidantly attached individuals were more likely to endorse a script in which trusting their partner would result in being hurt.

Baldwin and Meunier (1999) conditioned participants' visualization of relationships in which they felt contingently versus noncontingently accepted by an other to different tones. These conditioned tones were played in the background while participants engaged in a lexical decision task involving if–then contingencies of acceptance and rejection. Different effects were found depending on the participants' "chronic attachment patterns" (p. 209). More specifically, when presented with a cue conditioned to a contingent relationship, preoccupied participants showed the activation of acceptance contingencies. Thus, just as the finding (Miranda et al., 2013) that a stable predisposing factor (dysphoria) interacting with activation of a representation of a significant other influenced self-evaluations, so similarly did Baldwin and Meunier (1999) find that a presumably stable predisposing factor (attachment pattern) interacting with activation of a representation of a significant other influenced if–then expectations in relation to others.

In still another example of an interaction effect between stable predispositions and activation of schemas, in a study on social anxiety. Baldwin and Main (2001) paired distinctive tones with thoughts of either social acceptance or rejection. Female participants then interacted with a male confederate while either one of the tones or a control tone was sounded repeatedly. Level of reported social anxiety was a function of the interaction between the nature of the tone (i.e., acceptance or rejection) sounded and level of self-consciousness. Highly self-conscious participants were more affected by the cues than low self-conscious participants.

Effect of transference on willingness to disclose, hostility, and goal persistence

Berk and Andersen (2008) have carried out an ingenious study that deals with many nuances of transference. They reported the following findings:

1. When a new person is described as resembling a significant other, the new person is remembered by participants as having features of the significant other, even when these features were not part of the description of the new person. In other words, as has been shown in other studies, transference occurs.
2. When the new person who resembles a significant other who is described by the participant as not satisfying his or goal of receiving affection, the participant is less willing to seek intimacy with the new person or self-disclose to that person. The opposite occurs when the new person resembles a significant other from whom the participant has received

affection. These findings are especially relevant to the clinical situation where disclosing intimate details about oneself is expected.

3. Participants also showed greater hostility toward the new person who resembled the significant other associated with not receiving affection.
4. After being told that producing a large number of responses on the Unusual Uses [of objects] test would increase the likelihood of being liked by the new person, when the new person resembled the non-satisfying significant other, participants persisted longer in the task compared to the condition in which the new person resembled the satisfying significant other.
5. When the new person resembled a significant other who was a non-satisfying family member, hostility toward the new person was significantly associated with persistence in the Universal Uses test. The opposite occurred when the new person resembled a satisfying family member. The authors interpret these findings as indicating anger at not receiving affection combined with persistence in trying to get that affection—certainly, a familiar clinical pattern.

The study raises interesting questions and suggests future research. For example, it is not uncommon to observe clinically the following pattern: first, the patient initially describes in the treatment an early significant figure very loving, but with the suggestion of overprotectiveness and indulgence; and second, the patient (usually male, in my experience) complains that his current partner is not sufficiently loving and caring. What often becomes clear in the course of treatment is that the patient's complaints about his partner are, in effect, complaints that she does not indulge him the way his mother did—although, of course, the patient does not express it this way. Further, part of the clinical picture includes: first, the patient's persistence in trying to get his partner to satisfy "needs" presumably met by mother; and second, hostility that accompanies the persistence, a pattern quite similar to the one shown by the participants in the Berk and Andersen (2008) study.

It would be interesting to determine in future research whether a subclass of individuals who describe their early significant other as providing affection, but also present evidence of overprotection and indulgence, would behave in the same way as the participants in the Berk and Andersen (2008) study who report their need for affection not being met. Such a study would be relevant to testing Freud's (1905[1901]) hypothesis that both over-deprivation and over-gratification are conducive to fixation, when that is understood in the following way: over-deprivation leads the individual to constantly seek to gratify a need of which she or he was deprived; and overgratification makes it difficult for the individual to relinquish the experience of being indulged. Thus, in both the cases the individual reacts to the transference figure with both hostility and persistence in trying to get him or her to gratify an early need or wish. In the case of over-deprivation, the individual's hostility is generated by the expectation that the transference figure will behave in a manner that is *similar* to his or her early significant other; and in the case of over-gratification, the individual's hostility is generated by the expectation that, at least in one area, the transference figure will behave in a manner *different from* his or her early significant other. Both have in common the expectation that the transference figure will not satisfy their experienced need or wish and both, therefore, react with hostility to the transference figure and persistence in seeking to have their experienced needs and wishes met.

Naturalistic studies of transference in the clinical situation

In the previous section, I discussed experimental research outside the clinical situation that demonstrate the role of transference in social perception and that investigated the factors that influence transference. In this section, I discuss research on transference and the therapeutic situation. Although, in accord with social psychological research, we think of transference as a phenomenon of everyday life, cutting across clinical and nonclinical situations, the fact is that the concept of transference arose in the psychoanalytic therapeutic situation and it is in that context that one should be best able to investigate its vicissitudes. Unlike the experimental work on transference described in the previous section, the research described below deals with transference in the therapeutic situation.

Degree of overlap between relationship themes in relation to therapist and in relation to other people

Luborsky and Crits-Christoph (1990, 1998) have carried out extensive work in an attempt to validate Freud's observations about transference through the use of the Core Conflict Relationship Theme (CCRT) method. The CCRT measure analyzes narratives or reported relationship episodes (primarily in the therapeutic situation) in terms of the individual's wishes or wants in relation to other people (wish, W), how other people react (Response from Other, RO), and how one reacts to these reactions (Response of Self, RS). According to Luborsky and Crits-Christoph (1990), "The CCRT looks much like Freud's (1912a) transference template" (p. 2).

The evidence they adduce in support of this statement is limited to reporting a parallel between, first, the patient's CCRT in relation to therapist and in relation to other people; and second, between the individual's CCRT in relation to memory of events about early parental figures and CCRT in relation to other people. Although Luborsky and Crits-Christoph's (1990) book is entitled *Understanding Transference*, it is mainly concerned with the CCRT method.

Do those findings provide support for the Freudian conception of transference? Before addressing this question, it would be useful to cite Luborsky and Crits-Christoph's (1990) definition of a transference template: "Transference template is a central relationship pattern that serves as a prototype, a schema for shaping subsequent relationships" (p. 252). Consider the first set of findings regarding the parallel between CCRT to therapist and to other people.

In one study first reported in the Luborsky and Crits-Christoph (1990) book and then reported in a separate paper, grandly entitled "The first empirical demonstration of transference in psychotherapy," employing the CCRT method, Fried et al. (1992) investigated the similarity between themes expressed in patients' narratives about their therapists and in narratives about others in their life. Degree of similarity was measured in the following way: Employing a 1 to 7 scale, judges who were unaware of which pairs were matched or unmatched were asked to rate degree of similarity between relationship themes expressed by patients in their therapist narratives and relationship themes expressed in their other person narratives (correctly matched pairs). The judges also rated degree of similarity of themes between therapist narratives and themes in other person narratives for randomly chosen cases (mismatched pairs). Averaging all three components of the CCRT, the mean similarity rating for correctly matched pairs was 3.5 and 3.0 for mismatched pairs, a statistically significant difference, but hardly an impressive one that would warrant the confident and assertive title of the paper. Indeed, the results could just as readily be read as not supporting strong claims regarding the overlap of relationship themes of therapist and other people. Further, although the ratings for the matched and mismatched pairs on the wish (W) and RS components were significantly different from each other, the ratings for the matched and mismatched pairs on the RO were not significantly different from each other. This negative finding is especially important insofar as an essential component of transference is experiencing the new person (i.e., the therapist) as behaving in ways similar to representations of significant others. Indeed, the RO component of the CCRT is the one most closely related to transference.

Employing a similar methodology as the above study, Connolly et al. (2000) reported that 33 percent of patients showed a significant relationship between their pretreatment main cluster profile (of interpersonal themes) and therapist profile; and 44 percent showed a significant relation between any cluster profile and therapist profile. Across the entire sample or 18 patients, the correlations between main cluster profiles and therapist profiles ranged from (.23 to .69 with a median of .14. As the authors note, "It is noteworthy that over 50 percent of patients did not reveal any significant relation between their pretreatment interpersonal theme and the theme described in narratives about the therapist" (p. 365). Neither this nor the previous Fried et al. (1992) study provides compelling evidence that the development of transference, at least when it is defined in terms of overlap of therapist themes and themes of others, is inevitable in psychodynamically oriented psychotherapy.

There are other problems with the assertion that the findings represent "the first empirical demonstration of transference in psychotherapy." For one thing, as the authors themselves note, patients' explicit narratives about the therapist do not tell us much about the kinds of more subtle behaviors that are taken by clinicians as expressions of transference. Second, there are plausible and more parsimonious explanations of the results than invoking transference. The main finding is that there is a modest degree of consistency across relationship themes (on the components of wish and response from self) in relation to therapist and to others. But, without appealing to the concept of transference, this is just what one would expect based on the hypothesis that at least some personality traits are relatively consistent across situations.

One has to ask whether and to what degree explanatory power is added by invoking transference. Thus, for example, if I am generous (or stingy) toward my therapist and also generous (or stingy) toward others in my life, in what way does that represent the process of transference? One needs to at least address that question. Or as an example closer to the CCRT measure, in what way does, say, my wish to be treated with respect by my therapist and also by others in my life involve transference? I am not suggesting that this question cannot be addressed. My point is that it needs to be addressed before one invokes transference as an explanatory concept or interprets this similarity between response to therapist and other as a demonstration of transference. One can question whether defining transference simply and entirely in terms of a modest similarity between expression of wishes and response from self in relation to therapist and others really captures the essence of what is meant by transference.

The essence of transference is transferring representations of relationship patterns acquired early in life onto current important figures including one's therapist, with the result that one's experience and expectations of current figures is shaped by these representations. Even if the results were more robust, simply demonstrating a general similarity between, say, the patient's wishes toward therapists and toward others outside the therapeutic situation hardly captures that essence. Further, there is no evidence presented that a "transference template" shapes subsequent relationships. If one defines transference too loosely, then any consistency in an individual's relationship patterns would be called transference, diluting and trivializing the concept.

I think the theoretical and clinical relevance of research on transference would be enhanced if one focused on certain sets of wishes and wants as well as expected response from others that, according to particular theories, are especially implicated in transference. For example, according to Freudian theory, one would expect that it is especially infantile wishes that are transferred onto the therapist. Or, as another example, according to self psychology, certain patients transfer onto the therapist a wish for perfect mirroring. Further, both sets of wishes are characterized by, first, their roots in the individual's relationship to parental figures in his or her early life; second, their impossibility of fulfillment; third, their role in psychopathology; and fourth, generally their subtle and indirect rather than direct expressions.

I am aware that such research is extremely difficult to carry out and that one, therefore, does what one can do. However, I think it is important to delineate and clarify the ways in which the findings support as well as fail to support, or are irrelevant to, the psychoanalytic concept of transference rather than alter and dilute the concept so that it is barely recognizable and then conclude that the findings support the originally formulated concept of transference. It would be useful to think of the research in this area as dealing with "something like" transference and then articulate how "something like" transference is understood and the ways in which the psychoanalytic concept has been modified.

I want to note that whatever the limitations of the CCRT research with regard to transference, as the work of Luborsky and his colleagues over many years has shown, the CCRT method has proved to be an important approach in research on the relationship themes both in and outside the therapeutic situation.

Transference interpretations and therapeutic outcome

As Ogrodniczuk et al. (1999) observe, "transference interpretations are one of the distinguishing features of dynamically oriented psychotherapy" (p. 571) and are widely considered to be "a core active ingredient" in psychoanalytic treatment (Hoglend et al., 2011, p. 697). Indeed, according to many analysts, whatever its other features, if a treatment takes account of and interprets transference and resistance, it can be considered a psychoanalytic treatment. Further, since Freud's writings on the topic and Strachey's (1934) classic paper, the received psychoanalytic wisdom has been that transference interpretations constitute the key component of psychoanalytic treatment and the key factor in therapeutic action. Some psychoanalytic theorists have come close to taking the position that non-transference interpretations are therapeutically futile and ineffective (e.g., Gill, 1994; Levine, 1997). And others have advised analysts, as a matter of analytic listening and technique, to take the perspective that virtually everything the patient says should be heard as a direct or indirect allusion to the transference (e.g., Gill, 1982; Levine, 1997). We are all familiar with the plausible—even convincing—theoretical arguments for the assumption that transference interpretations should play a special therapeutic role: for example, they deal with the here-and-now; they have emotional immediacy which is conducive to conviction and emotional insight; one cannot slay a dragon *en effigie*; only transference interpretations speak to the transference neurosis; and so on.

Despite the axiomatic status of the assumption of a special therapeutic role of transference interpretations and despite the plausibility of the above arguments, until recently, there has been little empirical evidence investigating that assumption. Indeed, because the assumption is so axiomatic, so central to a psychoanalytic conception of psychoanalytic treatment, and because the theoretical arguments have seemed so convincing to many, the special therapeutic role of transference interpretations has remained largely unquestioned, as if there were no need for empirical evidence. Further, I suspect that even if some analysts, particularly beginning analysts, did not focus near exclusively on transference interpretations, they would be reluctant to publicize it for fear that they would not be seen as a "real analyst."

So, what do the few studies that have been carried out tell us about the relationship between transference interpretations and therapeutic outcome? Before discussing the findings of these studies, it is important to note that most of them, not all, dealt with short-term dynamic psychotherapy. Hence, although the findings of these studies may be of interest in their own right, their implications for long-term psychoanalytic treatment are questionable. After all, it is long-term treatment that is the original context for psychoanalytic formulations of transference and of the relationship between transference interpretations and therapeutic process and outcome.

There is some evidence that the presence and intensity of transference may vary with duration of treatment as well as the frequency of sessions (Parish & Eagle, 2003). If this is so, it might well be the case that the effects of transference interpretations vary with duration of treatment. I am aware that some forms of brief psychodynamic therapy expressly focus on transference and transference interpretations. However, this may be an unwarranted and ineffective application of the use of transference interpretations.

A number of studies focusing on a wide range of disorders have shown an inverse relationship between frequency of transference interpretations and favorable therapeutic outcome in short-term psychodynamic psychotherapy (e.g., Connolly et al., 1999; Hoglend, 1993, 1996; Piper et al., 1991; Ryum et al., 2010). In one study dealing with patients diagnosed with avoidant personality disorder, a concentration on interpretive techniques (not just but including transference interpretations) in early sessions was associated with negative outcome as well as patient–therapist disaffiliative interactions (Schut et al., 2005). Further, therapists who persisted with interpretations had more hostile interactions with their patients.

A number of interaction effects have also been reported. For example, in the Ryum et al. (2010) study, a greater emphasis on transference interacting with lower therapeutic alliance was associated with poorer therapeutic outcome. McCullough et al. (1991) reported that transference interpretations followed by patient's affect was associated with improvement. However, this study was limited by a small sample size ($N = 16$). After reviewing the literature on transference interpretations with personality disorder patients, Ogrodniczuk and Piper (1999) arrived at the following three conclusions: (1) a strong therapeutic alliance is necessary for successful exploration of transference; (2) transference interpretations should be balanced with supportive work; and (3) the patient's quality of object relations and ability to work within the transference should be considered in making transference interpretations.

In a study limited by the sample size ($N = 15$), Hoglend (1996) reported that for personality disorder patients judged unsuitable for transference work, a high number of transference interpretations was associated with a negative therapeutic outcome. In the 1993 study by Hoglend referred to above with neurotic and major depressive disorder patients, frequency of transference interpretations was inversely related to long-term outcome two and four years after therapy termination for those patients with a history of high-quality interpersonal relations. This finding not only contradicts the received wisdom that less-disturbed patients (i.e., higher level of ego and interpersonal functioning) are more likely to benefit from transference interpretations, but also the finding reported by Connolly et al. (1999) that "high levels of transference interpretations were significantly associated with poor treatment outcome for patients with poor interpersonal functioning" (p. 485). It needs to be noted that the transference interpretations in the Connolly et al. study were made in early sessions of the treatment. It is possible that the impact of transference interpretations varies with their timing in the treatment.

In an important study with a relatively large sample ($N = 100$), employing a randomized design, and with a one-year treatment duration, Hoglend et al. (2006) assigned patients to a condition with a moderate level of transference interpretations and to one with no transference interpretations. There were no differences in outcome between the two groups. However, transference interpretations were more helpful for patients with poor object relations. As Hoglend et al. note, this finding is "contrary to mainstream clinical thinking" (p. 1745), but is consistent with reports by Piper et al. (1991) and Hoglend (1993) as well as an early finding of the Menninger project (Kernberg et al., 1972) that patients with ego weakness responded better to therapy with transference interpretations than to supportive therapy. As Hoglend et al. (2006) also note, the usefulness of transference interpretations with more disturbed patients is consistent with the effective use of transference focused therapy (TFP), an outgrowth of the Menninger project, with borderline patients (e.g., Clarkin et al., 1999).

Unlike most of the studies in this area, which focused on brief psychotherapy, the Hoglend et al. study of a one-year duration of treatment provided sufficient time for transference to develop, a factor that would seem to give their findings greater ecological validity. Hence, the main effect finding of no significant differences in therapeutic outcome between the modest level of transference interpretations group and no transference interpretations group is especially important insofar as it calls into question the widely accepted—virtually axiomatic—assumption in the psychoanalytic literature that transference interpretations constitute *the* indispensable ingredient of therapeutic action.

Analyzing additional data from the Hoglend et al. (2006) study, Johansson et al. (2010) reported on follow-up one year and three years post-treatment as well as the mediating role of insight in therapeutic outcome. With regard to the former, the positive effect of transference interpretations on interpersonal functioning for patients with a history of poor object relations held at three years posttreatment. For patients with high-quality object relations, there continued to be no differences in outcome for the transference interpretations and no transference interpretation conditions.

As for the relationship among transference interpretations, insight, and therapeutic outcome, the mediating effect of transference interpretations on insight increased with lower scores for quality of object relations. In other words, insight "explains a substantial proportion of the long-term effects of . . . transference interpretation in psychotherapy" (p. 445)—but only for patients with a relatively poor quality of object relations. Another important finding is that changes in insight occurred prior to improved functioning, ruling out the possibility that improved functioning led to increased insight.

I want to call attention to one finding that the authors mention in passing. Within the low-quality object relations transference group, a significant negative correlation was found between number of transference interpretations and outcome ($r = -.56$). The authors do not make much of this finding because, as they point out, "within group correlations may lead to erroneous conclusions about the effects of transference interpretations" (p. 446) and do not warrant conclusions about causal effects. That is, of course, true. For example, the negative correlation between number of transference interpretations and outcome may be because of a third unidentified factor. However, given the body of studies on the relationship between transference interpretations and therapeutic outcome, I do not think the finding should be ignored. At the very least, it adds to the skepticism—as do the major findings of the Johansson et al. (2010) study—regarding the received wisdom that transference interpretations are a necessary and indispensable ingredient of successful therapeutic outcome or that the more transference interpretations the better.

In a recent paper on the same sample of patients, Hoglend et al. (2011) reported a significant three-way interaction among treatment group Δ7 quality of object relations × alliance, "indicating that alliance had a significantly different impact on effects of transference interpretation, depending on the level of QOR [i.e., quality of object relations]" (p. 697). As they note, "contrary to our hypothesis and common clinical wisdom, transference work had the strongest specific effects with patients with low QOR scores within the context of weaker alliance. . . . For patients with a high alliance score and high QOR Scale scores, the specific effect of transference work was negative" (p. 702).

How do psychoanalytic hypotheses on transference interpretations measure up against the above findings? On the one hand, that the effect of transference interpretations on therapeutic outcome appears to be mediated by insight supports the traditional psychoanalytic claim regarding a central ingredient of therapeutic action. On the other hand, that these effects and the mediating role of insight holds mainly for patients with a relatively poor quality of object relations certainly appears to contradict the received wisdom (1) that transference interpretations are mainly useful with high functioning patients; and (2) that it is mainly such patients who are capable of insight and using it in the service of therapeutic change.

How does one explain these surprising and "contrary to clinical wisdom" findings? Although there is no definitive answer to this question, there are some factors one might consider in formulating a plausible account. More disturbed patients are more likely to bring to the therapeutic relationship the very problems and difficulties (e.g., fear of rejection, avoidance, overdependency, devaluation/idealization) that have interfered with their outside relationships and that, therefore, require a therapeutic focus. As Hoglend et al. (2011) note, "if the therapist does not address this [i.e., the problems as they are expressed in the therapeutic relationship] the patient may easily feel less understood and less contained by therapy, leading to deterioration in an already weak alliance" (p. 702). Contrastingly, in the case of patients with a higher level of object relations, where the alliance is strong and where there is a lower level of resistance, a therapist who offers a large number of transference interpretations "may appear to the patient to be narcissistically and needlessly focusing the patient's attention to the therapist" (p. 703).[12] As is the case with any study, there are, of course, limitations to the set of studies I have discussed, a consideration which suggests important areas for further research. For example, we know only about the frequency and nothing about such factors as the content, timing, and tone of the transference interpretations made in the studies. Certainly, not all transference interpretations are the same with regard to these factors. For example, although he does not employ the term transference interpretations, when Kohut (1984) discusses "optimal failure" or "optimal frustration," he suggests that the analyst respond to the patient's experience of the analyst's empathic failure first, by acknowledging such failure; and second, by linking the patient's experience of such failure to his or her feelings of rage and despair. These are clearly transference interpretations. The point here is that Kohut is suggesting that transference interpretations are especially called for and therapeutically useful when the patient experiences an empathic failure on the part of the therapist. Although not simple or easy to investigate, this is certainly a testable hypothesis.

Indeed, there is a small body of work indicating that ruptures in the therapeutic relationship, followed by repair, a sequence that parallels Kohut's optimal failure followed by addressing the patient's experience of the analyst's failure, is associated with a better therapeutic alliance and more positive therapeutic outcome (e.g., Muran et al., 2009; Safran et al., 2011; Stiles et al., 2004; Strauss et al., 2006). Although one would want to know more about the specific ways in which they are implemented, it is highly likely that repair includes interventions that would fall into the category of transference interpretations.

If my reasoning is correct, one could hypothesize that transference interpretations are likely to be more effective in response to disruptions in the therapeutic relationship.

Indeed, this hypothesis is implicit in Freud's (1912a) suggestion that positive transference need not be interpreted and that one should not interpret transference until it constitutes a resistance. The research findings on rupture and repair are congruent with Freud's suggestions. However, they can be subjected to more direct empirical test. In effect, Freud's suggestions as well as the rupture and repair research have to do with both the content and the timing of transference interpretations.

One should also note here the general congruence among Freud's suggestions, the rupture and repair research, Kohut's formulations on "optimal failure," and the finding that transference interpretations are more effective with patients who show a low quality of object relations.[13] For, as noted earlier, it is with precisely such patients that one is more likely to see ruptures, resistance, and experiences of the therapist's empathic failure in the therapeutic relationship (see Hoglend et al., 2011, p. 703).

Accuracy of interpretations and therapeutic process and outcome

A number of studies investigated the effects of accuracy of interpretations, including transference interpretations, on therapeutic outcomes. In one study by Crits-Christoph et al. (1988), accuracy of interpretations was operationally defined in terms of clinical correspondence of interpretations to the patient's CCRT. They reported that accuracy of interpretations regarding wishes and experienced responses from others was significantly but modestly related to outcome, even when quality of helping alliance was controlled for. In another study, defining accuracy of interpretations in the same way, Crits-Christoph et al. (1993) found that therapist interpretations congruent with the patient's wishes and experienced response from other predicted changes in the therapeutic alliance.

Although not explicitly referring to accuracy of interpretations, the work of Weiss and Sampson (1986) and their colleagues on whether the analyst's interpretations are compatible or incompatible with the patient's unconscious plan can be understood as relevant to the issue of accuracy of interpretations. Weiss (1993) has proposed that patients in treatment have an unconscious plan to disconfirm certain pathogenic beliefs and further, that interpretations can be reliably judged in terms of degree of "plan compatibility." Operationally defining accuracy of interpretations in terms of degree of plan compatibility, Norville et al. (1996) found in a small sample of seven cases a significant relationship between ratings of plan compatibility of interpretations and therapeutic outcome immediately after termination of therapy and at a six-month follow-up. Also employing a small number of cases, Silberschatz et al. (1986) reported that compatibility with the patients' plan rather than transference versus non-transference interventions correlated with patient progress (see also Silberschatz et al., 1989, 1993).

One can also understand much of Weiss and Sampson (1986) and their colleagues' work on test-passing and test-failing in the context of transference interpretations. They have generally found that in contrast to interpretations that are independently judged as constituting test-failing, test-passing interpretations tend to be followed by, among other consequences, reduced anxiety and emergence of warded-off contents. One can employ this design to investigate specifically the effects of transference interpretations rated by independent judges as constituting test-passing versus test-failing on therapeutic outcome. To be noted here is that test-passing interpretations can be understood as more accurate in the sense that they correspond to the patient's main concerns.

As a final example of a study on the relationship between accuracy of interpretations and therapeutic outcome, analyzing data from the National Institute of Mental Health Treatment of Depression Collaborative Research Program (Elkin et al., 1989), Crits-Christoph et al. (2010) reported a significant interaction between type of treatment (interpersonal therapy [IPT] versus cognitive therapy [CT]) such that accuracy of interpretations in relation to the Wish (W) component of the CCRT predicted reduction of depression only for the IPT group and accuracy of interpretation in relation to the (W) and RS predicted positive change in social adjustment, also only for the IPT group. (The RO component approached significance.) For the CT group, higher accuracy scores were significantly associated with *poorer* outcomes. It is not clear why this is so.

As I noted, the above studies deal with the accuracy of all interpretations, not only transference interpretations. However, I have taken the time to describe these studies because employing a similar design, one can investigate various aspects of transference interpretations, including their accuracy, on therapeutic process and outcome. However, these types of studies are generally naturalistic ones rather than randomized control studies that entail the experimental manipulation of transference interpretations versus no transference interpretations, as in, for example, the Johansson et al. (2010) and Hoglend et al. (2011) studies.

As Johansson et al. (2010) note, naturalistic studies reporting on within-group correlations do not generally allow assessment of causal effects. However, what they lose in capacity for causal attribution, they partly make up for in ecological validity. Thus, whereas experimental manipulations of number of transference interpretations can tell us whether, as a main effect, frequency of transference interpretations influence therapeutic outcome, and what other factors it interacts with in influencing outcome, important information in itself, they do not tell us anything about the influence of such factors as the content, timing, accuracy, and the style of transference interpretations. To investigate these factors, we also need to include naturalistic studies and reliance on judgments and ratings of clinical data. As Hoglend et al. (2011) note, this is also the case in studying the therapeutic alliance, something that is "naturalistically" there in the clinical data (and is assessed through clinical ratings) rather than something that can be (ethically) experimentally manipulated.

First-person reports of psychoanalytic treatment

Although hardly qualifying as systematic research, I include first-person accounts of treatment experiences in two different psychoanalyses. Such accounts constitute a sort of mini-experiment in nature on the question of different transference patterns emerging with different analysts. There are very few first-person reports of such experiences, in particular, of the different transference patterns that emerge in the different analyses. I know of only three such reports: Guntrip (1975); Kohut (1979); and Hurwitz (1986). I found the Hurwitz paper the most detailed and informative of the three. So, I begin with that paper. Hurwitz describes his analysis with two training analysts he refers to as Dr. X and Dr. Y. His first four-and-a-half-year analysis with Dr. X was nearing termination when Dr. X became seriously ill and died. Hurwitz then undertook a second analysis with Dr. Y.

Hurwitz describes Dr. X in the following way:

> From the beginning, I found the experience to be anxiety-provoking. Dr. X seemed cool and aloof, self-consciously standoffish (as I felt he should be). I was uneasy with what I sensed to be an air of impatience about him. Very quickly I developed the sense that I was under the scrutiny of a very stern man, a man of conviction, not to be messed with. My associations were to an orthodox rabbi who terrified me as a child.
>
> (p. 445)

Hurwitz recounts incidents throughout the analysis in which he experiences Dr. X as "sarcastic and condescending" and making interpretations as "pronouncements," and in which he, Hurwitz, would respond with "defensive rage and defiance." This behavior was responded to by Dr. X with either silence or interpretation of Hurwitz's "oedipal strivings, jealousy, and competitiveness, my wish to defeat the powerful father; as a provocation to be beaten which I wanted in order to relieve my guilt stimulated by my patricidal wishes" (p. 446). Hurwitz reports frequently not feeling understood and writes: "I often thought I was angry with Dr. X in response to his frustrating and infuriating ways" (p. 446).

As he became more familiar with Mahler's and Kohut's work, Hurwitz writes, "there was a resonance with what I sensed to be important issues having to do with separation, recognition, and the maintenance of self-esteem" (p. 446)—issues that Hurwitz notes, "seemed to be missing" (p. 446) in his analysis. Dr. X viewed Hurwitz's introduction of "these issues as an attempt to evade directly confronting my oedipal conflicts" (p. 447).

When Hurwitz told Dr. X that there was something about his style that he was reacting to, Dr. X replied "you'd respond that way no matter who was in this chair;" and when Hurwitz persisted by asking "you don't think it has anything to do with you?," Dr. X's reply was "Nothing" (p. 447). Hurwitz began to accept Dr. X's view of what was going on and began to feel and express "warm, appreciative feelings" (p. 448) toward him—which Dr. X responded to by jokingly telling Hurwitz that he felt these feelings "because the hour's up" (p. 448).[15]

Hurwitz's reactions to this interaction are quite important. Unsurprisingly, he feels hurt. As Hurwitz writes, he understands Dr. X's supposedly joking interpretation as: "I was just a lot of hot air. The only reason I felt that way [i.e., the warm, appreciative feelings] was because I was about to escape" (p. 448). When Hurwitz communicates his reactions to the "joke," he feels chided for being "too sensitive." What is especially interesting is that Hurwitz agreed with this assessment and "heard the chiding as a call to grow up, not to be 'such a little boy'" (p. 448). Identification with the aggressor is almost complete.

After Dr. X's death, Hurwitz began a second analysis with Dr. Y who was quite different from Dr. X in a number of ways. "He was not aloof, distant, or guarded. I did not experience his interpretations as pronouncements at all. He offered them as possibilities for me to consider" (p. 449). Hurwitz felt that he "could feel more of what was going on in [Dr. Y]" (p. 450), which "was very important in helping me to understand how not to drown in my own reactions" (p. 450). Hurwitz experienced Dr. Y as "much more attuned to preodipal and narcissistic issues" (p. 450) and experienced a good deal less anxiety in the analytic sessions.

Hurwitz briefly describes two memories that were interpreted both by Dr. X and Dr. Y. The first memory from age four, shortly before his father is going to be shipped overseas, involves Hurwitz being teased (by an offer of candy) and bullied by some boys and repeating that experience over the next two days. Dr. X interprets this memory in terms of guilt and need for punishment in relation to the pleasure of oedipal triumph in anticipation of his father being shipped overseas. When Hurwitz brings up this memory in his second analysis and says that there is something about this memory that he does not understand, Dr. Y responds: "Perhaps you were lonely"—a response which led to a "flood of memories of that time . . . I recalled an awful sense of loneliness which I had repressed. The sense of incomplete understanding was gone" (p. 451).

The second memory from age eight, after Hurwitz's father has returned from overseas and shortly after a baby sister was born, is of watching his mother tend to his sister in a bassinet. Dr. X's interpretation "focused on regressive responses to the castration anxiety stimulated by the situation" (p. 451). Dr. Y's response to the same memory was "perhaps you thought it was love" (p. 452), which Hurwitz reacts to with a much fuller sense of that memory; my jealousy, my rivalry, my love, my longing, and my loneliness" (p. 452). Hurwitz also reports with regard to both memories that Dr. Y's interpretation "opened the way for additional and fuller understanding of these same memories on an oedipal level" (p. 452).

Hurwitz then goes on to discuss the different transference patterns stimulated by the two different analysts. His descriptions are important enough to cite in detail. He writes that:

> The transferences stimulated in response to Dr. X were primarily those of the severe rabbi, the persecutory, vengeful, powerful, oedipal father, admired, feared, hated, loved, but kept at a distance. Superego projections were almost constant. Dr. X's physical appearance was close enough to my father's to have been a stimulus in this direction. Dr. X's style and theoretical stance were also important triggers. His stand that preoedipal conflicts and loving feelings for him (the father) were primarily a regressive avoidance to the central oedipal struggle, was, I think, oversimplified, limited the effectiveness of my analysis with him in dealing with these issues, and was an additional source of frustration. His style limited the maternal transference to a sense of being teased. What is, I think, most important to note in all of this is that my reactions would have been interpreted by Dr. X as confirming his theoretical point of view, as I understand it.
>
> My identification with Dr. X was very much an identification with the aggressor with a high titre of ambivalence (Meissner, 1979). I began to note a change in my style of doing therapy and analysis in which there was an uncomfortable tendency to repeat actively what I felt I was experiencing passively. I had become the dutiful son of the tyrannical father and the transmission to the next generation was under way. The sense that I have alluded to of something missing in my relationship with Dr. X was complicated and related to splitting of these issues from the transferences already mentioned.
>
> The transference responses to Dr. Y were far more complex. The persecutory oedipal father was very much there, but less insistently

> stimulated. There was also a loving, idealized father and maternal grandfather who served as ego ideal, guides, and models for identification. Above all, there were the complex maternal transferences—the mother who carried me in her womb, who suffered to give me life, loving and supporting, disappointing and castrating, always longed for but never quite available. It is important to note that Dr. Y's appearance and habits also played a role in the transferences stimulated. Dr. Y was short, as was my mother and as was my maternal grandfather. Dr. Y smoked and drank coffee, both of which were passions of my mother and my maternal grandfather during my early years. Dr. Y's style was less intrusive, his theoretical stance more open, broader, and less stimulating of defiant and provocative stances on my part. He offered a perspective that provided a depth and texture to my understanding that went beyond a schematic outline, and his personal availability allowed for a more mature identification (Meissner, 1979). In my transference responses to him and my sense of what happened in my analysis with him, Dr. Y would find, I think, confirmation of his theoretical formulations. Over time, I became aware of changes in my own style of analyzing which were congruent with my sense of what was occurring between Dr. Y and myself.
>
> (pp. 452–453)

If anyone has had any doubt that the behavior and personality of the analyst have a strong influence on shaping the nature of emerging transference patterns, Hurwitz's account should put that doubt to rest.

Guntrip's (1975) report of his analyses with Fairbairn and Winnicott is, in a number of ways, strikingly parallel to Hurwitz's experiences. Indeed, Hurwitz writes that Guntrip's account "struck a resonant chord" (p. 460). Despite his theoretical emphasis on the importance of the personal relationship in psychoanalytic treatment, Fairbairn is described by Guntrip as formal, "more orthodox" and as "more of a 'technical interpreter'" (p. 146). Throughout the analysis, similar to Dr. X in Hurwitz's account, Fairbairn's focus was virtually exclusively on oedipal issues. Guntrip describes his negative transference to Fairbairn, reacting to him as his "dominating mother." Guntrip's experience of Winnicott is very different and is there from the very start: In contrast to Fairbairn's formal consulting room and formal manner, Winnicott's consulting room is "simple, restful in colors and furniture" (p. 149); and he would "stroll in with a cup of tea in his hand and a cheery 'Hallo'" (p. 149); at the end of the session, Winnicott "held out his hand for a friendly handshake" (p. 149). Paralleling Hurwitz's experience with Dr. Y, Winnicott focused on Gruntrip's very early life rather than on oedipal issues. Also and perhaps most important, Winnicott's interpretations were "alive" and spoke personally and directly to Guntrip's subjective experience. It is no surprise, therefore, to read that whereas Guntrip experienced Fairbairn as a dominating mother, he experienced Winnicott as a good mother. Guntrip's experience is similar to reports of other patients' experience of Winnicott. For example, Anderson (2014), who interviewed a number of Winnicott's former patients, quotes one of them as saying "Winnicott was the best mother I ever had" (p. 376). And Margaret Little, one of the interviewees, tells Anderson that Winnicott "recognized my psychotic anxieties and provided the 'facilitating environment' and the 'good enough' holding that I needed" (p. 378). What seems to emerge from the various descriptions of these analysands of Winnicott is their experience of his personal caring and authenticity. It appears that Winnicott the pediatrician, the analyst, the theoretician, the author of many papers, and the everyday individual all seem to converge on the same person. He emerges as a man of one piece.

What is striking about the above personal reports is the relationship between the analyst's theoretical beliefs and his personal beliefs and behavior. For example, although there seems to be a harmonious relationship between Winnicott's theoretical writings and personal therapeutic behavior, this seems to be much less the case in regard to Fairbairn. Thus, as noted, while Fairbairn writes about the importance of the analyst being a "good" object, Guntrip experienced him as a dominating mother (in contrast to experiencing Winnicott as a good mother) and as someone who focused somewhat rigidly on oedipal issues rather than Guntrip's core experiences.

Finally, I come to Kohut's (1979) "The two analyses of Mr. Z," which is obviously quite different from the above accounts. For one thing, there seems to be a consensus that Mr. Z is Kohut himself. But even if there were an actual Mr. Z, Kohut's report is of two purported analyses with the same analyst, albeit the same analyst with different theoretical perspectives. Indeed, it is clear that Kohut's intention is to employ the fictitious two analyses of Mr. Z as a vehicle to illustrate clinical and theoretical changes in his own thinking. Nonetheless, it is useful to discuss "The two analyses of Mr. Z" as if there were, in fact, two different analyses by two different analysts. When viewed this way, there are clear parallels to the Hurwitz and Guntrip accounts. In the first analysis of Mr. Z, the emphasis is on oedipal issues and castration anxiety and so-called preoedipal aims were understood "as a defense against oedipal competitiveness and castration fear" (p. 8). Kohut describes the emergence of "a regressive mother transference" characterized by "defended grandiosity and his demands that the psychoanalytic situation should reinstate the position of exclusive control, of being admired and being catered to by a doting mother" (p. 5).

In the supposed second analysis with Mr. Z, Kohut no longer viewed or interpreted Mr. Z's narcissistic demands as regressive defenses, but as important in their own right and as underlain by "chronic despair" (p. 12). Most important in the present context, Kohut reports significant changes from the first to the second analysis in his attitude toward Mr. Z's behavior. In the first analysis, Kohut expected that Mr. Z would "relinquish his narcissistic demands and grow up" and saw him as "resisting change or as opposing maturation because [he] did not want to relinquish [his] childish gratifications" (p. 12)—an attitude that Kohut refers to as a "health—and maturity—morality" (p. 12). In the second analysis, Kohut understood Mr. Z's self "as desperately—and often hopelessly—struggling to disentangle itself from the selfobject, to delimit itself, to grow, to become independent" (p. 12).

Although Kohut does not explicitly address the question of whether different transference patterns emerged in the two analyses, his comments suggest that this was indeed the case. For one thing, it is highly likely that the analyst's expectation in the first analysis that Mr. Z relinquish his childish gratifications and grow up—his "health—and maturity—morality" —would find expression in his manner and behavior and would activate a transference pattern in which the analyst is experienced as a stern, demanding parent, much like the way Hurwitz experienced Dr. X and Guntrip experienced Fairbairn. Kohut's suggestion that this was, indeed, the case is seen in his report that for a long period of time, Mr. Z blew up in rages against Kohut partly in response to his "interpretations concerning his narcissistic demands and his arrogant feelings of 'entitlement'" (p. 5).

Kohut reports that in the second analysis, Mr. Z developed an idealizing transference of short duration, "replaced by a mirror transference of the merger-type" (p. 11), which was characterized by the patient becoming "self-centered, demanding, insisting on perfect empathy, and inclined to react with rage at the slightest out-of-tuneness with his psychological states, with the slightest misunderstanding" (p. 11). Although, as Kohut observes, Mr. Z's rage was similar to the rage expressed in the first analysis, Kohut's attitude toward and understanding of it were different. By the time the second analysis had begun, Kohut had relinquished his "health—and maturity—morality" and now understood Mr. Z's rage, not as the behavior of a "spoiled child" whose demands were not being met, but as "the struggles of his feeble self to define itself" (p. 12). Kohut's shift in attitude led to Mr. Z "feeling supported by the analyst" (p. 14), which enabled him to explore hitherto unexplored areas of his life. There is much more material that Kohut discusses, but the point I want to emphasize in the present context is the different transference patterns that emerge as a function of the different attitudes, behaviors, and perspectives of the analyst.

Kohut comments with regard to the second analysis that Mr. Z displayed relatively little evidence of "transference distortions." He goes on to suggest that, in an important sense, the patient cannot, so to speak, afford to misperceive the analyst. For "in order to be able to proceed with the task of perceiving the serious pathology of the selfobject of childhood, the patient has to be certain that the current selfobject, the analyst, is not again exposing him to the pathological milieu of early life" (p. 13), in other words, is not likely to retraumatize him.

Like Gill (1982, 1994), although for different reasons, Kohut is suggesting that transference can develop with a minimum of transference distortion. It appears that for Kohut the essence of transference is not a "false connection" characterized by the attribution to the analyst of characteristics of parental figures, but rather looking to the analyst to meet developmental needs (such as the need for empathic mirroring) that were not adequately met early in life. This understanding of an important aspect of transference is virtually identical to Freud's (1905[1901]) earlier noted description of transference in the following way: "if someone's need for love is not entirely satisfied by reality, he is bound to approach every new person whom he meets with libidinal anticipatory ideas" (p. 100).

As Kohut observes, on this view of transference, distortion in the form of attributing to the analyst characteristics of parental figures is not a prominent feature. Indeed, an implication of this conception of transference is that, in certain respects, the patient experiences the analyst as *potentially different* from early parental figures. Consider the idealizing and mirroring transference patterns described by Kohut. In both the transference patterns, the patient hopes that the analyst—unlike his or her parents—will permit his or her needs for idealization and empathic mirroring to be met. The patient's rage emerges when he or she experiences the analyst as not meeting these needs, which, as Kohut notes, often cannot be realistically met (e.g., experience of perfect mirroring). If there is distortion here, it lies in the patient's often unrealistic fantasy that the analyst will be the exact and perfect opposite of his or her parents, that is, will be perfectly idealizable and will provide perfect mirroring.

A similar de-emphasis on transference distortion is also found in the work of Weiss and Sampson (1986) and their colleagues. According to their Control–Mastery theory, patients come to treatment hoping that the therapist will be different from traumatizing parental figures, and unconsciously present tests to the therapist to determine whether this is, indeed the case. Implicit in this formulation is the idea, similar to Kohut's, that the patient cannot afford a seriously distorted perception of the analyst—too much is at stake. If the patient is going to feel safe enough to confront painful material, he or she must first determine whether conditions of safety obtain. That is, the patient must feel that he or she will not be retraumatized at the hands of the therapist.

Thus, distortion does not play a prominent role in the Control–Mastery theory conception of transference. The emphasis is on the patient's poignant hope that the therapist will behave differently from parental figures and enable the patient to disconfirm and relinquish pathogenic beliefs that, according to Control–Mastery theory, are at the core of psychopathology. Although transference in the traditional sense is de-emphasized, there is nevertheless much room in clinical work for the patient and therapist to mutually examine their interactions, particularly with regard to issues of test-passing, test-failing, and conditions of safety.

In short, according to both self psychology and Control–Mastery theory perspectives, transference consists largely in casting the therapist as a parental figure, but one, the patient fervently hopes, who will be radically different from one's actual parents in the sense that (1) he or she will meet unmet developmental needs (self psychology); and (2) will be someone who, through establishing conditions of safety, will disconfirm unconscious pathogenic beliefs (Control–Mastery theory). In both theories, the assumptions appear to be made that the patient is essentially searching for a "good object" and that, given his or her powerful fear of retraumatization, can make largely accurate assessments of whether the therapist is, indeed, a "good object."

In a series of studies, Pfeffer (1961, 1963, 1993) reported that few years after the termination of the analysis, even successfully analyzed patients tend to experience preanalytic symptoms and recurrence of the "transference neurosis." However, both phenomena tend to be transitory and replaced by "a representation of the analyst as a nonconflicted object" (p. 323). This finding is congruent with Farber and Geller's (1993) report that long after termination, former patients tend to invoke an image of the therapist at various times of distress. This suggests not so much resolution of the transference, but rather transformation of the therapist into a benevolent object who is internalized and whose representation can provide needed support.

Implications of research findings for psychoanalytic theories of transference

In discussing the implications of empirical research for psychoanalytic conceptions of transference—or, for that matter, for any aspect of psychoanalytic theory—a key consideration is the question of ecological validity (Kazdin, 2006). That is, to what degree are the research findings applicable to real-life situations, including the therapeutic situation? This is an exceedingly important question. Early attempts to demonstrate repression in the experimental laboratory possessed little ecological validity and were justifiably ignored by psychoanalytic theorists and clinicians. It is likely that the lack of ecological validity of much early empirical research purporting to investigate psychoanalytic concepts and formulations has contributed to a disturbing tendency for psychoanalytic theorists and clinicians to dismiss out of hand any empirical research, a precedent set by Freud's dismissive reaction to Rosenzweig's (1997) letter informing him of some research findings that supported psychoanalytic ideas.

Unfortunately, the one extreme of automatic dismissal of empirical research findings is often matched by the other extreme of uncritical interpretations of research findings and a cherry-picking habit of citing only findings that appear to support psychoanalytic propositions. I think it is important to thread one's way between these two extremes and address empirical research findings in a critical and disciplined way.

The effects of representations of significant others on the experience of new persons

At the core of the traditional conception of transference is the idea that one tends to attribute to new persons characteristics of one's representations of significant figures. Anderson and her colleagues have shown that, defined this way, although priming representations of the significant other as well as similarity between representations of significant other and new person enhance the transference process, neither is necessary to produce it. The chronic accessibility of representations of significant others itself is sufficient to generate transference. These findings provide general support for the proposition that transference is a ubiquitous phenomenon. Most broadly, one can say when we encounter a new person, we tend to assimilate to some degree the experience of that new person to preexisting representations of significant others.

However, these findings address only one aspect, although a core one, of the psychoanalytic conception of transference. Although research findings provide support for general propositions regarding the ubiquitousness and "intelligence" of unconscious processes, most of them do not speak directly to the specific psychoanalytic conception of the dynamic unconscious. Similarly, with regard to transference, the findings of Andersen and her colleagues appear to provide support for the general hypothesis that we tend to attribute to new persons characteristics of our representations of significant others in our life. This is an important finding, which constitutes a foundation for the further empirical investigation of transference phenomena.

However, these findings do not address certain aspects of transference that are of special psychoanalytic interest. For example, in the psychoanalytic context, the respective roles of interacting individuals is hypothesized to influence both the threshold for eliciting transference responses and the particular nature of the transference patterns that are elicited. For example, the roles of patient and therapist or employee and employer or student and teacher are hypothesized to more readily elicit parental or authority transference patterns associated with authority figures or parental or attachment figures than, say, the role of peer. Further, the transference interactions between patient and therapist (or employee and employer or student and teacher) are embedded in a motivational context characterized by each individual in the interaction having a set of needs, motives, and expectations regarding the other.

Thus, as noted earlier, central components of a psychoanalytic conception of transference include not only attributing characteristics of significant others to the "new person," but also looking to the "new person" to meet one's wishes and needs as well as having a set of expectations as to whether these wishes and needs will be met and a set of defenses that reflect, among other things, the conflictual status of these wishes and needs—all of which may operate on an unconscious level.

These latter aspects of transference are, of course, difficult to investigate directly in the experimental laboratory. However, they can be studied indirectly. For example, building on Andersen et al.'s (1995) finding that similarity between significant other and new person facilitates transference, one can investigate the effects on transference of not only similarity of characteristics, but also similarity of roles between significant other and new person. One would also need to broaden one's operationalization of transference beyond falsely remembering descriptions of early significant other as belonging to a target new person to include such ecologically valid components of transference as attributing similar attitudes toward one's early significant other and toward the new target person and expectations of the current target person that are similar to expectations of early significant others with regard to how they will respond to one's expression of needs and wishes.

In the research of Andersen and her colleagues, the focus is on the attribution of characteristics of a significant other to a new target person one has never encountered before. However, in "real-life" situations outside the clinical context, that are nevertheless are of great clinical importance, transference also entails transferring characteristics, motives, expectations, and so on, from one familiar past significant other (e.g., parental figure) to a familiar current significant figure (e.g., one's spouse) rather than to a new person in a literal sense. This is a fertile area for future research.

A common clinical example of this phenomenon is a man's attribution to his wife of characteristics, expectations, etc., belonging to representations of his mother. Further, according to psychoanalytic theory, this transference phenomenon is not simply a matter of attribution of characteristics or, more broadly, of assimilation of new experience to preexisting schemas, but is deeply motivated. That is, the man looks to his wife to meet certain needs and wishes that were met by mother—or that he *wanted* to have met by his mother. Furthermore, insofar as these needs and wishes are embedded in conflict and defense, his desire to have them met by his wife can be highly ambivalent.

From a psychoanalytic perspective, the attribution of characteristics of mother to wife is not just a "cold" cognitive fact, but is saturated with affect and has significant affective consequences. For example, the assimilation of the experience of wife to the preexisting schema of mother may result in the experience of wife as a forbidden incestuous object and therefore inhibit sexual feelings toward her (Freud, 1912b). It is not uncommon to observe in male patients a radical change in sexual feelings when girlfriend becomes wife or when wife gives birth to a child and becomes a mother. In the case of one male patient, sexual attraction to his girlfriend was radically transformed virtually overnight into sexual inhibition and loss of sexual interest immediately after the wedding day (see Eagle, 2007, 2013). This dynamic can be understood as every bit an expression of a transference phenomenon as transference in the clinical situation.

Let me describe a concrete instance of a garden-variety transference phenomenon in a therapeutic session: my patient informed me that he had a new job, but did not tell me much more about it. When I noted that, he said that because my arms were crossed and I looked "stern," he was reluctant to tell me how high his salary was lest I be envious and critical of him (as far as I was aware, I did not experience either feeling). His subsequent associations were on the themes of his father's lack of confidence in him, chronic criticism, and competitiveness with him—themes that were central throughout the treatment.

As in the Andersen et al. studies, my patient had attributed to me characteristics of his representations of a significant other, his father. However, unlike the Andersen et al. studies, my patient's attributions were made in an interactional context, included interactional schemas and entailed selective attention to cues (e.g., my arms crossed) that were congruent with and served to support his attributions and interactional schema (i.e., if I am successful, my therapist [and] father will be envious and critical).

Effects of representations of significant others on self-evaluations

Although the above studies deal with the effects of representations of significant others on experience of a new person, as we have seen, activation of representations of significant others can also influence how one views oneself. Further, the activation of representations of *particular attitudes* of significant others (e.g., approving or disapproving) is an important factor in influencing how one views oneself. What are the implications of these latter findings for a conception of transference?

These findings extend the concept of transference in the following ways: The transference attributions one projects on to the other not only influence how one experiences the other, but also then feeds back to influence how one evaluates and experiences oneself. Thus, the activation of, say, the representation of a disapproving authority figure is likely to influence not only one's experience of the other as disapproving, but is also likely to lower one's evaluation of oneself. Hence, the effects of projecting characteristics of a significant other on to a new person who plays some important role in one's life are not limited to how one experiences the new person, but also extend to how one experiences oneself.

Baldwin (1997), along with others, has argued that one's sense of self "derive[s] in large part from if–then expectations about the contingencies of interpersonal interaction; that is, expectancies about how other people will react to one's behaviors" (p. 326). A question that arises is the degree to which there are individual differences in the degree to which expectancies themselves remain relatively fixed or vary with the activation of representations of different significant others.

From this perspective, the concepts of self-esteem and self-evaluation refer not only to self-representations, but are essentially interactional schemas. Thus, low self-esteem or poor self-evaluation would be one component of an interactional schema that would also include representations of a disapproving or rejecting significant other. In the language of Sullivan (1947), the concept of self is the product of "reflected appraisals" of significant others. The attachment patterns of attachment theory represent other instances of self-evaluation as a component of interactional schemas. For example, an avoidant attachment pattern includes the components of the representation of the early attachment figure as rejecting, the expectations of rejection at the hands of a current attitude figure, and a representation of self as unworthy.

An important question that arises regarding these studies on the effects of activating representations of approving or disapproving significant others on self-evaluation (as well as other research discussed) is their ecological validity. Self-evaluation is measured in these studies by various self-report instruments; and shifts in self-evaluation are operationally defined in terms of changes in numerical values on the measuring instruments. There is the question of what Kazdin (2006) has referred to as the "arbitrary metrics" of numerical values on measuring instruments of this kind.

Also, we know little regarding the lastingness of the effects on self-evaluation. It is very likely that these effects are highly transitory and do not last beyond the duration of the experiment. The critical question that arises is what relationship these highly transitory changes in self-evaluation bear to real-life self-evaluation, which is often long-lasting and chronic. Thus, although level of self-esteem may fluctuate as a function of various factors, including the temporary activation of representations of significant others, the most common pattern one encounters in clinical work is chronically accessible feelings of low self-esteem that are relatively resistant to change.

Indeed, this state of affairs is often an important motive for coming to treatment. It may well be that different chronically accessible levels of self-esteem entail different and equally chronically accessible representations of significant others. For example, chronic low self-esteem may involve the chronic activation of a representation of a disapproving or rejecting other. From this perspective, as noted, low self-esteem is not simply a function of representations of self, but is essentially an interactional schema that includes representations of self in interaction with representations of the attitudes of significant others toward oneself. To put it another way, chronic low self-esteem can be understood as an expression of one's attitude toward oneself so long as one recognizes that one's attitudes toward oneself, to an important degree, consist in internalized and chronically accessible representations of the negative attitudes of significant others.

As I have already suggested, I am essentially describing the Sullivanian view of the self as the "reflected appraisals" of significant others. However, to some extent, this point of view is also implicit in Freud's concept of the superego and Fairbairn's (1952) concept of internalized object. Both concepts share in common the properties (1) that they are schemas or structures that reflect the attitudes and values of parental figures; (2) that these attitudes and values, once they have become internalized, are part of one's personality structure; and (3) that it is the activation of these schemas or structures that influence, among other things, the individual's self-evaluation, including feelings of self-esteem and self-worth.

As we have seen, the research in this area is formulated in terms of the effects of activation of representations of significant others on various responses, including on experience of a new person and on self-evaluations. The research then focuses on demonstrating that activating representations of different significant others (e.g., authority figure versus non-authority figure) as well as different attitudes of significant others (e.g., approving versus disapproving) will have different effects on how one experiences a new person or how one evaluates oneself. However, from the psychoanalytic perspective noted above, insofar as they are internalized, some representations of significant others are essentially components of one's personality structure (a superego structure in Freudian theory and an internal object in Fairbairnian theory). Hence, from this perspective, transference is essentially the projection of part of oneself onto another, with the result that one experiences that other in accord with one's projections. Another way to put it is to say that one experiences the other as having the same attitudes toward oneself that, whether acknowledged or unacknowledged, one also has toward oneself.

The situation gets somewhat more complex insofar as there are different parts of oneself as well as different interactional schemas that one can project onto the other. And here is where the cues emitted by the other are likely to exert an influence on how one experiences the other. This influence lies in the fact that different cues emitted by the other tend to activate internalized representations of different attitudes of significant others.

Although projections of one's representations of significant others influence one's experience of a new person, it is important not to exaggerate that influence and to keep in mind that one's experience of the other is influenced not only by transference projections, but also by actual behaviors and characteristics of the other.[17] (This, of course, is what Gill was insisting that we recognize.) Indeed, critical process and outcome goals of psychoanalytic treatment include the decreasing role of transference projections and the increasing role of actual characteristics of the other in influencing how one experiences that other. It would be interesting to determine whether such changes are associated with positive therapeutic outcome.

Generalization of changes in transference to outside figures

One of the issues that is not sufficiently addressed in the psychoanalytic literature and that would benefit from research is the question of the generalization of changes in the patient's representation of the analyst to other significant figures in his or her life. Kohut (1984) writes that in successful treatment, the patient can avail himself or herself not only of the "good enough" empathic understanding of the analyst, but also of the support and empathic understanding expressed, for example, in a friendly arm on one's shoulder. Kohut's description can be read as suggesting that in successful treatment, it is not so much that transference has been resolved, but rather that it has been transformed into something akin to a satisfying and supportive relationship. The important question is the degree to which other important relationships have been similarly transformed.

Stereotyped template "versus" situation cues

As we have seen in the above, from a psychoanalytic perspective, one can understand many of the research findings on transference in terms of the effects of activating superego or internal objects on attitudes toward oneself. In the Baldwin et al. (1990) study, the schema of a disapproving authority figure was activated through experimental manipulation (i.e., priming). However, in the clinical situation, an individual's deeply engrained and chronically available schema of an authority figure as disapproving may be projected onto the therapist without any external manipulation. That is, from a psychoanalytic perspective, the individual may attribute to the therapist an attitude of disapproval without the presence of an external priming cue activating the schema of disapproving authority figure (although Gill, 1994, would argue that some external priming cue would have to be present that the patient "plausibly" construes as disapproving). However, recall Andersen's conclusion that whereas priming may contribute additively to transference (defined as attributing characteristics of a significant other to a new person), it is not necessary due to the "chronic accessibility" (i.e., deeply engrained status) of certain schemas.

One way to put it is to say that for some people the association between authority figure and disapproval is so strong that the mere representation of an authority figure automatically triggers expectation of disapproval, whether or not the authority figure emits any such cues. Also, given the wide range and ambiguity of cues that people emit, individuals with a high associative strength between authority figure and disapproval will find it relatively easy to select and construe certain cues in the other that activate and serve to "confirm" the chronically accessible schema, just as was the case with my patient who not only selectively attended to, but also construed the cue of my arms being crossed and my supposedly serious expression as indicating envy and disapproval.

It is likely that even before the therapeutic session began, my patient expected at some level an envious and disapproving reaction on my part to the news of his new job and high salary. Of course, that is what it means for a schema to be chronically accessible. And given such chronic accessibility of representations of authority figures as envious and disapproving (i.e., given its low threshold for activation), my patient selected precisely those cues—and construed them in a way—that conform to his "chronic" and deeply engrained expectations. Identification of my patient's chronically accessible schemas and recognition of the ways in which they influence his reactions to me does not mean, contrary to Gill, that I am setting myself up as an arbiter of reality. Nor does it mean that the way to address the presence and influence of these chronically accessible schemas is through authoritative pronouncements—a tendency on the part of some analysts to which Gill rightly objected. Rather, these issues can and should be addressed collaboratively. Indeed, ideally, they should enter the patient–therapist collaboration through the patient's thoughts, feelings, and reactions rather than through the interpretation of the *Menschenkenner* with special knowledge available only to him or her.

As we have seen earlier, a point of contention between a classical and a more relational conception of transference lies in the classical claim (often implicit) that the patient's attributions of characteristics, attitudes, etc., to the analyst are essentially expressions of a stereotyped template formed early in life and as such, are relatively independent of the analyst's actual characteristics, attitudes, etc., particularly if the analyst is a blank screen who remains opaque to the patient. Hence, on this view, the patient's experience of the analyst is likely to be viewed as expressions of an inner stereotyped template, quite independent of the therapist's characteristics and emitted cues (recall Hurwitz's analyst, Dr. X saying: "You'd respond that way no matter who was in the chair").

In reacting against this exclusive emphasis on chronically accessible schemas (i.e., stereotyped templates) and neglect of cues emitted by the therapist in the classical theory of transference, contemporary relational theories sometimes tend to go the opposite extreme in overemphasizing the role of therapist cues and minimizing the influence of chronically accessible schemas. As we have seen from the research of Andersen and her colleagues, the activation of representations of significant others is an additive function of both their chronic accessibility and of the presence of priming, with chronic accessibility playing a stronger role. This can be understood as a specific example of a general trait × situation interaction, with chronic accessibility constituting the dispositional trait-like factor and priming constituting the situation factor.

A reasonable hypothesis is that just as both chronic accessibility and situational factors influence the activation of representations of significant others, so similarly is this the case with regard to activation of self-schemas. As Baldwin et al. (1990) put it, "A person's sense of self at any given moment is surely influenced by a broad range of factors, including stable self-concepts, recent experiences, social roles, and various context effects" (pp. 435–436). Further, the context effects that are especially important in influencing activation of self-schemas are likely to include "how the person believes he or she would be regarded by significant others" (Baldwin et al., 1990, p. 436).

In other words, according to this perspective, self-schemas are powerfully influenced by the particular representations of significant others that are activated. Indeed, there is likely to be a circular causal chain in which activations of representations of significant others influence self-evaluations or self-schemas, which, in turn, feed back to influence the activation of representations of significant others. Or, the process can start with particular self-schemas activating particular representations of significant others, which, in turn, feed back to influence activation of particular self-schemas. The latter process can be seen in states of depression wherein particular self-evaluations (low self-esteem) may selectively activate negative representations of significant others.

The process is somewhat more complicated insofar as the representations of a given significant other that are activated can include that other in different roles and in different relationships to oneself. For example, the representations of the same significant other can include the other as rejecting or accepting, as loving or demeaning, as approving or disapproving, and so on.

One can think of the blank screen role of the classical analyst as constituting an attempt to eliminate or at least minimize the influence of situational factors (i.e., cues emitted by the analyst) so that whatever occurs in the analytic situation (e.g., the patient's free associations) can presumably be attributed primarily to "inner" dispositional trait-like factors "within" the patient (e.g., wishes, fantasies, defenses, conflicts, transference patterns, etc.) "uncontaminated" by contributions from the analyst. Employing the language of Andersen and her colleagues, one would say that the function of the blank screen is to create conditions that would reveal the patient's inner structure that is chronically accessible whether or not it is primed by external cues (i.e., situational factors). Of course, even if it were possible to create an interpersonal condition in which no cues are being emitted by the other—clearly an impossibility—the *role* of the therapist and the entire context of the patient coming for help are powerful situational primes that would tend to activate particular sets of representations (e.g., parental significant others rather than, say, representations of peers). Thus, being in the role of patient is likely to activate not only representations of particular significant others, but also particular self-schemas, namely, those related to the context of being distressed and seeking treatment.

It follows that the self-schemas that one will see most clearly in the treatment situation will be those that are chronically accessible, that are activated by the treatment situation (i.e., by the individual's role as patient), by the idiosyncratic cues emitted by a particular therapist, and by the patient's construals of these cues. One may have less access to behaviors and self-schemas that would be activated by roles and contexts that are not normally represented in the treatment situation. Furthermore, the patient's narratives of his or her behavior, thoughts, and feelings in situations outside the treatment may well be influenced by the context of the treatment situation as well as the patient's experience of cues emitted by a particular therapist.

One is reminded of the pattern observed in tape-recorded sessions of Rogers (Masling & Cohen, 1987). Early in treatment the patient's verbal contents were divided approximately equally between sexual themes and issues related to self. After a period of time, the frequency of sexual themes markedly diminished, whereas the frequency of self themes increased. Most important, the frequency of sexual and self themes were lawfully related to Rogers' differential cues (e.g., uttering "Hmm" versus silence) in response to each set of themes. It appears that despite Rogers' explicit *nondirective* approach to therapy, his responses were subtly shaping the contents the patient brought up in the therapeutic sessions. This sort of phenomenon along with the earlier considerations discussed raise the question of to what degree the transference patterns of a particular patient will vary with the particular therapist and the cues emitted by that therapist, most importantly, cues contributing to the patient's sense of how he or she is regarded by the therapist (Baldwin et al., 1990).

It is clear that classical theory emphasizes trait-like dispositions to the neglect of situational cues, whereas contemporary theories tend to emphasize situational cues to the neglect of stable trait-like dispositions. Just as was the case some years ago in the trait versus situation controversy in the context of personality theory, the resolution of this debate lies in the recognition that for any given behavior, the dispositional and the situational interact and that the relative influence of the two sets of factors will vary with the particular behavior in question and the nature of the dispositional and situational factors (e.g., Endler & Magnusson, 1976).

Complicating matters further, one needs to add the factors of the individual's selective attention to particular situational cues as well as how he or she construes these situational cues—which, in turn, are likely to at least partly reflect chronically accessible trait-like dispositions. One is reminded of the story of the optimistic and the pessimistic child being put in a room full of horse manure. The pessimistic child is miserable, whereas the optimistic child is gleefully digging into the manure. When asked why he is so happy, he replies "With all this horse manure, there must be a pony somewhere."

Conclusions

What conclusions, even if tentative ones, can we draw about transference based on the foregoing theoretical and clinical formulations and critiques as well as empirical research findings?

1. One conclusion seems quite firm: There is no such thing as a fully opaque blank screen analyst who, because he or she emits no cues, is experienced solely on the basis of the patient's projections. Rather, every analyst or therapist emits cues, which are likely to play some part in the patient's experience of him or her.
2. The reactions to this reality have ranged from arguing for the analyst's relative anonymity (e.g., Friedman's, 1998, "keeping the noise down") to favoring explicit self-disclosure (e.g., Ehrenberg, 1995). There are no systematic studies on the relationship between self-disclosure and therapist process and outcome. Particularly relevant in the present context, there are little or no systematic data—only anecdotes and claims—on the effects of self-disclosure and analytic neutrality on transference patterns, that is, on how the therapist is experienced by the patient.
3. There is little evidence that, as Freud (1912a) maintained, transference is always linked to the patient's erotic life. Transference patterns identified in both empirical research and clinical descriptions involve a wide range of different affects and different aspects of the individual's psychological life.
4. There is much evidence that one's transference reactions to another person, including the therapist, is not simply a stereotyped template, but is strongly influenced by the behavior and attitudes of the other person. Different behaviors and attitudes of different new persons may activate different representations of significant others and therefore, may result in different transference patterns. The first-person reports of Hurwitz, Guntrip, and Kohut provide eloquent testimony to that likelihood.
5. There is also much evidence that the other's behaviors and attitudes influence not only one's transference patterns, but also one's self-evaluations. For example, cues from the other that the individual experiences as disapproving influences his or her self-esteem. Such evidence supports Kohut's formulation regarding the relationship between the

analyst's empathic mirroring and the patient's quality and level of self-esteem. It also reminds us that silence and a "blank screen" stance, which may constitute powerful cues that may have an impact on the patient's self-evaluation.

6. Based on conceptual analysis as well as clinical evidence and empirical research, there are few convincing reasons to view transference as necessarily constituting a form of resistance. Certain transference phenomena that have been interpreted as resistance can be meaningfully understood as fear of retraumatization and the need to establish conditions of safety. They can also be understood as "habitual relationship patterns" (Schachter, 2001) learned early in life.
7. There is only a moderate overlap in relationship themes between narratives about the therapist and significant others outside the therapeutic situation. The overlap that is found concerns the patient's wishes and response to self; there is no significant overlap in the component of experienced response of the other, the component most directly related to the concept of transference. This finding is at variance with the assumption that the patient experiences the therapist's reactions to his or her conflicted wishes as similar to the significant other's reactions to these wishes. Transference defined as the transfer of characteristics and expectations of significant figures on to the therapist is a ubiquitous phenomenon in the therapeutic situation.
8. There is some minimal evidence (minimal because of lack of studies) that accuracy of interpretations, including transference interpretations, is positively related to therapeutic outcome. More research is needed in this area.
9. There are mixed findings with regard to frequency of transference interpretations and therapeutic outcome. One set of studies shows that frequency of transference interpretations is related to poorer therapeutic outcome; and one well-designed study with a relatively large *N* and a one-year duration of treatment found no significant difference between frequency of transference interpretations and therapeutic outcomes. Surprisingly and "contrary to mainstream clinical thinking" (Hoglend et al., 2006, p. 1745), there was a significant interaction effect such that patients with poorer object relations benefited from transference interpretations, whereas patients with more mature object relations did not. This is an important finding that has direct relevance to clinical technique.

However, research on the relationship between frequency of interpretations and therapeutic outcome does not deal with such significant aspects of transference interpretations as their content, timing, and tone, aspects that all clinicians would agree are likely to have a greater impact on the therapeutic process than sheer frequency. As Hobson and Kapur (2005) have cogently argued, because "different psychoanalytic therapists mean very different things by the expression 'transference interpretations,' it follows that we should be circumspect about generalizing from research on the therapeutic effectiveness of interpretations when what is meant may differ widely from study to study" (p. 275). An investigation of these aspects of transference interpretations would certainly enhance the ecological validity of research in this area. Nevertheless, the fact that there were no significant differences in outcome between moderate frequency of transference interpretations and no transference interpretations raises questions regarding the axiomatic assumption that analysis of the transference is the sine qua non ingredient in successful psychoanalytic treatment. Because of the importance of this assumption in the psychoanalytic conception of transference, research is needed to further explore this issue.

One needs to distinguish here between the claim that analysis of the transference is a defining component of psychoanalytic practice, in the absence of which it would no longer be *psychoanalytic* treatment (a "sociological" observation regarding the nature of psychoanalytic practices) and the quite different empirical claim that analysis of the transference is a necessary ingredient of positive therapeutic outcome in psychoanalytic treatment. Of course, those who identify analysis of the transference as a defining component of psychoanalytic treat-ment are not just being descriptive, but also prescriptive insofar as they believe that it is a necessary ingredient in positive therapeutic outcome. Indeed, that is the basis, they would argue, for viewing it as a defining component. Nevertheless, the two should not be conflated. Even if all analysts focused on analysis of the transference in their practice, it would not necessarily follow that doing so is a critical factor in successful treatment. At the very least, there is little support for the assumption that analysis of the transference as *the* sine qua non of successful treatment.

10. Although most of us are confident that we understand what is meant when we use the term "transference" or see references to it in the literature, a careful examination of how the term is used suggests that our confidence is not always justified. The term "transference" is used in a variety of ways and refers to different behaviors and processes, among which are:
    (a) The attribution of characteristics and expectations associated with representations of early significant others to new persons.
    (b) The attribution of characteristics and expectations associated with representations of early significant others to current familiar significant others (e.g., spouse).
    (c) The attribution of characteristics and expectations associated with representations of current significant others to new persons (as in the Andersen & Baum, 1994, study).
    (d) The attribution of characteristics and expectations associated with representations of one set of current significant others to a different set of significant others.
    (e) The selective attention to cues emitted by either the new person or current significant other that facilitates and justifies the attribution of characteristics and expectations associated with representations of early significant others to the new person or current significant other.
    (f) The construal of these cues in accord with representations of early significant others.
    (g) Looking to the new person or current significant other to meet unmet developmental needs (e.g., the need for love, need for empathic mirroring).
    (h) Looking to the new person or current significant other to meet infantile wishes (e.g., incestuous wishes, wish for perfect mirroring).
    (i) As exemplified in the CCRT research, any commonality of themes with regard to what one wants from the therapist and what one wants from others outside the therapeutic situation. (As discussed earlier, this kind of consistency is just what one would expect on the basis of a trait conception of personality and does not especially require the concept of transference. In any case, this is a highly diluted concept of transference.)

11. The extant research on transference interpretations tells us little or nothing regarding their content as well as the patient's material that prompted these interpretations. With regard to the former, we do not know the criteria for what constituted a transference interpretation. My fear is that any comment made by the therapist about the patient–therapist interaction and relationship may have been identified as a transference interpretation. Ulberg et al. (2014) have developed a therapy process rating scale referred to as Transference Work Scale (TWS) reported as having good to excellent interrater agreement and which generates subscales on timing, content, and valence of transference interpretations, along with response from the patient. Future studies of the effects of transference interpretations should take account of these different features to maximize clinical ecological validity. I think it is fair to say that the verdict is not in regarding the relationship between transference interpretations and therapeutic outcome.
12. Given the many different definitions and conceptions of transference, over the years the suggestion is periodically made that the concept of transference should be abandoned and replaced by a term that is more theory-neutral and that is not as weighted down by questionable assumptions. The most sustained argument for going in this direction has been made by Schachter (2001) who suggests that we employ the term "habitual relationship pattern" to replace the term transference. In support of this suggestion, Schachter argues that there is little evidence for the basic assumption that the etiology of the patient's feelings and fantasies about a current person (the therapist in the clinical situation) lies in early childhood. The term "habitual relationship pattern" is intended to convey a focus on the here-and-now interactions between patient and therapist, with no commitment to its etiology in childhood experiences.

    Although the term "habitual relationship pattern" is a more neutral term than transference, it is not clear that it resolves or bypasses the issues inherent in the concept of transference. For one thing, as is the case with the concept of transference, a *habitual* relationship pattern clearly implies origins in the past that are not restricted to the here-and-now. As is also the case with the transference concept, insofar as it is a trait-like concept implying marked cross-situational stability, it is not clear that the concept of habitual relationship pattern provides adequate room for the influence of situational factors such as cues emitted by the other person, including the therapist (see the different relationship patterns with the different analysts described in Hurwitz's and in Guntrip's accounts).

Schachter (2001) notes the similarity between "habitual relationship pattern" and Bowlby's (1980) term "internal working model" (IWM) and Stern's (1985) concept of "representations of interactions generalized" (RIGs). However, the concepts of IWMs and RIGs refer to representations that are shaped early in life and that are relatively resistant to change, thus conceptualized as products of the very "infant determinism" Schachter wants to avoid. The question of the degree to which IWMs are trait-like, that is, stable over time and across situations, or temporally and situationally responsive has been a controversial issue in attachment theory and research. Indeed, although there is evidence of stability of attachment patterns over time, such stability is found mainly when there is also environmental stability, a situational factor. Thus, although the relative stability of attachment patterns appears trait-like, a closer look suggests that it possesses what one might refer to as an interactional stability. That is, a particular attachment pattern interacting with a relatively stable environment is likely to remain relatively stable over time. Contrastingly, a particular attachment pattern interacting with an unstable environment is likely to be relatively unstable over time.

Similar considerations arise with regard to the question of stability of attachment patterns across situations when situation is understood in terms of characteristics of one's attachment figure, which in the adult, also reflects the individual's object choice. As noted, there is some debate in the attachment literature as to whether attachment pattern is best understood as an interactional concept (i.e., one's attachment pattern with a specific attachment figure) or a trait-like concept (i.e., one's generalized attachment pattern across different attachment figures).[16]

My own view is that we should either drop the term transference or, if and when we do employ the term, make clear what we mean by it. I think there is much to be said in favor of discarding the term transference and instead focusing on exploration of and understanding the nature of the patient–therapist interactions (see Gill, 1994; Ponsi, 1999).

We will, I suspect find that different patients and different patient–therapist pairs show different patterns of interaction. Some patients may impose a stereotyped template on their experience of the therapist; other patients may show little evidence of doing so. Some patients may be exquisitely sensitive and responsive to cues emitted by the therapist; others may be *relatively insensitive and unresponsive* to such cues. By understanding one's aim as the exploration of the nature of patient–therapist interactions one hopefully limits the impact of one's theoretical assumptions (e.g., the patient is transferring onto the therapist expectations and representations of early parental figures) on how one perceives and understands the nature of these interactions.

13. One of the potential problems accompanying at least certain kinds of transference interpretations lies in their implication that the patient's reactions to the therapist are not really about the therapist, but are reactions to early parental figures transferred on to the therapist. Indeed, this is virtually made explicit by Dr. X who tells Hurwitz "You'd respond that way no matter who was in this chair." This may be experienced, as one of my patients put it, as a "cop out," as the therapist's way of avoiding confronting his or her own behavior, as a way of saying to the patient: "Your reaction has nothing to do with anything I said or did." (See Greenson's, 1967, account of his unwitting departure from a neutral stance in relation to a patient's comments about Franklin Roosevelt.)

    Given the current vagueness of the term, Dr. X's interpretation and, say, Kohut's "optimal failure" interpretations would both be seen as transference interpretations. Any research or clinical formulation that lumps together these interventions as "transference interpretations" is not likely to tell us much that is useful. It would be much more useful to refer to interpretations of patient–therapist interactions and then specify the kind of patient–therapist interaction one has identified and the specific nature of the interpretation made by the therapist.

14. Without getting bogged down by such vague and ambiguous terms as "transference interpretations" or "analysis of the transference," we may be able to avoid such arbitrary "rules" such as only analysis of the transference matters and be better able to determine to what extent and for which patients (as well as which patient–therapist pairs) active exploration of patient–therapist interactions are associated with positive

therapeutic outcome. We may also be better able to investigate such matters as whether an exploration of certain kinds of patient–therapist interactions (e.g., those that have been referred to as ruptures [see Safran, Muran, & Eubanks-Carter, 2011] or optimal failures or negative transference) are more therapeutically effective than exploration of other kinds of patient–therapist interactions (e.g., those characterized as constituting a strong therapeutic alliance or contributing to an experience of conditions of safety) for certain patients and patient–therapist pairs. By clarifying terms such as transference so that they may be more readily linked to what can be observed in the clinical situation and by recognizing that there are likely to be important individual and contextual differences in the nature of patient–therapist interactions, we may also narrow the gap among theory, clinical processes, and empirical research.

Notes

1. Note that although Freud seems to be stating here that the therapeutic relationship itself is a therapeutic ingredient, he makes it clear in his other writings that he views the therapeutic relationship mainly as a vehicle for the operation of the critical therapeutic ingredients, namely, interpretations leading to insight and awareness.
2. According to Freud (1915[1914]), like transference love, falling in love in general is also based on infantile object choices.
3. Despite his theoretical position, in Guntrip's (1975) account of his analysis with Fairbairn, he is described as rather remote and engaged in a good deal of interpretation primarily concerned with oedipal issues. This apparent gap between theoretical writings and personal qualities and behavior as a therapist is undoubtedly not uncommon, but somewhat of a taboo topic in the psychoanalytic literature.
4. It is somewhat odd that Freud does not discuss the possibility, inherent in his concept of fixation, that over-gratification as well as over-deprivation can result in an indiscriminate search for love. This logic also applies to Fairbairn's comments on infantile dependence insofar as the separation anxiety and restriction of relationships to overly dependent ones that he describes may be because of a combination of an overindulgence of dependency needs and a failure to encourage and reinforce normal independence. (See Masterson & Rinsley, 1975, who argue that this pattern plays an etiological role in the development of borderline personality disorder.)
5. Given this perspective, it is understandable that the form of psychopathology with which Fairbairn is most concerned and which he believes is at the core of

all psychopathology is the schizoid personality structure. Not surprisingly, what is identified as the core of psychopathology by different theorists varies with their theories of personality and human nature. Thus, for Fairbairn, the schizoid condition is at the core of all psychopathology; for Freud, it is id–ego conflict; for Kohut, it is self-defects; and for attachment theorists as well as relational analysts such as Mitchell, it is maladaptive interactional structures.

6. The lessening of transference projection and distortions and getting to experience the analyst as he or she really is would, one would expect, also constitute a goal for classical treatment. However, this goal would appear to be hampered by the opaque blank screen stance of the analyst. That is, how does one get to experience another more realistically when he or she aims to be as opaque as possible.
7. It should be noted that despite the sharp differences between Freudian and Kohutian views, there is a common emphasis on the "replacement" of infantile or archaic wishes and needs with more mature ones. However, from the Freudian perspective, it is mainly wishes that are "replaced" through renunciation and/or sublimation; and from a self-psychology perspective it is mainly needs that are "replaced" by virtue of strengthening of self-cohesiveness.
8. Bacal (1998) has raised the question of why one should not refer to "optimal responsiveness" rather than "optimal frustration"? I think there are good reasons for the latter term. However, as Bacal's question suggests, from Kohut's perspective, the term "optimal frustration" has the virtue of not raising the specter of gratification and, indeed, as the above-quoted passage from Kohut indicates, being read as essentially equivalent to "abstinence."
9. It is interesting to observe that there is at least some family resemblance between Freud's notion of relinquishment or sublimation of ungratifiable infantile wishes and the idea of relinquishment of the ungratifiable wish for perfect mirroring. The difference between Freud and Kohut—an important one—is that whereas Freud claims that infantile wishes are life-long and not easily relinquished, self-psychology theorists such as Basch (1986) maintain that once self-cohesiveness is strengthened, the wish for perfect mirroring, which, according to Basch, is not inherently pleasurable, fades away of its own accord. That is, it is no longer experienced as a vital need.
10. As well as, perhaps, other reasons, such as shortening the duration of analytic treatment and de-emphasizing the primacy of insight.
11. French (1933) was quite interested in conditioning and wrote a lengthy paper devoted to identifying convergences between psychoanalytic and Pavlovian theories.
12. I am reminded here of an old comedy skit in which Elaine May plays the part of a Viennese-accented psychoanalyst and Mike Nichols is the patient. He announces in a session that he will miss the Christmas day session because he wants to be with his family. The analyst obviously feels rejected and is emotionally devastated by this announcement, but covers over and clothes her reactions in presumably professional and "objective" transference interpretations. The result is a hilarious satire on the concept of transference.

13. One can speculate that Kohut's approach is therapeutically effective because it deals with narcissistic patients suffering from self-defect, that is, more disturbed patients.
14. From a strictly conditioning perspective, this is such a blatant instance of negative reinforcement of the patient's expression of warm, appreciative feeling.
15. It needs to be kept in mind that in the research of Andersen and her colleagues, although participants falsely attributed characteristics of a significant other to a new person, for the most part, their memory of the new person was accurate.
16. I am reminded of a scene in the novel, *The accidental tourist* (Tyler, 1985). The wife of the protagonist who leaves her for another woman asks him whether he still loves her. He responds that he does. Why, then, she asks, are you leaving me? His response is that he likes the person he is when he is with the other woman.

Chapter 2

Countertransference

There are two literatures on the topic of countertransference, one published in psychoanalytic journals and the other published in psychology journals. As one might expect, the latter is characterized by an emphasis on research and on measurement of countertransference. Although the articles in the psychological literature necessarily refer to psychoanalytic papers and books on the topic—after all it is in that literature that the term countertransference first appears—there is virtually no reference in the psychoanalytic literature on countertransference to any articles in psychology journals. It is as if the former did not exist. Indeed, it is likely that psychoanalysts who have written about the topic do not know of the existence of the psychological literature on countertransference.

The organization of this chapter is as follows: I begin with the psychoanalytic literature on countertransference and then follow with a discussion of the psychological literature, much of which is taken up with research on the topic of countertransference. I then consider the implications of the research findings for how one understands countertransference and the role it plays in treatment process and outcome.

Definitions of countertransference in the psychoanalytic literature

Freudian conception of countertransference

Freud first uses the term countertransference in a 1909 letter to Jung in which he refers to the latter's amorous and sexual involvement with Sabina

Spielrein (McGuire, 1974). He writes in a somewhat fatherly way that he understands the experiences of sexual temptation in relation to the patient, and that such experiences "help us to develop the thick skin we need and to dominate 'countertransference,' which is after all a permanent problem for us; they teach us to displace our own affects to best advantage" (McGuire, 1974, p. 230). Thus, in this first reference to countertransference, Freud's focus is on the analyst's erotic feelings toward his or her patient and, in particular, on the danger of the analyst acting on these feelings.

In the same letter to Jung, Freud writes, "The way these women manage to charm us with every conceivable psychic perfection until they have attained their purpose is one of nature's greatest spectacles" (McGuire, 1974, p. 231). Thus, as de Urtubey (1995) notes, at this point in his thinking, countertransference for Freud referred primarily to male analysts' erotic feelings and temptations in response to the female patients' seductions; and "dominating what the countertransference means for Freud, that the (male) analyst will not succumb to the (female) patient's seductions" (de Urtubey, 1995, p. 684). Nothing is said about other possible countertransference constellations or about the analysts' other feelings and responses (e.g., hostility) to the patient that may interfere with the treatment.

In Freud's 1910 paper, the classical concept of countertransference became broadened to refer to material "which arises in him [i.e., the analyst] as a result of the patient's influence on his unconscious feelings" (p. 144). Freud further notes the need for the analyst "to recognize and overcome this countertransference in himself" in view of the fact "that every analyst's achievement is limited by what his own complexes and resistances permit" (pp. 144–145). Countertransference needs to be resolved either through self-analysis or returning to a regular analysis. In other words, as the prefix "counter" suggests, the countertransference of the analyst is a reaction to and parallels the transference of the patient. In both the cases, it must be recognized, analyzed, and resolved if therapeutic progress is to occur.

In his 1912b paper, Freud states that the analyst's emotional stance and attitudes should be similar to that of the surgeon. As he puts it, "I cannot advise my colleagues too urgently to model themselves during psychoanalytic treatment on the surgeon, who puts aside all his feelings, even his human sympathy, and concentrates his mental forces on the single aim of performing the operation as skilfully as possible" (p. 115). Freud's justification for requiring emotional coldness in the analyst is that "it creates the most advantageous conditions for both parties: for the doctor a desirable protection for his own emotional life and for the patient the largest amount of help that we can give him today" (p. 115). Another justification, as noted in Chapter 1 on transference, is the importance of the analyst presenting himself or herself to the patient as a (blank) screen on which the patient can project his or her preoccupations, conflicts, fantasies, wishes, etc. According to this rationale, were the analyst to show or express his or her own personal feelings, it would not be clear to what extent the patient's attributions to the analyst were entirely his or her own projections or were influenced by the analyst's expression of his or her feelings. After all, the safest way of avoiding the danger of revealing one's feelings is not having them, or at least not expressing them.[1]

The other rationale for advising the stance and attitude of the surgeon for the analyst is that adopting this stance will minimize the risk that the analyst's central role of an objective observer, someone whose primary tasks are to gain knowledge of the patient's unconscious contents and processes and communicate such knowledge to the patient, will be compromised.[2]

Although Freud appeared to define countertransference as a reaction to the patient's transference, his surgeon metaphor advising a general attitude of "emotional coldness" implies that any experience of emotions, whether it arises in response to the patient's transference or independently of it, would be seen as countertransference. Also, if countertransference is understood as reflecting the analyst's unresolved conflicts and "neurotic residue" (de Urtubey, 1995, p. 684), it is not clear why its manifestations would be limited to reactions to the patient's transference. The mere presence of the patient, including his or her gender, ethnic background, how he or she looks, talks, and dresses, and so on, insofar as they are redolent of figures from the analyst's past or as they trigger certain thoughts and feelings, may elicit unresolved conflicts and the analysts' "neurotic residue." This may all occur independently of and prior to expressions of the patients' transference.[3]

Contemporary conceptions of countertransference

Under the impact of influential work by Heimann (1950), Little (1951), Racker (1968), and others, countertransference was reconceptualized in a number of ways; first, it was now "totalistically" defined "to cover all the feelings which the analyst experiences toward his patient" (Heimann, 1950, p. 88; Kernberg, 1965); and second, rather than an occasional blip in the treatment, the analysts' emotional responses toward the patient were seen as ubiquitous and inevitable. Along with the redefinition of countertransference came the claim that rather than representing an impediment to treatment, countertransference "represents one of the most important tools for [the analyst's] work." In particular, "the analyst's countertransference is an instrument of research into the patient's unconscious" (Heimann, 1950, p. 81). Thus, the radical shift from viewing countertransference as an impediment to an indispensable therapeutic tool, in particular, an indispensable tool to understand the patient's unconscious mental states.[4] (See also the works of Langs, 1980, and Searles, 1979, on countertransference.)

As noted in the beginning of Chapter 1, recognition of the centrality of transference was viewed as the "common ground" that cut across different psychoanalytic theories (Wallerstein, 1992). Quite remarkably given the literature on countertransference already by 1992, when the edited book by Wallerstein was published, there was not a single reference to countertransference in the book's index. Only three years later, Gabbard (1995) wrote that recognition of the therapeutic usefulness of the analysts' countertransference constituted the "common ground" that cut across different psychoanalytic theories. Although the centrality of transference and analysis of the transference did, indeed, constitute a common ground during a long period of psychoanalytic history, the "common ground" claim for countertransference could only reasonably be made following a reconceptualization of the concept and an altered perspective on it.

To a certain extent, this shift in understanding countertransference from impediment to indispensable therapeutic tool parallels the shift from viewing the transference primarily as resistance to viewing it also as an indispensable therapeutic tool, but only to a certain extent. From a psychoanalytic perspective, one can readily understand that although transference may be a form of resistance, understanding and interpreting the transference, that is understanding and interpreting how the patient experiences the analyst, would be at the center of the therapeutic work. However, a similar logic or rationale is not apparent with regard to the analyst's countertransference, even when it is understood as the totality of his or her thoughts and feelings about the patient. One then needs to ask in what ways the analyst's attention to his or her thoughts and feelings triggered by the patient serves as an indispensable therapeutic tool.

One needs to separate out the different aspects of the reconceptualization of countertransference. One aspect, a definitional one, is reconceptualizing it "totalistically" as referring to all the analyst's feelings toward the patient. A second aspect is that the analyst's emotional responses to the patient are ubiquitous, even inevitable. A third aspect, an empirical claim of the role of the newly defined countertransference in the clinical process, is that rather than an impediment, it is an indispensable therapeutic tool; and the fourth aspect is the more specific empirical claim that the most important way that the analyst's countertransference feelings represent a therapeutic tool is as a reliable guide to the patient's unconscious mental contents.

Although the above redefinition and claims are presented as intertwined, they are, in fact, somewhat separate in the sense of being logically independent of each other. For example, the fact that emotional responses to the patient are ubiquitous and inevitable does not preclude the possibility that they are largely generated by the analyst's unresolved conflicts and therefore, generally constitute therapeutic impediments. A "totalistic" conception of countertransference does not, in itself, necessarily imply that "all the feelings which the analyst experiences toward his patient" represent "one of the most important tools for his work" (Heimann, 1950, p. 81). They may or may not, depending upon a number of factors, including the nature and intensity of these feelings, how they are expressed, the patient's character structure, the nature and strength of the alliance, and so on. The claim that analyst's feelings toward the patient represent an important therapeutic tool requires a separate argument that needs to be made along with supporting evidence.

Further, even if it could be shown that the analyst's emotional response to the patient "represents one of the most important tools for his work" (Heimann, 1950, p. 81), that, in itself, would not warrant the further conclusion that the specific way in which the analyst's emotional responses to the patient represent an important therapeutic tool is that they serve as an instrument that can reliably reveal the patient's unconscious mental contents. Again, they may or may not. That claim, too, requires a separate argument and relevant evidence.[5]

It is possible, after all, that the analyst's emotional response to the patient may constitute an important therapeutic tool in ways other than as a guide to the patient's unconscious. For example, the analyst's emotional response may enhance his or her caring and dedication to the patient and to the therapeutic process. And contrastingly, if the analyst's emotional response to the patient is intensely negative or suffused with boredom, it is likely to represent an impediment to the treatment rather than a therapeutic tool. But this more commonsensical way in which the analyst's emotions may serve as a therapeutic tool is not what Heimann and others have in mind. In their view, even intensely negative emotional responses to the patient constitute an important therapeutic tool because these responses serve as a guide to the patient's unconscious mental states.

In any ordinary interaction, reliance on one's own emotional response to the other as a guide to what the other is thinking and feeling may not only be useful, but can also lead to disastrous miscommunication. Based on one's emotional response to the other's behavior, one may attribute motives to the other that do not match the other's feelings or intentions. Because of this possibility and particularly if one cares about the relationship, a self-aware person reflects on his or her emotional response; questions its relationship to the other's actual feelings and intentions; and, if necessary and deemed useful, communicates his or her feelings to the other, with an eye toward examining their "match" to the other's feelings and intentions. This process is not always successful, but it certainly more greatly enhances the possibility of accurate and constructive communication than the blanket assumption, often implicit, that one's own emotional response is a reliable guide to the other's feelings and intentions.

Interestingly, the implicit and unquestioned assumption that in any given interaction, one's emotional response to another is a reliable guide to the other's feelings and intentions characterizes the cognition and affect of borderline patients. Thus, if I feel insulted and "dissed," you must have these feelings and intentions toward me (see Gabbard & Horowitz, 2009, for a clinical example). Particularly, under the impact of strong emotion, the borderline individual's capacity to insert an intervening questioning and reflective step is limited (see Bateman & Fonagy, 2006).

The possibility or perhaps likelihood that what holds for ordinary interactions also may hold for the analytic situation is often denied or minimized by the arguments that unlike most interactions, (1) the analyst achieves "rapport on a deep level" with the patient (Heimann, 1950); (2) through identification with the patient, the analyst is able to tap into what the patient feels (Racker, 1968). As Racker (1968) puts it, the "thoughts and feelings which emerge in him [i.e., the analyst] will be, precisely, those which did not emerge in the patient, i.e., the repressed and the unconscious" (p. 17); (3) because the analyst does not experience "violent emotions of any kind, of love or hate . . . [that] impel towards actions rather than towards contemplation," he or she can rely on his or her own emotional response (Heimann, 1950, p. 82); (4) unlike others, "when the analyst in his own analysis has worked through his infantile conflicts and anxieties (paranoid and depressive), so that he can easily establish contact with his own unconscious, he will not impute to his patient what belongs to himself" (Heimann, 1950, p. 83); (5) as a variation of (4), because the analyst is less repressed than the patient, he or she has access to unconscious material that the patient does not have (Racker, 1968); and (6) in a state of evenly hovering attention, the analyst's unconscious functions like a telephone receiver that can register and pick up the patient's unconscious (Freud, 1912a). Indeed, Freud (1933[1932]) wrote that after taking account of various anecdotes, "there remains a strong balance of probability in favor of thought-transference as a fact" (p. 43). These are just samples of the arguments for the claim that, unlike ordinary interactions, the analyst's emotional response to the patient serves as a reliable guide to the patient's unconscious.

One assumes, although it is not always made explicit, that it is the analyst's attention to and reflection on his thoughts and feelings, rather than the thoughts and feelings per se, that constitute a therapeutic tool. Such a reasonable perspective would perhaps represent a point of convergence between classical and contemporary conceptions of countertransference insofar as attention to and reflection on one's emotional responses to the patient are deemed important in both perspectives. However, reflection on one's thoughts and feelings can lead one to conclude, on any given occasion, that they do not represent an accurate guide to the patient's mental state, but rather more fully represent one's own unresolved conflicts. Thus, it is somewhat disturbing to read Racker's (1968) unqualified assertion that for the well analyzed analyst, "the thoughts and feelings which emerge in [the analyst] will be, precisely, those which did not emerge in the patient, i.e., the repressed and the unconscious" (p. 17). It is also disturbing to read

Levine's (1997) assertion that there is a pragmatic value in assuming that even those thoughts and emotional experiences that clearly arise within the analyst from the analyst's own personal life and have seemingly little to do with the specific patient at hand—for example, when the analyst's personal life events intrude upon the hour to such an extent so as to encroach upon or even override his or her capacities to analyze effectively—can be presumed to have a patient-related component that contributes to their appearance in a given hour in a particular way (p. 48).

In both of the above cases, what is emphasized is not the potential value of the analyst's attention to and reflection on his or her thoughts and feelings, with an eye toward considering their *possible* relative usefulness or lack of usefulness in understanding the patient's mental state. Rather, what seems to be asserted is that the analyst can simply *assume*, without any further examination or reflection, that his thoughts and feelings are "precisely those which did not emerge in the patient" or, more modestly, that they always and necessarily have a "patient-related component." Quite remarkably, the latter assumption is advised even when "thoughts and emotional experience that clearly arise within the analyst from the analyst's personal life and have seemingly little to do with the specific patient at hand" (Levine, 1997, p. 48). Also note that countertransference has been implicitly broadened to include not only all of the analyst's feelings and thoughts toward the patient, but also all of the analyst's feelings and thoughts in the analytic situation even when they are concerned with the "analyst's personal life events" which so preoccupy him or her that they "encroach upon or even override his or her capacities to analyze effectively" (Levine, 1997, p. 48).[6]

How do theorists who adopt the above point of view justify this claim? What processes do they posit that would enable this to take place? Some theorists do not address these sorts of questions at all, but simply assert that such and such is the case in one way or another. However, some theorists do attempt to address these questions. As we have seen, Racker (1968) writes that if well analyzed (e.g., fewer repressions) and identified with the patient, the feelings and thoughts arising in the analyst will be those the patient has repressed. In effect, Racker proposes that through the process of identification, in particular, through the analyst's identification with the patient's repressed unconscious, he or she gains access to the latter. Thus, this is no ordinary identification or empathy with another's conscious experiences, but with the other's unconscious, that is, with what the other has *not* consciously experienced, indeed, has defensively kept from conscious experience.

To complicate matters even more, insofar as countertransference is understood as an unconscious process, it is not entirely clear what Racker can mean when he refers to the "thoughts and feelings, which emerge in [the analyst]" [and] will be, precisely, those which did not emerge in the patient, that is, the repressed and the unconscious? If countertransference is unconscious, in what sense do these thoughts and feelings *emerge* in the analyst? Racker seems to suggest that because the analyst is less repressed than the patient, he or she has greater access to thoughts and feelings that would ordinarily be repressed. But, if the analyst does, indeed, have access (which presumably means phenomenal access to experiences) to a set of thoughts and feelings (that are the product of identification with the patient), in what sense can all this be understood in the context of countertransference as unconscious?

One possible response to these questions, one suggested by Freud's (1912b) metaphor of the analyst's unconscious as a telephone receiver, is that the thoughts and feelings that "emerge" in the analyst, even if fleetingly, and to which he or she has direct conscious experiential access, require *deciphering and interpretation* for their unconscious meaning to be understood (similar to the patient's free associations, manifest content of dreams, and drive derivatives). In this view, it is not the specific thoughts and feelings that emerge in the analyst that will be precisely, those that the patient has repressed, but rather the unconscious meanings of these thoughts and feelings that will presumably be, precisely, the unconscious meanings the patient has repressed, and of which, therefore, he or she is unaware. According to this view, the specific phenomenal content of the analyst's thoughts and feelings could be quite different from the contents the patient would experience were he or she not engaged in repression. Rather, the unconscious meanings to which the analyst's thoughts and feelings point to, once deciphered and interpreted, would serve as a guide to the unconscious meanings repressed by the patient.

This seems to be something like what Freud had in mind when he referred to the unconscious of the analyst communicating with the unconscious of the patient and when he employed the telephone receiver metaphor. He (Freud, 1912b) writes: "the analyst must turn his own unconscious like a receptive organ towards the transmitting unconscious of the patient. He must adjust himself to the patient as a telephone receiver is adjusted to the transmitting microphone. Just as the receiver converts back into sound waves the electric oscillations in the telephone line which were set up by sound waves, so the doctor's unconscious is able, from the derivatives of the unconscious which are communicated to him, reconstruct that unconscious, which has determined the patient's free associations. But if the doctor is to be in a position to use his unconscious in this way as an instrument in the analysis, he must himself fulfill one psychological condition to a high degree. He may not tolerate any resistances in himself which hold back from his consciousness what has been perceived by his unconscious" (p. 115).

Freud's telephone receiver metaphor would seem to suggest that to reconstruct the unconscious of the patient, the analyst must decipher not only the unconscious meanings of the patient's free associations, but also the unconscious meanings of the thoughts and feelings that emerge in him or her. In short, even from the perspective of those, like Racker, who believe that the analyst's thoughts and feelings serve as a guide to the patient's unconscious, a careful examination of this position suggests that matters are far more complex than the simple idea that the analyst's conscious thoughts and feelings somehow mirror the patient's unconscious; and therefore, all the analyst need do is turn to his or her thoughts and feelings to discern the patient's unconscious.

As we will see in Chapter 3 on projective identification, one reason the analyst's thoughts and feelings are believed to serve as a guide to the patient's unconscious is the assumption that the patient projects his or her mental contents not only *on to* the analyst, but also *into* the analyst, that is, *puts them* into the analyst. This difference in prepositions has a major impact on meaning. For the former can be understood as the familiar process of consciously or unconsciously attributing to another one's own thoughts and feelings (see Chapter 1 on transference). What it means, however, to put one's thoughts and feelings *into* another can only be understood as a fantasy rather than the familiar cognitive process of attribution to another. But if talking about one person putting mental contents into another refers to a fantasy, why should it influence the analyst's thoughts and feelings at all? Only if the patient's fantasy of putting his or her thoughts and feelings into the analyst in some way triggers or exerts some influence on what the analyst thinks or feels, would it make sense to claim that the analyst's attention to his or her thoughts and feelings provides any information about the patient's mental contents. Unless one believes in mental telepathy or unconscious communication through some mysterious extrasensory means, one person's fantasy in relation to another person per se does not influence what the latter thinks or feels. Hence, if the patient's fantasy is to influence or trigger the analyst's thoughts and feelings, it must be accompanied by cues emitted by the patient, however subtle they may be. Further, the analyst must, at some level, pick up and respond to these cues, even if he or she is not aware of doing so. As far as I can see, this is the only reasonable meaning that talk about the patient putting mental contents *into* the analyst can have.

As we will also see in Chapter 3, this is, in effect, what Ogden (1979, 1982) proposes when he describes the phase of "interpersonal pressure" in projective identification. Ogden is referring here to the patient's unconscious attempt to induce in the analyst the very feelings and thoughts the patient has projected. One can, of course, only succeed in inducing certain feelings and thoughts in another by emitting cues, that is, by behaving in a certain way—again, unless one postulates mental telepathy or some other mysterious process.

To return to and summarize the main point here: attention to one's thoughts and feelings about another person or triggered by another person can serve as a guide to one's (conscious or unconscious) mental contents only if these mental contents have some impact on oneself. Put another way, a necessary condition for the claim that the analyst's countertransference can serve as a reliable guide to the patient's unconscious thoughts and feelings to have any semblance of validity is that the latter must at least have some impact on the analyst's mental state. And this can come about only if the patient's thoughts and feelings are accompanied by patient cues that the analyst registers.

But—and herein lies the rub—this is only a necessary but not sufficient condition for the claim that countertransference is a reliable and even indispensable guide to the patient's mental contents. It is one thing to register and react to someone's cues. It is, however, another thing to claim that one's reaction to these cues invariably or even regularly serve as a guide to the identification of the other's mental states. And this is so because one's reactions to another's cues always entail one's own construals of these cues and the personal history and "apperceptive mass" that underlie these construals. To assume otherwise is to replace the conception of the analyst as a blank screen with a concept of the analyst as nothing but a mirror who passively "receives" the patient's thoughts and feelings and contributes none of his or her own thoughts and feelings that are the product of his or her own idiosyncratic history and personality. If one takes the contemporary conception of countertransference to its *reductio ad absurdum* logical extreme, one could conclude that for the analyst to achieve understanding of the patient's unconscious mental states, all he or she need to do is simply examine his or her own thoughts and feelings triggered in the interaction with the patient.

Heimann (1950) attempts to address the issue of the effect of the analyst's own contributions to the countertransference on its validity as a guide to the patient's unconscious. She writes that "in the comparison of feelings roused in himself with his patient's associations and behavior, the analyst possesses a most valuable means of checking whether he has understood or failed to understand his patient" (p. 82). Heimann seems to be saying here that the analyst assesses the degree to which his or her emotional response to the patient really does provide a key to the latter's unconscious by somehow comparing or looking at the relationship between his or her emotional response and the patient's associations and behavior. This, already, represents a softening of the stark unqualified claim that "the character of the countertransference corresponds to the nature of the patient's unconscious impulses and defenses". Be that as it may, however, Heimann does not elaborate on how this comparison would operate. What is especially problematic here is that it is the analyst's own interpretations of the patient's free associations and behavior that are expected to tell him or her "whether he has understood or failed to understand his patient." And insofar as it is the patient's free associations and behavior that play a significant role in triggering the analyst's emotional response, and insofar as the analyst's interpretations of the patient's free associations and behavior are embedded in that emotional response, how and in what ways are the analyst's attention to and interpretations of the patient's free associations and behavior expected to help him or her decide whether his emotional response constitutes understanding or failing to understand his or her patient? Heimann does not address these complex issues.

The conception of countertransference I have described is not limited to the early work of Racker and Heimann. In a 2015 paper, Ogden interprets a main message of Bion's (1967) "Notes on memory and desire" that the analyst must forgo any attempt to gain information about the patient based on "sense impressions because such an attempt is 'a hindrance to the psychoanalyst's intuition of the [patient's] reality with which he must be at one'" (Bion, 1967, p. 136). For Ogden, as illustrated in a clinical vignette he presents, being at one with the patient's psychic reality is essentially an expression of a love relationship, even if an "analytic love relationship" (p. 300). Ogden ends his paper by concluding that the significance of Bion's article lies in the fact that "it supplants awareness from its central role in the analytic process and, in its place, instates the analyst's (largely unconscious) psychic reality of the present moment by becoming at one with it" (p. 305). In other words, the main task of the analyst is not to gain knowledge and understanding of the patient through observation and "sense impressions." Rather, the task of the analyst is to intuit (based largely on unconscious processes) the unconscious psychic reality of the current interaction with the patient. In short, this is another version of the stance that the analyst comes to understand the patient not primarily through observation and listening, but through attention to his or her thoughts and feelings elicited in the interaction with the patient. Ogden's emphasis on the analyst's "reverie" as a vital source of understanding is his specific version of this general formulation. It is not clear from Ogden's paper what the analyst does with the understanding he or she has presumably achieved from the "reverie" experience.

The challenges to the classical conception of countertransference constitute but one aspect of a broader challenge to the classical conceptions of the analytic stance, of the patient's transference, and of the relationship between patient and analyst. More specifically, challenges arose with regard to the conception of the analyst as a "blank screen" for the patient's projections and as an objective observer who, without the possibly contaminating effects of his or her own emotions, could "read" the patient's unconscious. In rejecting this image, it was noted, for example, by Heimann (1950), that emotional responses to the patients were ubiquitous, even inevitable. Just as the patient's emotional responses to the analyst were ubiquitous and inevitable, so was this also true for the analyst vis-a-vis the patient. One can understand these developments as a legitimate and constructive expression of some kind of increasing "democratization" or humanization of the analytic relationship and a softening of the image of the authoritative (authoritarian?), austere, and objective *Menschenkenner* who could see into the unconscious mind of the patient. Indeed, at one point, in the hands of Ferenczi, the "equalization" of the analytic relationship took the form of mutual analysis.[7]

The next or perhaps accompanying step taken was to reject the idea that the analyst's emotional responses to the patient were necessarily contaminating. Indeed, this idea was turned on its head in the assertion that the analyst's emotional responses represented an indispensable therapeutic tool rather than a contaminating factor. In short, a recognition of the untenability of the blank screen image of the analyst, and of the inevitability and ubiquitousness of the analyst's emotional responses to the patient went a long way to undermining the classical conception of the analyst as objective observer whose knowledge base provided him or her with privileged epistemological access to the patient's mental life. And yet, and with great irony, the claim of privileged epistemological access to the patient's unconscious has been essentially resuscitated in new guise and with a new basis for such access. Now, it is not primarily the analyst's theoretical knowledge that enables him or her to peer into the patient's unconscious. This claim, in any case, while perhaps sustainable during the period of hegemony of classical theory and ego psychology, became increasingly difficult to maintain in the face of theoretical pluralism.

The new claim is that the well analyzed analyst's "thoughts and feelings which emerge in him will be, precisely, those which did not emerge in the patient, i.e., the repressed and the unconscious" (Racker, 1986, p. 17). Or, as Heimann (1950) puts it, "the character of the countertransference corresponds to the nature of the patient's unconscious impulses and defenses operative at the actual time" (p. 84). Thus, a new foundation is created for the familiar claim of the analyst as *Menschenkenner* who continues to have a kind of privileged access to the patient's unconscious, this time, through his or her identification with and emotional response to the patient.

Like most individuals or groups who have achieved a privileged position, the analyst has found a new way to retain that position in the very process of seeming to relinquish the old foundation for it. Indeed, in certain respects, there is now a firmer, more solid, basis for the analyst's claim. For, after all, theoretical pluralism and the possibility of contrary empirical evidence in relation to one's presumed theoretical knowledge can serve to weaken one's claim that one's theoretical knowledge serves as a reliable basis for understanding the patient's unconscious. Contrastingly, if it is really true, as Racker (1968) proposes, that the thoughts and feelings that emerge in the analyst well be precisely those that make up the patient's unconscious, and if it is really true, as Heimann (1950) maintains, that "the character of the counter-transference corresponds to the nature of the patient's unconscious impulses and defenses." (p. 84), then the new basis for understanding the patient's unconscious is on for firmer footing than the basis it has replaced. For, the surgeon metaphor, notwithstanding, insofar as all analysts, whatever their theoretical persuasion, have some emotional response to their patient, it follows that we now have a transtheoretical reliable tool for having access to the patient's unconscious.

The problem with this rosy picture is that it is constructed on a house of cards. As noted earlier, although there is little doubt that in any human interaction, including the interaction between analyst and patient, one's emotions and thoughts in relation to the person with whom one is interacting can serve as a guide to that person's mental states, including mental states of which he or she is not fully aware, one's thoughts and feelings may just as readily *not* serve as such a guide. For psychoanalysis to rely on the analyst's emotional response to the patient as its sole or main credential, its "common ground" for understanding the patient's unconscious mental states, is, indeed, a thin and shaky foundation. This is especially the case given the fact that no specific processes are identified that would make that claim plausible or convincing. Many of the current writings on countertransference seem to go from the observation that in any given interaction, one's emotional responses to the other may reveal something about the other's unconscious/unacknowledged mental states to the hyperbolic claim that it can regularly and reliably do so.

Countertransference and analytic love

In Chapter 1 on transference, I cited Freud's (1912c) statement that "if someone's need for love is not entirely satisfied by reality, he is bound to approach every new person whom he meets with libidinal anticipatory ideas" (p. 100). Freud is essentially saying that because the need for love persists in individuals deprived of love, they seek love in every new relationship, including the therapeutic one. This component of transference entails the patient looking to the analyst (as well as other significant figures) to gratify needs for love that were not sufficiently met in childhood.

How does Freud suggest the analyst respond to this aspect of transference? From Freud's perspective, although a patient can realistically expect his or her analyst to provide such things as professional expertise, interest, and caring, he or she cannot reasonably expect the analyst to meet unmet needs for love. Further, the indiscriminate (approaching every new person with "libidinal anticipatory ideas") and unrealistic nature of the patient's wish for love would make it evident to Freud that the patient's wish for love is essentially an infantile wish that cannot be realistically met (at least not by the analyst). Freud's "answers" here fit into his general point of view that the patient's infantile wishes need not to be gratified, but repudiated or sublimated.

Freud (1915[1914]) warned against the danger of the analyst yielding to the temptation of the patient's erotic seduction. He also warned against the analyst's temptation to gratify rather than analyze. Insofar as the patient's most persistent efforts to receive gratification is in the realm of love, Freud's warnings against gratification essentially consist in warnings against returning the patient's love. In short, Freud believed that the analyst could not (and should not) gratify the patient's unmet needs and wishes, including the wish or need to be loved by the analyst.

For the analyst to attempt to gratify the patient's wish to be loved would be seen by Freud as an egregious instance of countertransference, understood as an impediment to the treatment. For many years, this was simply taken for granted by analysts. And then, at some point, papers began to appear that spoke of a special kind of love, *analytic love*, that the analyst felt for his or her patient. This was not sexual love, but what one might call sublimated love, implicitly expressed in everyday analytic work. So, this talk of analytic love was presumably not so much a matter of doing something different, but a matter of the attitude with which one carried out one's therapeutic work and of construing what one was doing as analytic love.

The first expression of that construal of the analytic situation that I recall reading was in a paper by Loewald (1960) wherein he writes that "the analyst assumes a stance of objectivity and neutrality the essence of which is love and respect for the individual and individual development" (p. 229). Although Loewald analogizes between analytic and parental love, he is obviously referring here not to what we ordinarily mean by love, including parental love (parents do not generally have a stance of objectivity and neutrality toward their children), but to a kind of love that is somehow neutral and objective.

More recently and in a relatively short space of time, a number of papers began to appear on the topic of analytic love. Some illustrative examples include a paper by Friedman (2005a) entitled "Is there a special psychoanalytic love?" accompanied by a discussion of the paper by the philosopher Martha Nussbaum and a reply by Friedman; a chapter by Wolson (2011) entitled "The seminal therapeutic influence of analytic love: A pluralistic perspective;" a book by Bach (2006) entitled *Getting from here to there: analytic love, analytic process*; a paper by Novick and Novick (2000) entitled "Love in the therapeutic alliance;" a book by Steingart (1995) entitled *A thing apart: Love and reality in the therapeutic relationship*; a paper by Shaw (2003) entitled "On the therapeutic action of analytic love"; and an entire issue of the journal *Psychoanalytic Inquiry* (Shaw, 2007) devoted to the topic "The analyst's love: Contemporary perspectives."

One of the questions that arises with regard to this literature is: Why now? Why the recent reconceptualization of regular analytic work as analytic love and why the recent stance that, in some way, analysts love their patients, that it is alright to do so, and that it is even inevitable in the work they do with patients—even if analysts may differ with regard to how they define love in the analytic situation? Among the reasons for why now, one can point to a number of possible factors, including the increasing influence of relational psychoanalysis and the two-person psychology perspective it has ushered in; presumed differences in the type of patients seen in psychoanalytic treatment who presumably require the dedication implied in the term analytic love; the emphasis in self psychology on empathic understanding—which can be seen as having a family resemblance to analytic love; the new respectability of relationship factors, including corrective emotional experiences; and the identification of the analyst as a "good" object as a critical ingredient in positive outcome (Fairbairn, 1952).

There may be an additional factor. As we know, the pool of patients available for traditional analysis, including the frequency, rigor, time, and expense it demands, has shrunken precipitously. There are undoubtedly a number of reasons for this state of affairs, including perhaps changes in the predominant form of psychopathology and a marked drop in the status and prestige of psychoanalysis in the culture, which, in turn, has meant that many people who in the past might be eager to undergo psychoanalysis are simply not interested in doing so. They are simply not willing to invest time, energy, and money in engaging in a project about whose value and efficacy there is much skepticism expressed in the larger culture.

Given this state of affairs, we find the psychoanalytic community responding by relaxing and altering the austere image and rigor of traditional psychoanalytic situation characterized by deprivation and abstinence and transforming it into one in which the patient is loved by the analyst, even if it is a special kind of love—analytic love. I am not suggesting that the analytic community has consciously and deliberately launched a public relations market campaign to soften the image of psychoanalytic treatment and render it more attractive to prospective patients. It is clear that nothing of this sort has taken place. I am suggesting that the recent prominence of analytic love may reflect a response to a current state of affairs characterized by the relative unavailability of analytic patients and the beleaguered status of psychoanalysis.

As for how analytic love is understood, as noted, this varies somewhat among analysts. In her commentary on Friedman's (2005a) paper, Nussbaum (2005) compares his concept of analytic love to Adam Smith's (1776/2009) "judicious spectator" (p. 378). Very tellingly, Nussbaum (2005) addresses the following questions with regard to the very notion of analytic love: "Does the analyst really need the patient? Would the analyst's life have a gap in it if the patient was no longer there, or came to grief? Does the relationship with the patient really make the analyst vulnerable?" (p. 378). She also implicitly asks how it is possible to love all one's patients. One is reminded of Spitz and Wolf's (1946) observation that love is not possible when objects are interchangeable. Nussbaum goes on to identify the following questions a patient might pose:

> Will you grieve if something happens to me, or will you just go merrily on your professional way? Do you have the kind of hope for my progress that entails fear as its correlate? I mean, do I keep you up at night? And just as I am inclined to be jealous of other patients and, even more, of those family members that occupy your attention and affection when I am not there, are you ever jealous of my friends, my lover, my children? In short, do you really love me?
>
> (p. 380)

I would add to this list of questions one, perhaps deemed too crass by Friedman and Nussbaum to ask: "Will you continue to offer analytic love even if I no longer pay you?"

Bach (2006) writes that his love for his patients is not essentially different from his love for his children and friends. This kind of analytic love, certainly different from Friedman's conception described by Nussbaum as that of a "judicious spectator" would seem to suggest a "Yes" answer to the first set of questions posed by Nussbaum (e.g., would my life have a gap if you were no longer there? Does the relationship make you vulnerable?). It does not seem likely that most analysts, even those who profess analytic love for their patients, would endorse Bach's statement.

A question that arises is the relationship between analytic love and analysis and resolution of the transference. As Friedman (2007) observes, from the perspective of transference, the analyst is aware that he or she is not the "real" object of the patient's love. According to Friedman, this recognition makes it safer for the analyst to experience analytic love for his or her patient. However, a question one might want to raise—one implicit in Nussbaum's comments—is to what degree is the patient the "real" object of the analyst's analytic love. And further, how does one analyze the transference and help the patient resolve the transference when one believes and feels that one loves the patient?

A common assumption made in analytic work is that in the course of adequate resolution of the transference the patient comes to recognize that it is not the analyst who is the "real" object of his or her love, but a stand-in for an object in the patient's life. Is this also the case with regard to the analyst's love for the patient? If the answer is a negative one, we end up in the peculiar circumstance in which whereas we expect the patient to resolve transference love (as a function of gaining insight into the link between the analyst and earlier figures), we do not expect the analyst to resolve his or her love for the patient presumably because it is not transference (or countertransference) love, but—it is difficult to find the right word here—something like realistic love for each patient rather than a displaced stand-in for the patient. The irony here is that what starts out as a consideration that presumably narrows the affective gap between the patient and analyst—after all, both are smitten with love, even if different kinds of love—ends up with increasing the affective distance between the two. To put it perhaps too crudely, whereas the transference nature of the patient's love will ultimately be recognized as a displaced love, the analyst's love, even if more judicious and reserved and qualified as analytic love, is, within its limits, the real thing.

There is a clearly discernible relationship between the new legitimacy of analytic love and the reconceptualization of countertransference. When the image of the ideal analyst is that of a surgeon-like objective observer, acknowledgement of anything like love for one's patient would be seen as an egregious instance of an interfering countertransference. Contrastingly, according the analyst's emotional responses to his or her patients are not only acceptable, but also ubiquitous, inevitable, and even indispensable for the treatment why rule out the likelihood of love for one's patients?

As noted earlier, one can say that rather than carrying out analytic treatment in a radically different way, the term analytic love is primarily a matter of recategorizing what one has been doing all along and of a different attitude toward one's therapeutic work. This is not very convincing. For one thing, it is difficult to draw a clean line between one's therapeutic work and one's categorization of, and attitudes toward, one's work. Thus, if one construes one's work as an expression of analytic love, it cannot help but influence how one carries out that work. As for attitudes toward one's work, some have argued—coining the phrase "psychotherapy by attitude" (Sampson, 2005)—that one's general attitude toward one's therapeutic work (e.g., one tends to think of one's approach as casual and conversational) can, itself, have a therapeutic impact.

Consider Bach's (2006) statement that his love for his patients is not essentially different from his love for his friends and his children. It would seem utterly impossible for that construal of and attitude toward one's therapeutic work to fail to have a real influence on that work. Further, how can work construed in that way and motivated by the experience of love that is not essentially different from one's love of one's friends and children not be different, in important respects, from the work of an analyst who, say, construes his or her work as an objective and detached observer or a "judicious spectator."

Self-disclosure

It is clear that the "blank screen" conception of the analyst's stance is not tenable and, justifiably, has been replaced by a more interactional perspective. However, despite general agreement that the analyst's complete opaqueness is neither possible nor, even if it were possible, desirable, and despite general agreement on the inevitable interactional nature of the patient–therapist relationship, there is, nevertheless, a range of views as to just how opaque or revealing the analyst should be. On one end of the continuum are more traditional analysts who, although recognizing the inevitability of the analyst emitting cues, lean toward maintaining a significant degree of anonymity. As Friedman (1998) puts it, although some degree of inadvertent disclosure is inevitable, one might as well try to keep the noise down. At the other extreme, are analysts, often associated with the relational or interpersonal "school," who believe that explicit self-disclosure can be therapeutically useful (e.g., Ehrenberg, 1995; Renik, 1996). As far as I know, there is no systematic evidence suggesting that explicit self-disclosure is either consistently therapeutically useful or harmful. To be ecologically valid, any research on self-disclosure would have to take account of such factors as the specific nature of what is disclosed (e.g., how intimate and personal), its tone and timing, and the context of the disclosure.

My own view, for which I have no systematic evidence, is that the many ways in which the analyst's *inadvertent* self-disclosure is expressed, including his or her affective presence (Stechler, 2003), is likely to be more therapeutically consequential than specific episodes of explicit self-disclosure. I would speculate that although there may be circumstances in which intentional self-disclosure may be useful, the most therapeutically significant form of self-disclosure is the day in and day out *inadvertent* self-disclosure that is expressive of one's attitudes and affects toward and empathic understanding of the patient, in short, is expressive of who one generally is as a person and who one is in relation to the patient. I have been struck by the importance of Stechler's (2003) concept of affective presence. One reveals a great deal about oneself and, in particular, a great deal about one's attitudes about a particular person with whom one is interacting by the degree to which one is affectively present. Further, I suspect that in many interpersonal interactions, both within and outside the therapeutic situation, one generally has an intuitive feeling of the degree to which the person with whom one is interacting is affectively present. This is generally true in all reasonably significant relationships and is especially true and important in the therapeutic relationship.

I have wondered about the timing of explicit self-disclosure and have entertained the hypothesis that at least some episodes of intentional self-disclosure in the therapeutic situation are more likely to occur when the therapist has difficulty being affectively present and, therefore, attempts to reestablish an affective connection with the patient through explicit self-disclosure. This hypothesis is quite testable. Independent clinical judges would rate the therapist's degree of affective presence. The prediction would be that degree of affective presence would be significantly associated with episodes of explicit self-disclosure.

Research on countertransference

Let me turn now to empirical research on countertransference. It is quite remarkable, but not surprising, that in the extensive psychoanalytic literature on the topic, virtually no attention is paid to the possibility of systematic empirical research regarding various claims and assertions regarding countertransference. Although difficult to do in a way that is clinically meaningful, it is possible to carry out empirical research on various aspects of countertransference. For example, one can investigate the degree to which and under what circumstances the analyst's emotional responses to his or her patient serve as a reliable guide to aspects of the latter's unconscious mental life. However, one will not find such research in the psychoanalytic literature. Rather, it is characterized by claims, assertions, debates on definitions, redefinitions, and what one might refer to as resolution of issues by definitional assertions. Thus, countertransference is variously defined as the analyst's conflictual reaction to the patient, which leads to blind spots, and is, therefore, an impediment to the treatment versus countertransference defined as the totality of the analyst's emotional responses to his or her patient which serve as an indispensable guide to the patient's unconscious mental states.

In view of this situation, it is no surprise that much of the empirical literature on countertransference begins with an attempt to clarify two related issues: first, some agreement on its meaning; and second, its measurement. As Fauth (2006) observes, it is difficult to carry out research on a construct unless there is reasonably clear agreement as to what the construct means and how one measures it. He goes on to note that "the overly inclusive nature of the totalistic definition [i.e., all of the therapist's emotional responses to the patient] is problematic, . . . rendering the term countertransference practically meaningless" (p. 17), and suggests adopting the "moderate" definition offered by a number of theorists and researchers: the "therapist's idiosyncratic reactions . . . to clients that are based primarily in the therapist's own personal conflicts, biases, or difficulties (e.g., cognitive biases, personal narratives, or maladaptive interpersonal patterns)" (p. 17). He goes on to write that "these reactions can be conscious or unconscious and triggered by transference, client characteristics, or other aspects of the therapeutic situation (e.g., termination), but not by extratherapy factors" (p. 17).

Following Hayes (1995) and Hayes et al. (1998), countertransference can be categorized into five main components: origins, triggers, manifestations, management, and affects. As Rosenberger and Hayes (2002) write: "most of the empirical research on countertransference, particularly in the last 20 years, has been driven by the moderative perspective" (p. 264).

Measures of countertransfence

Measures of countertransference employed in research (whether or not labeled as such), which entail implicit operational definitions of the concept, have included the following instruments and therapist behaviors:

1. Therapist avoidance behavior (Bandura et al., 1960)
2. Therapist withdrawal of personal involvement (Yulis & Kiesler, 1968)
3. Therapist state anxiety following listening to audiotapes of a seductive patient (Hayes & Gelso, 1991)
4. The Countertransference Factors Inventory (CFI) which measures five variables: self-insight, empathic ability, self-integration, anxiety management, and conceptualizing ability (Van Wagoner et al., 1991)
5. Therapist's distorted perception of patients (McClure & Hodge, 1987)
6. Supervisor's assessments (Williams et al., 1997)
7. Self-report Countertransference Questionnaire (Betan et al., 2005)
8. Inventory of Countertransference Behavior (ICB), which relies on supervisor ratings and includes a positive subscale of 10 items (e.g., enmeshed or overly supportive therapist behaviors) and a negative subscale of 11 items (e.g., punitive, avoidant, or aggressive behaviors; Friedman & Gelso, 2000)

9. Feeling Word Checklist (FWCL), which includes 30 emotion words that therapists can check in relation to their patient (Holmqvist & Armelius, 1996, 2000)
10. Therapist Appraisal Questionnaire (TAQ), which assesses how therapists are with their patient on three scales: challenge, threat, and harm (Fauth & Williams, 2005; Williams & Fauth, 2005)
11. Ratings of Emotional Attitudes toward Clients by Treaters (REACT; Najasits et al., 1995) which is a 40-item self-report measure in which therapists rate their emotional responses to a patient on a Likert scale. The instrument yields four factors: (1) in conflict with self; (2) focus on own needs; (3) positive connection; and (4) in conflict with patient.
12. Therapist Response Questionnaire, which consists of 79 items tapping a wide range of therapist thoughts, feelings, and behaviors in relation to their patients (Betan et al., 2005; Zittel & Westen, 2003)
13. Transference and countertransference: A survey of attitudes (Mendelsohn, Bucci, & Chouhy, 1992).

Countertransference and therapeutic process and outcome

There have been a number of studies on the relationship between countertransference reactions operationally defined in various ways and aspects of therapeutic process and outcome. I will summarize some representative examples below.

Countertransference as avoidance

In an early study involving two therapists, Cutler (1958) reported that when patients talked about material in sessions that were linked to the therapist's blind spots, as identified by their close associates, the therapists tended to avoid that material. Note that therapist avoidance of conflictual material constituted the operational definition of countertransference in this study, a behavior, as we will see, that is also the criterion of countertransference in a number of other studies. For example, Bandura et al. (1960) reported that therapists who showed less anxiety in relation to patient hostility tended to use more approach responses to expressions of patient hostility, whereas therapists who showed greater anxiety tended to show more avoidant responses. As another example, Hayes and Gelso (1993) found that therapist homophobia was associated with avoidance behavior in response to a videotaped vignette of a gay patient. This was not found for the videotaped vignette of a heterosexual patient. (See Hayes, 2004, for an outline of a program of research on countertransference.)

Therapist's emotional tone and patient's response

There are a number of studies on the relationship between the therapist's emotional response to the patient and various aspects of patient's responses. In one early study, the more anger and certainty in doctors' voices during an initial interview, as determined by audiotape ratings, the fewer the number of patients who followed through on treatment of their alcoholism (Milmoe et al., 1967).

Therapist bereavement and patient's experience of empathy

In one study on bereavement therapy, therapists' reports of missing a deceased loved one were inversely related to patients' perceptions of the therapist's empathy (Hayes et al., 2007). Contrastingly, the more therapists reported having resolved their grief, the more patients perceived the therapist as empathic. The authors interpret the therapist's missing the deceased loved one as an instance of unresolved grief and, therefore, of unresolved conflict, an interpretation which allows them to conclude that countertransference in the form of unresolved conflict is related to the therapist's empathy as experienced by the patient. However, it does not seem reasonable to assume that continuing to miss a deceased loved one is an instance of unresolved conflict. The results can be plausibly accounted for in a more parsimonious and commonsensical way, namely, that when the therapist is distracted and preoccupied (in this case, preoccupied with feelings of missing a loved one), the patient will experience him or her as less fully emotionally present, that is, as less empathic. What is particularly interesting about this study is that insofar as it dealt with bereavement therapy, it is plausible to assume that at least to some significant degree, the therapist's feelings of missing a deceased loved one may have been triggered by the patient's references to his or her own bereavement. Hence, one can perhaps say that in this study, when patient material dealing with their bereavement elicits the therapist's own continued feelings of bereavement and loss, the patient is likely to experience the therapist as less empathic (see also Hayes & Gelso, 1991).

Wounded healer concept

Contrastingly, when therapists report that they have resolved their grief, and where, therefore, it is safe to assume that the patient bereavement material is less likely to elicit the therapist's feelings of grief, he or she will be more likely to focus on the patient rather than his or her own bereaved feelings and will, therefore, be more likely to be experienced as empathic by the patient. (Note that this interpretation of the findings tends to contradict the current "common ground" assumption that the therapist's focus on his or her feelings serves as a reliable and indispensable aid to understanding the patient.) The authors interpret this finding in terms of what they refer to as the "wounded healer" phenomenon. That is, they assume that the therapist who has experienced loss and has been able to resolve and come to terms with loss and grief is more likely to be experienced by the patient as empathic than the therapist who has not resolved his or her grief or loss. Because their sample was limited to therapists who had experienced loss and grief, they do not hypothesize about how therapists who have not experienced loss and grief would be experienced by patients in bereavement therapy.

The larger question here is whether the therapist's experience of traumas and conflicts similar to the patient's is likely to make him or her a more empathic or less empathic therapist. In one study on counseling students relevant to this question, Trusty et al. (2005) reported that contrary to the assumption that individuals with a secure attachment pattern would make the most effective counselors (Lopez & Brennan, 2000; Pistole, 1999; Pistole & Watkins, 1995), low scores on measures of attachment avoidance and high scores on attachment anxiety were associated with the highest level of empathy. Similar to Hayes et al. (2007), Pistole and his colleagues discuss their findings in terms of the wounded healer concept, at the core of which is the idea that therapists who have experienced trauma and personal distress and have been able to acknowledge and integrate these experiences are more likely to show greater empathy and sensitivity toward their patients (Cushway & Tyler, 1996).

The wounded healer concept also receives support from other studies, including the findings that negative perceptions of family of origin are associated with higher level of counseling skills and that the majority of therapists interviewed identified their experiences in dealing with difficulties in their family of origin as an important factor in their therapeutic effectiveness (Watts et al., 1995; Wilcoxon et al., 1989). The wounded healer concept along with the related findings are consistent with a general impression that many of us have to the effect that, at least to an important extent, people who become mental health professionals have experienced significant early struggles with conflict and distress in their family of origins, including the experience of becoming parentified children and who have dealt with these struggles with some degree of success are better able to manage their countertransference and empathize with their patients. The critical issue may not be so much whether the patient's material triggers the therapist's emotional responses, including distressing responses such as anxiety, but rather, as Hayes, Gelso, and Hummel (2011) have noted, the degree to which the therapist is aware and is able to *manage* his or her emotional responses.

Therapists' responses to different diagnostic categories

The findings of a number of studies suggest that therapists react differently to patients as a function of the nature of the latter's pathology. Employing the Countertransference Questionnaire, Betan et al. (2005) reported that therapists' emotional responses to patients were associated with the patients' Axis II pathology. For example, Cluster A disorders were more associated with therapists' feelings loading on the criticized/mistreated factor; Cluster B disorders with therapist feelings loading on overwhelmed/disorganized, helpless/inadequate, and sexualized factors; and Cluster C disorders with therapist feelings loading on the parental/protective factor. Borderline personality disorder, in particular, was associated with the therapist feelings loading on the special/overinvolved factor, and narcissistic personality disorder was associated with therapist feelings loading on the disengaged factor and also with feelings of anger, resentment, distracted, avoidant, being devalued, and wishes to terminate.

As the authors note, a limitation of the study is that the data are entirely self-report rather than, say, observations of therapist behavior in the clinical situation. Thus, although therapists reported negative feelings toward a patient, we do not know to what degree such feelings were expressed either inadvertently or intentionally. That is, we do not know how the therapists manage these feelings in the therapy situation.

Individual differences among therapists

The question of how therapists manage their feelings in the therapy situation is but one aspect of the broader question of individual differences among therapists with regard to therapeutic process and outcome. The classical conception of countertransference, in particular, implicitly lends itself to a consideration of individual differences. That is, the implication is that the degree and nature of therapists' countertransference, including their blind spots, will vary with the degree and nature of their unresolved conflicts. This is less the case in the psychoanalytic literature on countertransference defined totalistically. Thus, when Heimann (1950) states that "our basic assumption is that the analyst's unconscious understands that of his patient" (p. 82) or that "the analyst's emotional response to his patient within the analytic situation represents one of the most important tools for his work" (p. 81), she suggests that this is true for all analysts. And similarly, when Racker (1968) states that the analyst's feelings and thoughts will be "precisely" those repressed by the patient, he also suggests that this is true for all analysts, at least all well analyzed analysts. This neglect of individual differences seems to be a holdover from the implicit assumption that held sway for many years, namely, that given the blank screen stance of the analyst, all well analyzed analysts (which often meant analyzed by an analyst of an "acceptable" psychoanalytic institute) were interchangeable.

The fact is, however, that not all therapists are equal and interchangeable in their responses to patients and therapeutic effectiveness. Until recently, little attention has been given to the topic of individual differences among therapists, which has been virtually a taboo subject (see Eagle, 2009). This is especially notable given the recognition that analysts do, indeed, have emotional responses to their patients and given the likelihood that the nature and intensity of these responses will exert a significant influence on therapeutic process and outcome.

One would expect that the recognition that analysts, do indeed, experience emotional responses to their patients, that at least some of these responses are likely to be idiosyncratic to the particular therapist, and that these responses play an important role in the therapeutic process would pave the way for an equal recognition and investigation of the individual differences among therapists. However, this has not been the case. The assumption that all well analyzed analysts are equally able to rely on their emotional responses to "read" the patients' unconscious saves one from openly confronting this potentially fraught and taboo topic of individual differences among analysts.

Interestingly, in a very different context, the interchangeability of therapists is also an implicit assumption in randomized control studies comparing psychotherapy outcome among different therapeutic approaches. In such research, individual differences among therapists are not included as a variable that might be related to outcome. As Silberschatz (2015) observes, there is unwarranted assumption in randomized control trials research—that there is uniformity among all therapists who share a theoretical orientation. As far back as 1966, Kiesler referred to the erroneous assumptions that patients sharing a diagnosis and therapists sharing a theoretical orientation are homogeneous variables as "uniformity myths." And even further back, in 1957, in his classic paper on "The two disciplines of scientific psychology," Cronbach already pointed out the mistake in treating individual differences within groups being compared to each other as error variance.

Differential effectiveness among therapists

A number of studies have shown that differences between therapists' effects on outcome are consistently greater than differences between treatment effects (e.g., Luborsky et al., 1985; Wampold, 2001). Indeed, in one study, "the therapists whose clients showed the fastest rate of improvement had an average rate of change 10 times greater than the mean for the sample" (Okiishi et al., 2003, p. 373). Further, differences in effectiveness among therapists are found even when delivery of treatment is manualized and standardized (Huppert et al., 2001). In other words, despite attempts for uniformity of therapeutic approach, how the treatment is implemented bears the personal stamp of the therapist. Indeed, in a study of manualized cognitive therapy for depression (Castonguay et al., 1996), Goldfried and

Wolfe (1998) reported that although quality of the therapeutic relationship and patient's emotional involvement were associated with positive therapeutic outcome, therapist adherence to treatment manual was associated with negative therapeutic outcome. In a meta-analysis, Webb et al. (2010) reported that treatment adherence accounted for less than 1 percent of psychotherapy outcomes. This should not be surprising. For after all, whatever the therapeutic approach, psychotherapy is a human interaction between individuals and is carried out by specific individuals in distinctive ways as a function of not only theoretical commitment, but also their personality characteristics and personal history.

The issue of treatment adherence is a complex one in a number of ways. As Owens and Hilsenroth (2014) observe, one can investigate treatment adherence between clients (adherence consistency across clients), between therapists (adherence consistency across therapists), and within clients (adherence consistency across sessions). In a study on within-client treatment adherence in a psychodynamic treatment approach, Owens and Hilsenroth reported a positive association between within-case variability and therapy outcome (it accounted for 10 percent–11 percent of the variance), measured in terms of symptom change as well as a broad range of patient functioning. They account for their results in terms of *adherence flexibility*, which, they speculate, "could reflect therapists' efforts to be responsive to the emerging context of the therapy session as well as the needs of clients by increasing or decreasing theory-specific techniques" (p. 285).

Differences in therapeutic alliance

Individual differences in therapeutic outcome are mediated, among other factors, by differences in therapists' ability to form a positive working or therapeutic alliance with their patients, a factor that is consistently related to therapeutic outcome (Baldwin et al., 2007; Horvath, 2011; Levy et al., 2015; Ryum et al., 2010). And indeed, Baldwin et al. (2007) reported that patients who had therapists having, on average, high alliance scores had better therapeutic outcomes than patients whose therapists, on average, had low alliance scores. Further, for any given therapist, there were no differences in therapeutic outcome between patients with low versus high alliance scores. Hence, patient variability in alliance scores did not influence outcome. Rather, it was therapist variability that accounted for the relationship between alliance and outcome. That is, it was *differences between therapists* that accounts for the alliance–outcome correlation. Some therapists whose patients characteristically rate them high on therapeutic alliance have better outcomes, whereas other therapists whose patients characteristically rate them as low on therapeutic alliance have poorer therapeutic outcomes.

In an effort to replicate and extend Baldwin et al.'s (2007) findings, Zuroff (2010) carried out a study on outpatients who were diagnosed with major depressive disorder. He found that patients whose mean scores on the Barrett-Lennard Relationship Inventory (B-L RI), which measures "the patient's perception of the extent to which the therapist provides positive regard, empathy, unconditional regard, and congruence" (p. 687), were improved more quickly as shown by a Composite Maladjustment Index (CMI) than therapists whose mean sores on the B-L RI were low. This was also true for measures of self-critical perfectionism (SC-PFT), a factor that is linked with vulnerability to depression. Further, these results were found equally across cognitive behavioral therapy, interpersonal therapy, and a placebo clinical management condition.

In an interesting investigation of individual differences among therapists by Silberschatz (2015), the problems, conflicts, and treatment goal plans of patients (i.e., plans to disconfirm a pathological belief) in brief psychodynamic psychotherapy were assessed by clinical judges based on intake interview. Clinical judges independently rated compatibility between the patient's plan and therapist interventions. Degree of plan compatibility of therapist interventions was highly predictive of various measures of therapeutic outcome, accounting for approximately 25 percent of the outcome variance. Further, patients who were treated by therapists and who received higher plan compatibility ratings tended to view their therapies more positively, achieved greater self-understanding and self-control, and reported feeling more supported by their therapists (29 percent to 44 percent of variance explained). The study demonstrates the importance of individual differences in "the extent to which therapists are responsive to their patients' plans—that is, disconfirm core pathogenic schemas— . . . a strong predictor of treatment outcome and of patients feeling positively about their therapy experience" (p. 9). Clearly, therapists whose interventions received high plan compatibility ratings were experienced by their patients as more empathic and supportive, who, in turn, achieved a better therapeutic outcome.

The findings of the Silberschatz study represent still another demonstration that not all therapists are equally empathic and equally understand their patients. These findings also suggest the untenability of the claim that the feelings and thoughts of all therapists will accurately reflect their patient's mental states. This may well be true for some therapists and some patients and not true for other therapists and other patients. What is also important about the findings of this study, in the context of thinking about countertransference, is that they suggest that the more effective therapists are not those therapists whose thoughts and feelings mirror the patient's unexpressed thoughts and feelings, but rather those therapists who tend to understand the patient's dynamics, conflicts, and needs and who better enable the patient to feel understood and supported. The whole idea of empathic understanding entailing mirroring, including in the context of infant–mother interaction, seems misplaced. A sensitive and responsive mother who tries to understand and comfort her crying infant does not mirror her infant, that is, she does not also cry. Rather, she attempts to understand the source of her infant's distress and provide a response that will contain and comfort her infant. This is also the case with the empathic and sensitive therapist. In both the instances, the therapeutic response entails, in Racker's (1968) language, a complementary rather than a concordant identification. (However, see Eagle's, 2000, discussion of whether complementary identification should be viewed as an identification at all.)

It is not at all clear that therapists even have thoughts and feelings that are precisely those of the patient's, whether expressed or unexpressed, nor why that should be viewed as a therapeutic desideratum. Rather, the conclusion that research findings (as well as clinical experience) point to is that the elements that make for a positive therapeutic outcome include (1) the therapist's understanding of the patient, based on empathy as well as a more cognitive grasp of the patient's dynamics, conflicts, needs, and plans; and (2) the therapist's success in expressing his or her understanding in a way that enables the patient to feel understood, to explore, and to feel safe and supported as well as engaged in a mutual process.

What are some of the personal features that distinguish effective from less effective therapists? There are undoubtedly a host of individual differences, factors, such as age, years of experience, and gender, and so on that may influence therapeutic outcome. However, in the present context of a chapter on countertransference, I want to focus on the therapist's atttitudes toward and emotional responses to the patient. The factors that are associated with therapist effectiveness include accurate empathy (Miller et al., 1980); a high level of interpersonal functioning, genuineness, respect, and concreteness (Valle, 1981); warmth and friendliness, affirmation and understanding, helping and protecting, and an absence of belittling and blaming (Najavits & Strupp, 1994); flexible, honest, reflective, supporting, and affirming (Ackerman & Hilsenroth, 2003); and valuing of intellectual goals (Lafferty et al., 1989). As one might expect, therapist depression, withdrawal, and feeling overwhelmed (Ricks, 1974), and negative ways of relating to patients, including managing, belittling and blaming, ignoring and neglecting, and attacking and neglecting (Najavits & Strupp, 1994) are characteristic of less effective therapists; and what Zuroff (2010) refer to as the "Rogerian conditions of positive regard, empathy, unconditional regard, and congruence" are characteristic of effective therapists.

Although "Rogerian conditions" (which are essentially relationship factors) may themselves contribute to positive outcome (i.e., as a corrective emotional experience), as Freud (1912a) recognized in his reference to the importance of positive transference, they may also facilitate a positive therapeutic alliance and enhance the effectiveness of other interventions (e.g., interpretation and ensuing insight; see Levy et al., 2015). Further, a positive therapeutic alliance can also be therapeutic in itself as well as facilitate the patient's reception of other interventions. And from the other side of the therapeutic dyad, a therapist who is able to provide the "Rogerian conditions" may be more likely to provide empathic and accurate interpretations, which, in turn, may enhance the therapeutic alliance and facilitate the patient's reception of the therapist's interpretations.

There is some evidence that the therapist's attachment pattern may influence both therapeutic process and outcome. For example, Schauenberg et al. (2010) found that higher therapist attachment security was associated with both better alliance and outcome in more disturbed patients. Tyrrell et al. (1999) found that positive therapeutic outcome was associated with complementarity of attachment patterns between patient and therapist rather than identity between the two (e.g., avoidant paired with enmeshed/

preoccupied rather than avoidant paired with avoidant). When the "match" is one of complementarity rather than identity, there is likely to be less collusion between patient and therapist (e.g., avoidance of intimacy issues when both patient and therapist are avoidant) (see Mohr, Gelso, & Hill, 2005; Rubino et al., 2000; Sauer, Lopez, & Gormley, 2003). Rubino et al. (2000) reported that both patient and therapist attachment patterns play a role in therapist empathy and depth of interpretation in response to potential alliance ruptures.

There is evidence that therapists' ratings of their own personal characteristics and self-experiences, both in their personal and professional life, are lawfully related to therapeutic outcome. Further, there is also evidence that the particular self-rated personality characteristics that are predictive of therapeutic outcome (operationally defined in terms of level of psychiatric symptoms) vary with whether the treatment is psychoanalysis or long-term psychodynamic psychotherapy. For example, compared to patients for long-term psychodynamic psychotherapy, patients for psychoanalysis reported fewer symptoms at follow-up with therapists whose professional manner was less affirming. As another example, compared to patients for long-term psychodynamic psychotherapy, patients for psychoanalysis reported fewer symptoms with therapists who reported being less aloof and more forceful as personal characteristics (Heinonen et al., 2013).

In addition to studies on the relationship between individual differences in therapist characteristics and therapeutic process and outcome, there is at least one analogue study indicating that encouraging therapist self-analytic exercises led to an increase in empathy and positive feelings toward the patient (Schlesinger & Wolitzky, 2002). It would be interesting to investigate whether there are interaction effects on process and outcome between therapist individual characteristics (e.g., attachment pattern) and use of self-analytic or self-reflective exercises.

In short, individual differences in therapist characteristics, feelings, attitudes, and behaviors may be associated with differential therapeutic outcomes through their differential influence on such interrelated factors as the development of a positive therapeutic alliance, the accuracy of interpretation (as a product of greater capacity for accurate empathy), and greater patient trust and receptivity to the therapist's interventions. There may also be training experiences that interact with therapist characteristics.

Implications for current conception of countertransference

What are the implications of the above findings for contemporary psychoanalytic discussions of countertransference? There is evidence that characteristic attitudes, emotions, and behaviors of therapists cut across different patients. The therapist who is characteristically empathic, warm, and supporting is likely to be so across a wide range of patients despite provocations, role responsiveness, and interpersonal pressure. And, contrastingly, the therapist who exudes a sense of disengagement, rejection, and blaming is likely to express these attitudes characteristically and especially so when subject to provocation, the pressures of role responsiveness, and interpersonal cues from the patient. Of course, there are a host of questions that merit further investigation. For example, do effective therapists have as many negative countertransference reactions as ineffective therapists, but are better able to acknowledge, reflect on, and manage these reactions?

Some of the above findings can be understood as lending a significantly modified and diluted version of Racker's (1968) claim that through identification with the patient, the therapist's emotional responses may serve as a guide to the patient's unexpressed mental content. The more modest claim, for which there may be some support, is that based on having experienced and integrated traumatic events similar to those experienced by the patient, the therapist may be more likely to identify with and understand the patient. The contrast between this more modest and plausible formulation and Racker's hyperbolic claims that the therapist's thoughts and feelings will be "precisely" those repressed by the patient is striking.

I cannot help but comment on the degree to which exaggerated, unqualified, and often implausible claims, similar to the one made by Racker, populate the psychoanalytic literature, particularly the literature on countertransference and projective identification. One factor, I believe, that at least partly accounts for this tendency is a failure to address or even show any interest in possible specific processes or mechanisms that might be involved in elucidating a particular claim. For example, Racker does not seriously consider the question of what specific processes could make possible a rather implausible state of affairs in which my thoughts and feelings are precisely those that you have repressed. Or as another example, in all the talk about one person putting thoughts and feelings *into* another person, little or no interest is shown in trying to identify possible processes through which that could conceivably occur. Instead, references are made to Freud's (1912b) metaphor of the analyst as a telephone receiver, or his assertion that the analyst's unconscious communicates with the patient's unconscious, or, on occasion, vague references to "direct communication" (Spillius & O'Shaughnessy, 2012, p. 366) or even to mental telepathy. The impression created is that analysts are dealing with deep and mysterious phenomena and processes that do not lend themselves for further identification, investigation, and elucidation.

It seems to me that as this discussion suggests, despite whatever limitations they may have (and there are certainly such limitations), the value of including empirical research studies in discussions of psychoanalytic concepts, formulations, and claims lies not only in the specific findings of such studies, but also in their role as a model for a questioning attitude, a reliance on evidence, greater precision of thinking, and greater modesty of claims. This becomes apparent in contrasting the psychoanalytic literature on countertransference with that of the empirical research literature. For example, one goes from a bewildering array of definitions and redefinitions of countertransference in the psychoanalytic literature to agreement on a relatively clear definition of the term, which, in turn, permits a program of research in which different investigators are pretty much on the same page.

The studies I have discussed not only reveal individual differences in therapists' attitudes, behaviors, and emotional responses to their patients but, of great importance, also demonstrate that these individual differences are lawfully related to therapeutic effectiveness among therapists. Quite remarkably, the psychoanalytic literature is virtually silent on this topic. There is no explicit discussion in the contemporary psychoanalytic literature of the relationship between countertransference and therapeutic outcome. Ironically, it is the implications of the classical definition of countertransference that alerts us to the importance of individual differences among therapists through its emphasis on the therapist's unresolved conflicts and blind spots, as well as the negative impact of these conflicts and blind spots on therapeutic effectiveness. And, as we have seen, it is a variation of the classical definition that is employed in empirical research on countertransference.

One cannot help but wonder whether the totalistic conception of countertransference, particularly the assumption that the therapist's countertransference reactions mirror the patient's unconscious thoughts and feelings, serves to protect the psychoanalytic community from confronting the taboo and fraught topic of significant individual differences in therapeutic effectiveness among analysts. In that sense, the worry that the new conception of countertransference (as well as projective identification) may be used to "blame" the patient for one's own troubling reactions (and thereby fail to confront these reactions) may well turn out to be a justifiable one. Instead of encouraging the therapist to examine and manage his or her emotional reactions to the patient, the message communicated to the therapist in many psychoanalytic discussions of countertransference, whether intended or not, is that he or she can rest assured that these reactions represent a mirror of the patient's mind.

At one point, Gill (1994) writes that because the concept of transference is so confused in the psychoanalytic literature, it might be wise to drop the term and simply refer to the patient's experience of the therapist and the therapeutic relationship. The case for taking a similar step and dropping the term countertransference in favor of referring to the therapist's experiences of and responses to the patient and therapeutic relationship is even stronger. One could then investigate the relationship between those experiences and responses to various aspects of therapeutic process and outcome, including the relationship between therapist and patient experiences, less encumbered by debates about definitions and arbitrary assumptions regarding the nature of these relationships.

Notes

1. Freud's interest in demonstrating that the patient's free associations and other material produced in the analytic session are not influenced by the analyst also reflects his abiding concern with the problem of *suggestion.*
2. A not uncommon reaction to reading Freud's recommendation of emotional coldness is to note that he did not react that way at all to his patients, accompanied by accounts of his feeding and lending money to patients. This striking discrepancy between work and deed, if these stories of Freud's behavior are accurate, is disturbing. It raises questions as to how common such contradictions between word and deed are, and whether one can one get much of an idea of what an analyst is like in the clinical situation based on his or her theoretical writings. In any case, in the present context, the important point to be stressed

is that over many years, analysts were strongly influenced by and emulated not the Freud who lent money to or fed his patients, but the Freud whose "recommendations on analytic technique" and other writings they read in their training.

3. I am reminded of a likely apocryphal story that as I remember was told about Isakower at the New York Psychoanalytic Institute. Isakower, who was quite short, greets a new patient in his waiting room. When all 6 foot 8 of the patient stands up, Isakower looks up at him and says, "Come in anyway."
4. After referring to the "completely unfeeling and detached" (p. 81) analyst and to Freud's surgeon metaphor, Heimann (1950) writes: "on the other hand, there is an opposite school of thought, like that of Ferenczi, which . . . acknowledges that the analyst has a wide variety of feelings toward his patients" (p. 81). Heimann (1950) also notes and disagrees with the recommendation that the analyst "should at times express them openly" (p. 81). As Makari (2008) has pointed out, Ferenczi objected to what he felt was the increasingly intellectualized and austere conception of psychoanalysis and argued that affective factors, particularly those embedded in the analyst–patient relationship needed to be given greater prominence. In 1924, Ferenczi and Rank published *The development of psychoanalysis*, in which they argued that psychoanalytic technique "had fossilized . . . and become an overly intellectualized process of educating patients about the contents of their unconscious" (Makari, 2008, p. 352). Although Ferenczi and Rank's position was rejected by the psychoanalytic powers at the time, as the Heimann reference to Ferenczi indicates, it continued to reverberate through the years and has continued to influence psychoanalysts' clinical thinking.
5. One can add that this also holds for the claim that analysts' emotional responses serve as a reliable guide even to the patient's *conscious* mental states.
6. Levine's position parallels Gill's (1994) equally arbitrary stance that everything the patient reports in the clinical situation should be thought of as a direct or indirect reference to the transference.
7. The democratization and equalization of the analytic relationship appeared to have its limits. For unlike countertransference, no general claim is made that the patient's emotional responses to the analyst can serve as a reliable guide to the latter's unconscious. The closest one gets to that is Gill's (1994) insistence that rather than constituting distortion, the patient's transference reactions represent a plausible construal based on the cutes emitted by the analyst.

Chapter 3

Projective mode of cognition, projection as a defense, and projective identification

The concept of projective identification was cited with some frequency in response to my query on core psychoanalytic concepts. And, indeed, it is a concept that has figured prominently in the contemporary psychoanalytic literature, particularly in the writings of Klein and Bion and their followers. It is also a concept with which I have struggled mightily and which, it seems to me, constitutes a quintessential example of much that is problematic about psychoanalytic thinking and writing. For these reasons, I think it is important to include a chapter on projective identification. It is also important to include a discussion of projective identification in the broad context in which that concept is embedded, namely, a projective mode of thought and projection as a defense. Hence, the organization of this chapter is as follows: a discussion of the projective mode of thought, followed by a discussion of projection as a defense, and continued with an examination and critique of the concept of projective identification.

A projective mode of thought

The term projection refers not only to a particular defense mechanism, but also more broadly to a mode of cognition and thought, the essence of which is the tendency to experience objects in the external world in accord with one's inner thoughts, feelings, and preoccupations. A familiar example of an instrument that makes use of a projective mode of cognition is the Rorschach test (hence, the term "projective test"), which rests on the assumption that the percepts one sees in the ink blots reflect something about the inner world of the perceiver. Note that the instructions of the Rorschach test (i.e., asking the individual what the ink blots look like) as well as the ambiguity of the ink blots facilitate a projective mode of thought. An example of the external situation facilitating a projective mode of thought in the psychoanalytic context is the "blank screen" stance of the analyst. Here the assumption is made that a minimum of external cues emitted by the analyst will make it more likely that the patient's experience and perception of the analyst will reflect the patient's idiosyncratic cognitive and affective structures.

Another related psychoanalytic phenomenon that is assumed to entail a projective mode of thought is the transference, defined as projecting onto or attributing to another characteristic of one's representations of early figures, as well as one's affective reactions to these early figures. In ordinary everyday experiences, a projective mode of thought can influence experience of external stimuli in more subtle ways in the form of one's needs, feelings, preoccupations, etc., influencing not only one's attributions, but also one's selective attention and the salience and attractiveness of external stimuli (example of food shopping when hungry).

Projection and the construction of external reality

According to Klein (1975), projection as well as introjection are basic universal processes involved in the construction of external reality. Klein (1975) writes that the experience of the external world "is decisively influenced by projection" (p. 59). In discussing the contribution of introjections and projection "to the interaction between external and internal factors" (p. 250), she writes that "even in the adult . . . the judgment of reality is never quite free from the influence of his internal world" (p. 250).

It appears that Freud (1913[1912–1913]) takes a similar position as suggested by the following passage:

> projection was not created for the purpose of defense; it also occurs where there is no conflict. The projection outwards of internal perceptions is a primitive mechanism, to which, for instance, our sense perceptions are subject, and which therefore normally play a very large part in determining the form taken by our external world. Under conditions whose nature has not yet been sufficiently established, internal

> perceptions of emotional and thought processes can be projected outwards in the same way as sense perceptions; they are thus employed for building up the external world, though they should by rights remain part of the internal world. This may have some genetic connection with the fact that the function of attention was originally directed not towards the internal world but towards the stimuli that stream in from the external world, and that the function's only information upon endopsychic processes was received from feelings of pleasure and unpleasure.
>
> (p. 64)

Freud's above-cited passage leads Grotstein (1981) to write:

> This passage shows a cogent and decisive parallel between Freud's concept of projection with what would become Klein's concept of projective identification. That is, Freud substantiates Klein's idea that our image of the world is created via projective identification from sense impressions of the inner world.
>
> (p. 142)

How internal perceptions of emotional and thought processes that "are projected outwards" are employed "for building up the external world" is not made clear by either Freud or Klein. Indeed, Freud (1913[1912–1913]) writes that the role of projection in building up the external world occurs "under conditions whose nature has not yet been sufficiently established" (p. 64).

I think Grotstein (1981) is mistaken in equating Klein's and Freud's position on the role of projection in constructing external reality. Indeed, according to Freud, as seen in his concept of hallucinatory wish fulfillment, only very early in life does projection play a dominant role in one's construction of external reality. After the period of early infancy, the role of the projective mode becomes increasingly reduced and supplanted by the development of reality testing. An early expression of Freud's (1900) formulation of the role of a projective mode of thought in constructing reality is seen in his concept of hallucination of the breast. According to this formulation, after experiencing satisfaction of his or her hunger drives, when next hungry, the infant hallucinates the breast. This is a clear example of the projection of an inner need or wish onto the external world. In hallucinatory wish fulfillment, the need or wish, so to speak, "*creates*" the breast. On this view, it is only because the hallucinated breast does not succeed in reducing hunger that the infant is forced to turn to the actual breast in external reality. Or, to put it another way, the projected hallucinatory breast of primary process that is replaced by the actual breast in the external world. Thus, according to Freud, and in contrast to Klein, it is the diminished role of projection, which is dominated by the pleasure principle and the increased role of the reality principle that enable the infant to function in external reality.

Similar to Freud, Winnicott's (1958) formulation of the course of development is one in which the infant's experiences that he or she has created the breast are gradually replaced (through a process that Winnicott, 1945, refers to as "disillusionment" [p. 237]) with the experience of an external world that exists relatively independently of one's wishes and needs. Thus, for both Freud and Winnicott, the projective illusion that wishes and needs create objects that gratify these wishes and needs is gradually replaced by a conception of external objects that are relatively independent of one's needs and wishes.

One can say that normal development comes to be characterized by what Forguson and Gopnik (1988) refer to as "commonsense metaphysics," that is, the assumption that "there is a single world of objects, events, states of affairs, people, and other sentient beings which I (and others) experience perceptually and think about, that this world is independent of the thoughts and experiences I and others have of it" (p. 227).

"Commonsense metaphysics" is characterized by recognition of the constraints exercised by the external stimulus array in the building up of a picture of external reality. Despite individual differences in many areas of functioning, we are all constructed in such a way that a particular external stimulus array generates, for example, the same retinal image. And although retinal image is not the only factor determining the formation of a percept (Rock, 1983), it is not irrelevant. The point here is that there is an invariant relationship between certain inborn structures and external stimuli that are relatively independent of our projective tendencies and that cut across individual differences. The Gestalt psychologists referred to "autochthonous" factors in perception that are relatively independent of learning based on past experiences and, one can add, of our wishes and motives. These include, for example, figure–ground organization and the influence of spatial grouping in perception.

In his foundational chapter 7 of *The Interpretation of Dreams,* Freud (1900) wrote that because its primary function is reality testing, in contrast to memory, perception is relatively impervious to the influence of inner needs and wishes and primarily responsive to external input. Were that not so, perception would fail in its reality-testing function and seemingly paradoxically, in its ability to play a necessary role in gratifying our needs. One cannot identify objects necessary for gratification of needs unless perception is reasonably veridical.[1]

It is easy to lose sight of the importance of inborn structures and autochthonous factors in determining our perception of the external world, given the emphasis on the influence of needs and values on perception (recall the New Look era in perception research [e.g., Erdelyi, 1974; Eriksen, 1951; McGinnies, 1949], which was strongly influenced by psychoanalytic theory). However, it is important to keep in mind that virtually all the studies of the influence of needs and values on perception did not deal with the formation of the actual percept under normal conditions. Rather, they employed a variety of contrived conditions, such as ambiguous or impoverished external stimulus input, to facilitate projection; and they focused on such responses as recognition thresholds, judgments, and nonliteral imaginative responses rather than direct perceptual response.

There is little doubt that an internal emotion such as fear may predispose one to experience an external stimulus, particularly an ambiguous one, as menacing, whereas one would experience that same stimulus in a more neutral way when not in a fearful state. However, in normal circumstances, our emotions do not have a strong influence on the *formation of our percepts* of external stimuli. For example, we may have different feelings about an external object, say a chair. We may like it or dislike it, perceive it in various physiognomic ways such as friendly or unfriendly, warm or austere, aesthetic or unaesthetic, and so on. But, in virtually all cases, it remains a chair. Because just about everyone (in a given culture) would form the chair percept in response to the particular external stimulus array, the response "chair" would normally reveal little about individual differences in respondents' feelings, thoughts, etc. Such information emerges only under certain conditions, for example, when the external stimuli are ambiguous (as in the Rorschach) or when the individual is engaged in a nonperceptual task such as remembering or storytelling or free associating, all of which provide greater leeway for the role of the individual's imagination, and therefore are more likely to shed light on his or her preoccupations, styles of thinking and feeling, and so on.

A projective mode of thought may also be more readily apparent in the symbolic classification and functional organization of stimuli, as in the case of what Rapaport (1967) referred to as drive organization of cognition. For example, under conditions of high sexual arousal, certain stimuli, particularly ambiguous stimuli, may be classified as sexual, whereas they would be less likely to be classified that way under conditions of low sexual arousal; similarly for conditions of high versus low arousal of aggression and hostility. Under the former condition, a golf club, for example, might more readily be functionally classified as a weapon than under the latter condition.

It is important, however, to note that even when a golf club is classified as a weapon, the individual will likely continue to perceive the stimulus array as a golf club—which can also be used as a weapon. That is to say, in perceiving the stimulus array as a golf club, perception continues to carry out its reality-testing function. Were, however, the individual's hostility so intense that he or she could no longer perceive the stimulus array as a golf club, but only as a weapon, one would have to say that the reality-testing function of perception has been compromised by intense affect. Another way to put it is to say that the constraints on perception normally experienced by the external stimulus array have been overwhelmed by the sheer intensity of drive and affect. (One is reminded of a scene in a Chaplin film in which he makes a meal of his shoes under conditions of extreme hunger.[2]) (See Holt, 2009, on primary process modes of thought.)

There are subtle and nuanced ways in which our projective tendencies may influence cognitive responses to what is perceived. For example, there is evidence that when we perceive a word, not only is the representation of the word activated, but also an associative network in which it is embedded. The target word activates or "primes" a network of other words (and images) related to the target word associatively and even graphically. That is, the target word activates not only denotative meanings, but also, as noted earlier, a verbal network or what G. S. Klein (personal communication) referred to as a "connotative hierarchy." (See Anderson, 1983; Anderson & Bower, 1973/2014; Bleasdale, 1987.)

Further, although the connotations may not normally be consciously experienced, under appropriate conditions, for example, through recording recognition errors, one can show that they have been activated. That is, when people make recognition errors, they tend not to be random, but rather are related to the target word. Thus, if the target word is, say, "moon," the recognition error is more likely to be, say, "sky" than a word associatively or semantically unrelated to "moon." Further, if attention to the target word is reduced (i.e., via distraction), when presented with the target word "moon," the recognition error is more likely to be a graphically related word, such as "spoon" rather than a semantically related word (Eagle & Ortof, 1967).

In summary, although there may be invariances between particular stimulus arrays and perceptual structures such that virtually everyone (within a culture) will see a particular stimulus configuration as, say, a table or a chair, the percept will be enriched by a complex of personal responses and attributions that we bring to it, including its physiognomic properties, the connotative hierarchy it activates, our affective responses, our aesthetic judgments and evaluations, and so on, all of which entail a projective mode of thought that goes beyond the literal percept and that enlivens and animates our experience of the external world.

Transitional experiences as a projective mode of cognition and affect

Winnicott's (1953) concepts of the transitional object and transitional experience are quintessential examples of a projective mode of cognition and experiences that go beyond the literal. We are all familiar with the soothing and comforting properties that the well-worn raggedy blanket or teddy bear have for some toddlers. It is the toddler himself or herself who imbues these objects with soothing and comforting properties and then draws upon these projected properties for soothing and comforting. That is to say, the experience of the transitional object can be characterized as reflecting a projective mode of cognition. Winnicott (1953) famously writes that one does not ask the child: did you create these properties or are they independently there in reality? By forcing an answer to this question, Winnicott writes, one runs the risk of destroying the transitional experience. Winnicott goes on to say that as one matures into adulthood, transitional experience is spread out over the world of culture and art, a world in which a projective mode of thought is central.

Consider the aesthetic experience of listening to music. From an entirely literal and "objective" point of view, music consists only of sound waves of varying frequencies. And, of course, if one were to approach music literally as a collection of sounds, it would cease to be music. For the aesthetic experience of music to be possible, the collection of sounds must be "received" by and resonate with the listener as something a great deal more than a disparate array of sounds. There must be a readiness within the mind or the nervous system to resonate with the structure of the music and to imbue this structure with cognitive, affective, and aesthetic meaning. In an important sense, then, music exists in the transitional space between the subjective and objective. And to ask the question of whether I created the music or whether it is there in the notes is to destroy the aesthetic experience.

Indeed, when one listens to radically unfamiliar music which one is not ready to receive, one does tend to hear it as a disorganized cacophony of sounds, not as music. In this circumstance, it is the context and the setting —one is at a concert or it is recorded on a compact disc—that may play a role in one hearing the sounds as music, not one's subjective experience of them. However, and we have probably all had this experience, frequently upon repeated listening, what was painful cacophony or incoherent auditory sequences becomes music, that is, becomes an aesthetic experience. Consider, for example, the history of Stravinsky's *Rites of spring* or the history of one's experience in listening to, say, an Alban Berg string quartet. What happens with repeated hearings? The notes do not change. Rather, we slowly develop inner resonances and structures to "receive" and resonate with the external structure of the music—a meaningful aesthetic experience "magically" emerges.

One can argue that falling in love is also a transitional experience in the sense that one does not insist on an answer to the question: Did I wholly create the experienced attributes of the loved one or are they objectively present? It would be difficult to fall in love if one insisted on a clear and one-sided answer to that question. To put it another way, in falling in love, one attributes certain properties to the loved one or imbues the loved one with certain meanings and then falls in love with what one has partly created. Indeed, one frequent aspect of falling out of love is a sense of disillusionment and the often bitter conviction that the qualities and meanings once experienced were entirely one's own creation and were not really ever present in the object. One becomes, so to speak, excessively literal and "objective." In this state of mind, Winnicott's question is asked and is definitively and one-sidedly answered. In contrast to falling out of love, the transition from falling in love to loving or being in love is characterized by both a partial disillusionment in Winnicott's sense and an increasing conviction that at least some of the qualities and meanings one has attributed and imbued plus new ones are present in the loved one.

Similar processes can be described in relation to, in a manner of speaking, falling in and out of love with oneself. In the case of positive self-esteem, one may project on to one's self-image aspects of one's ego ideal. When, however, one falls out of love with oneself, for example, in a state of depression, one experiences oneself literally and objectively. The positive illusions about oneself described by Taylor and her colleagues (e.g., Taylor & Brown, 1994; Taylor et al., 2000) are replaced by "depressive realism" (Alloy & Abramson, 1988). In "Mourning and melancholia," Freud (1917[1915]) writes that the self-accusations of the melancholic person may well be justified insofar as "it is merely that he has a keener eye for the truth than other people who are not melancholic" and goes on to "wonder why a man has to be ill before he can be accessible to a truth of this kind" (i.e., the truth of his faults and inadequacies) (p. 247). In effect, Freud is saying that in a melancholic state, one sees oneself more objectively and literally.

Certain aspects of psychotherapy can also be viewed as a transitional experience involving a projective mode of cognition. As mentioned earlier, this idea is implicit in the concept of transference which is understood as the attribution or projection onto the therapist of representations of characteristics of early figures, particularly parental figures. However, psychotherapy can be seen as a transitional experience in a broader sense. The patient attributes to the therapist certain healing properties—much like the toddler attributes soothing properties to the raggedy blanket—and then calls upon these very properties that he or she has attributed in the object to be soothed and comforted. Indeed, it is not clear that psychotherapy would be possible if the patient were excessively literal and "objective" and incapable of a projective mode of cognition required for transitional experience, that is, were the patient to insistently ask the question: Did I create the healing properties of the therapist or are they there in the external world (i.e., actually present in the therapist)? It is likely that these are the sorts of considerations that Winnicott (1953, 1968) had in mind when he referred to the psychotherapy situation as a playground and as a transitional experience.

An implication of the above considerations suggests therapeutic limits to analysis of the transference. That is, if psychotherapy is to proceed, transference cannot be fully analyzed away to the point that the patient experiences the therapist in a fully literal and objective way, that is, in a Winnicottian sense, in a fully "disillusioned" way. I suspect that this is one aspect of what Freud (1912a) had in mind when he took the position that ordinary positive transference (as opposed to blatantly erotic transference) should not be analyzed. (However, see Brenner, 1979, who argued that "it is best for the patient if one approaches *everything* analytically" [p. 150], which, of course, includes positive transference.) Looked at from a coldly "objective" point of view, there is really no good reason for the patient to experience positive transference, particularly early in the treatment. And yet, without some modicum of positive transference, it is difficult to imagine how psychotherapy can proceed. See Friedman's (2007) discussion of deception in therapy in which the analyst does not explicitly disillusion the patient by informing him or her that his or her love for the analyst will not be returned.

If transference is, indeed, understood as the projection on to the therapist of characteristics of early parental figures, it follows that positive transference is based on the projection of positive characteristics of early parental figures. That is, however depriving and negative the patient's early experience may have been, without some positive experience with the parental figure, positive transference would not be possible. Another way to put this is to say that for the patient to imbue the therapist with healing properties, he or she had to have had some "healing" experiences with early parental figures. In this sense, the projection of the early "healing" experiences can be viewed as a *prerequisite* for psychotherapy rather than a phenomenon to be analyzed. I suspect that this is the implicit reasoning behind Freud's position regarding analysis of the unobjectionable positive transference. Also, as Gill (1994) and others have argued, not every aspect of the patient's experience of the analyst is a product of projection. Along with other reactions, most patients are generally capable of experiencing the benevolent intentions of the analyst.

Perception as a projective mode

I would suggest that it is not only aesthetic experiences, falling in love, and therapeutic experiences that are made possible by the projective mode of thought, but also everyday perception itself (Eagle, 1994). In an important sense, perception is a transitional phenomenon, involving the interplay between the inner and outer. In perceiving an object, we are, in a sense, constructing that object. That is, we are organizing external inputs—contours, angles, gradients, wavelengths, etc., which bear an invariant relationship to internal structure—into a consensually shared meaningful perceptual object—a chair, an automobile, or a person, which have already gone beyond the external stimulus array and become enlivened as socially shared objects.

Were we to organize the world at different seams (Goodman, 1960), our perceptual world would be a different one. For example, were we to select and construct the cues emanating from the world differently—say, as a bat does (Nagel, 1974)—we would experience a different world, the bat's world.[3] Of course, all this goes on automatically at a neurophysiological level and is not represented subjectively or phenomenally. That is, we are generally not aware of constructing the world; these processes are impenetrable to experience and we are aware only of the products of these processes. Thus, perception of objects as well as of events is a process that involves both inner attributions and constructions and external stimuli and cues. Our immediate phenomenal experience is, of course, of an independent external object or event and the question of did I create this or is it there in external reality does not normally arise. However, I am suggesting that the structure, not the phenomenology, but the structure, of perception is transitional in nature in the sense that it is both my creation and also determined by the external world.

In saying that in perception we construct the object, I am not contradicting my earlier statement that the formation or, indeed, construction of the percept is relatively immune to influence by one's needs and affects. For the percept is a construction in the Kantian sense that our experience of the external stimulus array is shaped (constructed) and constrained by our inborn apparatuses that yield particular categories of experience (e.g., causality, space, and time). (See Hoffman, 2016, for an interesting discussion of perception as a system selected for fitness, not veridicality.) These apparatuses are the product of evolutionary selection, which means that they are the product of adaptation to a particular environmental niche. It is this adaptive process that underlies normative relative autonomy and veridicality of perception.

An excessive influence of moods, needs, desires, wishes, and fantasies on perception, that is, on formation of the percept, would threaten survival. If, for example, whenever I was hungry, I perceived every object as food, and could not distinguish between food and nonfood objects, I would not survive very long. Whether or not infants ever actually hallucinate the breast (there is no evidence that they do), the important insight in Freud's formulation, in particular, his distinction between the pleasure principle and the reality principle, lies in the recognition that there are severe limits to the degree to which needs can influence perception without threatening survival. Thus, one cannot survive very long if one's primary means of attempting to gratify hunger is to hallucinate food.

The central point here is that whatever they are, if we are to survive, there must be a reasonably reliable match between our categories of experience, that is, the way we structure the world, and the nature of that world (the *Ding an sich*). This is as true for the bat as it is for us. Thus, the bat's echo system of navigation adequately matches an aspect of reality as adequately as our means of navigation "matches" another aspect of reality. Were that not the case, the bat would not survive.

It will be recognized that my comments parallel quite closely Hartmann's (1939) concept of the primary and secondary autonomy of the ego, as well as Rapaport's (1951) concept of the autonomy of the ego from the id. It will also be recognized that both Hartmann's and Rapaport's formulations are expressions of an adaptive point of view—which, quite fittingly, belongs to a broad evolutionary perspective (see also Holt's, 1967, discussion of ego autonomy).

One final point with regard to the role of projection and introjections is constructing external reality. As noted, Klein (1975) claims that projection and introjection are fundamental processes in the construction of external reality. Although the germ of truth in Klein's formulation is that a projective mode of thought does play a role in the construction of reality, her conception of projection focuses not on Kantian categories of experience, but on the death instinct and the projection of love and hate. As I have argued, it is precisely the adaptive relative freedom from this kind of projection that characterizes normal perception.

The two poles of perceptual experiences

Perceptual experience can break down at either the pole of becoming excessively my creation, as in hallucinatory experience that is relatively unconstrained by the external world, or it can become literal and de-animated, entirely determined by literal external physical features. In an extreme form of this latter kind of perceptual experience, objects and events lose their integrity and meaning and are experienced, in the case of objects, as separate and disconnected dimensions and, in the case of events, as separate and disconnected sequences and movements. Normally, we see objects and events in the environment as unified, a fact that neurophysiologists refer to as the "binding problem" and that Kant referred to as "the transcendental unity of apperception." But the experience of objects as unified depends upon intact brain functioning.

One finds both the extreme of near hallucinatory physiognomic perception as well as overliteral and lifeless perception—one might refer to them as extreme animism and de-animism—in certain forms of schizophrenia. For example, in *Autobiography of a Schizophrenic Girl* (Sechehaye, 1951/1994), Renee describes both kinds of experiences at different points of her schizophrenic breakdown. With regard to the latter de-animated kind of experience, she writes: "Pupils and teachers were puppets revolving without cause, without objective," and "I heard people talking but I did not grasp the meaning of the words. The voices were metallic, without warmth or color. From time to time, a word detached itself from the rest. It repeated itself over and over in my head, absurd, as though cut by a knife" (p. 7). She also describes the experience of "other children, heads bent over their work, [as] robots or puppets, moved by an invisible mechanism. On the platform, the teacher, too, talking, gesticulating, rising to write on the blackboard, was a grotesque jack-in-the-box" (p. 7). Renee's experience here is utterly "objective," literal and devoid of meaning. People's behaviors are experienced as "disconnected" movements without purpose rather than continuous and meaningful actions that are directed toward some purpose. There is no experience of *doing*, only of happenings and movements. It is not just the experience of purposive actions and events that has been lost. Although Renee still refers to persons (i.e., other children, pupils, and teachers), her hold on these meaningful percepts is tenuous and shaky—they are experienced as "robots or puppets, moved by an invisible mechanism."

An important question that arises with regard to Renee's de-animated experience is whether it should be viewed as the product of the loss of the projective mode of thought with the result that experiences become excessively literal and de-animated, or whether it should be viewed as a projection on to the external world of her experience of herself as lifeless, deadened, without agency, and controlled by "invisible mechanisms." Perhaps the two accounts converge when one considers that one consequence of the experience of inner meaninglessness and deadness is that the repertoire of what one can project on to the world is limited to meaninglessness and deadness and does not include the enlivening features of meaning, purpose, and motivated action, the built-in ways of experiencing the world. This, then, becomes equivalent to loss of the projective mode of thought.

At the other extreme of Renee's experience is an excessive physiognomic and animistic mode in which inner projections dominate her experience. While in a sanatorium, she describes the following experience: "I believed the wind blew from the North Pole, travelling over the icy Siberian Steppes, moaning and protesting in the forests; it was alive, monstrous, bending everything in its way" (p. 12). "At night I could not sleep, listening to the wind, sharing its howls, its complaints and despairing cries, and my soul wept and groaned with it. More and more I imagined the wind bore a message for me to divine" (p. 13); "the frozen wind from the North Pole wanted to crush the earth and destroy it" (p. 13). During this time, Renee also experiences her doll Riquette and other inanimate objects as alive. At the same time, the words for these objects become meaningless to her.

Both Renee's overliteral and lifeless as well as excessively animated perceptions entail loss of the transitional nature of experience. In the overliteral mode, the external world is imbued with nothing save deadness, with the result that it is experienced as fragmented and meaningless. In the excessive animistic mode, the external world, including the inanimate external world, is imbued with too much meaning, albeit autistic and destructive meaning. In a sense, the inanimate world is too alive with personal meanings of a frightening and destructive nature. Here, the projective mode of thought has gone wild, unconstrained by external stimuli. Although external stimuli register—Renee heard the howling wind—they are mainly triggers for terribly frightening personal meanings and messages. Between these two extremes of Renee's experiences lies normal perception which is both animated and fed by attributions of inner meanings as well as responsive to and constrained by the array of external stimuli (see Eagle, 1994).[4, 5]

Having set the framework for understanding the projective mode of cognition, I now turn to a discussion, first, of projection as a defense and then, projective identification. Before turning to these topics, it is important to note that, as we have seen, unlike projection as a defense and projective identification getting rid of unwanted mental contents or placing mental contents into another for safekeeping (whatever that might mean). As noted earlier, Freud (1913[1912–1913]) wrote "projection was not created for the purpose of defense" (p. 64). Rather, a projective mode of thought involves the influence on one's experiences, including giving meaning to external stimuli, through imbuing them with certain properties related to one's inner world of needs, concerns, imagination, interests, fantasies, and so on. The main thing that projection as a mode of thought has in common with projective identification and projection as a defense is the attribution of certain personal meanings to the external world. What it does not have in common with projective identification and projection as a defense is that it does not entail expulsion of inner contents on to the external world, including others in that world.

Projection as a defense

I turn now to the concept of projection as a defense, the essence of which is the unconscious attempt to rid oneself of unacceptable wishes, feelings, and thoughts by attributing them to others. Freud provides different illustrations of the use of projection as a defense. In one example, he writes: "The hostility, of which the survivors know nothing and moreover wish to know nothing, is ejected from internal perception into the external world, and thus pushed on to someone else" (Freud, 1913[1912–1913], pp. 62–63). As another example, in the context of discussing jealousy, temptation, and marital fidelity, he writes: "Anyone who denies these temptations in himself will nevertheless feel their pressures so strongly that he will be glad enough to make use of an unconscious mechanism to alleviate his situation. He can obtain this alleviation—and, indeed, acquittal by his conscience—if he projects his own impulses to faithlessness on to the partner to whom he owes faith" (Freud, 1922, p. 224).

Klein on projection as a defense

As we have seen, Klein has a great deal to say about projection as well as introjection as two fundamental psychological processes of mental life. It is not always clear when Klein is referring to projection as a mode of thought and when she is referring to it as a defense. According to Klein (1975), at its earliest and most basic level, projection as a defense comes into play to protect the infant against self-destructive impulses emanating from the death instinct. Klein (1975) writes: "The young infant would be in danger of being flooded by his self-destructive impulses if the mechanism of projection could not operate" (p. 238). Klein does not make entirely clear how projecting self-destructive impulses on to the object protects the infant from being flooded with them. There is little attention given to the nature of the processes involved. What seems to be clear is that Klein thinks of defensive projection as a *fantasy* of expelling some aspects of oneself (e.g., destructive impulses) into an external object, thus ridding oneself of them. Thus, on this view, the fantasy of expelling, say, destructive impulses, enables one to feel less destructive and "bad." However, as Klein goes on to observe, a negative consequence of the use of projection is the experience of the object as a "bad" object, as a *persecutor*. It appears that one has traded the danger of being flooded by self-destructive impulses for the danger of experiencing persecution from the object.

What confuses matters is that in the same context as that in which Klein talks about projecting unwanted mental contents, she also employs the term projection to refer to "the projection of love-feelings" (p. 69), which enables the infant to make mother "into a good . . . object" (p. 250). Here, Klein is no longer talking about projection as a defense as it is employed by Freud—why would one need to rid oneself of or expel "love-feelings"?—but rather as a projective mode of thought, a process through which one imbues objects in the external world with attributes linked to one's inner feelings. In contrast to the defense mechanism of projecting negative unwanted aspects of oneself, the projection of positive "love-feelings" on to the object does not result in the fantasy that one has rid oneself of these feelings. In her discussion of projection, Klein neither makes clear nor addresses these distinctions.

Klein also does not address another important distinction. Just as projecting onto or imbuing the object with "love-feelings" results in one's experience of the object as benevolent and loving, so similarly, does projecting one's hostility on to the object result in experiencing the object as hostile. Both are instances of the projective mode of thought. We have all had the experience of seeing the world as rosy and benevolent when in a positive and loving state and seeing the world as negative and gloomy when in a depressed and angry state. These are expression of state dependent cognition and affect, what one can refer to as affective or mood organization of cognition (see Bower, 1981, 1987).

The main point here is that experiencing the object and the external world in accord with one's inner thoughts and affects is an expression of a projective mode of thought *and not itself of projection as a defense*. To invoke the latter, one needs to show that the experience of the object as, say, hostile, is a product not simply of a projective mode of thought, but one that (1) is defensively *motivated* by the aim of ridding oneself of unwanted aspects of oneself; and (2) when effectively employed as a psychological operation, succeeds in blocking conscious experience of the projected unwanted aspect of oneself.

As we will see in the section on research on projection as a defense, there is much research evidence demonstrating the general tendency to attribute to others unwanted aspects of oneself and also some evidence that such attributions or projections serve to attenuate the impact of unwanted aspects of oneself. However, hypotheses regarding some of the specific processes through which this attenuation occurs are quite different from the psychoanalytic idea that projection helps one rid oneself of these unwanted aspects.

Transference and projection

According to the classical conception of projection as a defense, one projects one's unacceptable wishes on to another person and then experiences the other person as having those wishes. However, there is much evidence that one projects not only the unacceptable wish on to the other, but also self-critical attitudes. As shown in Baldwin and Keelan's (1999) research, individuals low in self-esteem are more likely to expect negative reactions from others. In the present context, one can say that they project self-critical attitudes on to the other and then are more likely to experience the other as critical. This important aspect of projection is overlooked or, at least, minimized in the classical account. In many situations, one projects on to the other not only, or perhaps, not primarily, an unacceptable wish, but one's critical and condemning attitudes toward that wish, and then experiences the object of one's projection as critical and condemning. This is essentially a description of a projection on to the other of one's *superego* evaluation, understood as the internalization of parental attitudes.

From a Fairbairnian perspective, one can understand this phenomenon as projecting one's internalized "bad" object on to the other, with the consequence that the other is now experienced as "bad" (i.e., rejecting, unloving). This process is often the most clinically significant aspect of projection. Whether it can be understood as a defense is questionable insofar as it may not be motivated by the aim of ridding oneself of self-critical attitudes. Further, the projection of self-critical attitudes onto another frequently does not succeed in attenuating these attitudes. Indeed, the experience of another person as critical of oneself may intensify one's own self-critical attitudes.

The projection of self-critical attitudes onto another person can be understood as the product of an *expectation* that the other will hold the same critical attitudes that one has toward oneself. Furthermore, this expectation may lead to the individual emitting cues that *induce* the other to feel and behave critically. Such behavior on the part of the other tends to confirm not only one's expectation about the other, but also the critical attitudes one has about oneself, creating a vicious circle (see Wachtel, 2014). The main point I want to make here is that the projection of self-critical attitudes onto another influences not only how one experiences the other, but also how one experiences oneself, partly through the behavior it may induce in the other.

The above formulation of projection has important implications for how one understands transference. In the classical perspective, the emphasis is on how the projection on to the therapist of parental attitudes influences the patient's experience of the therapist (e.g., like my parents, you, too, are disapproving of me). Given that these parental attitudes have been internalized, one can say that the patient has projected on to the analyst self-critical attitudes. A number of implications follow. One implication is that the patient's experience of how the analyst reacts to him or her and, in particular, how the analyst reacts to the patient's projections of self-critical attitudes is likely to influence not only how the patient experiences the analyst, but also how the patient experiences himself or herself.

The other possible implication is that the patient may be less concerned with the analyst gratifying infantile wishes than with looking to the therapist to *disconfirm* projected expectations, in particular, the expectation that the therapist shares the patient's self-critical attitudes.

I would hypothesize that transference interpretations that focus on the patient's attribution to the therapist of one's internalized parental attitudes toward oneself will be more therapeutically effective than interpretations that focus on the patient's demands for gratification of infantile wishes. There are a number of interrelated rationales for this hypothesis. There is evidence that episodes of rupture and repair are associated with positive therapeutic outcome (e.g., Muran et al., 2009; Safran et al., 2011). Control–Mastery theory research suggests that an important source of rupture lies in the patient's experience of the therapist as harboring the same critical attitudes that his or her parents had toward himself or herself. I would add—and this a testable hypothesis—that an important source of rupture lies in the patient's experience of the therapist as having the same critical attitudes that the patient has toward himself or herself. Hence, therapeutic interventions, including interpretations, that disconfirm these experiences are likely to constitute a "corrective emotional experience" that may repair the rupture. Following Strachey (1934), such experiences are also likely to soften the harshness of the patient's superego, that is, to attenuate his or her self-critical and self-punitive attitudes.

The kinds of interpretations I am describing also tend to encourage the patient to examine and reflect not only on his or her own mental states (i.e., critical attitudes toward oneself), but also on the mental states of the other (e.g., does my therapist have the critical attitudes toward me that I assume he or she has?). At their best, these sorts of interpretations may not only be conducive to self-understanding, but also may facilitate self-regulation.

Let me describe a clinical vignette that illustrates the affect-regulating value of reflective capacity. A patient would frequently attribute to others derogative attitudes toward her that reflected similar unacknowledged attitudes she had toward herself. Typically, she would respond with rage and attacks on the other, which led to stormy relationships with others. After a good deal of therapeutic work, she was able to step back and reflect both on the other's mental state (e.g., was the other, in fact, intending to be derogatory and dismissive?) and her own reactions (is my rage warranted by the other's intentions and behavior?). This enhanced reflective capacity enabled a marked reduction in uncontrollable and destructive rages. Later in the treatment, she was able to examine whether her attributions to others reflected derogatory and dismissive attitudes toward herself.

Before concluding this discussion, let me refer to a mundane personal experience having to do with the projection of self-attitudes on to others. I had made a commitment to be a discussant at a conference panel. About 10 days before the panel, which was to be held during my vacation, it became evident to me that attending the panel would be quite inconvenient and I began to think of an acceptable way to not attend the panel. A "solution" a friend suggested was to email my brief discussion to a colleague on the panel and ask her to read it. I felt quite guilty about this idea, put off contacting my colleague to ask her what she thought of this plan, and finally did so. She said she understood, would be happy to read the discussion, and assured me that it was a good idea. I felt quite relieved that the plan was acceptable to my colleague and that I would not have to travel some distance and disrupt my vacation just to read a 10-minute discussion.

However, I continued to feel somewhat guilty and wondered whether my colleague had some unexpressed reactions of disapproval, although there was nothing in the content or tone of her reaction that suggested disapproval. The question here is whether my lingering concern about my colleague's reaction was justified or whether it was due mainly to my attribution to her of my own disapproving attitudes toward my decision. The issue is somewhat more complex insofar as my disapproval of my decision reflects a general social "rule" that my colleague and I, both socialized in the same culture, likely share, namely, that generally speaking, one does not break a commitment for the sake of personal convenience. Hence, it is possible that my lingering concern regarding my colleague's possible disapproval may not have been entirely a matter of my projection, but at least partly because of our shared values.

I bring up the above incident because I believe that certain aspects of it may be relevant to the issues of transference and projection in the clinical situation. Let us say that in the above incident, I am a patient who is reporting the incident to my therapist, reluctantly, because I feel she will disapprove of my behavior. And let us say that my therapist interprets my reluctance and my attribution to her as a projection, that is, as reflecting my own self-critical attitudes that I attribute to her. And let us say further that I am reassured and relieved, at least, at the moment (as I was when my colleague agreed to read my discussion), because I understand the interpretation as suggesting that my therapist does not feel critical toward me and that I am being too hard on myself. In that sense, one can think of this interaction as constituting a "corrective emotional experience."

I wonder, however, if this is the full story, that is, whether the interpretation does justice to all that is going on and whether maximum therapeutic value has been realized from this interaction. What is not examined in this interaction is the possibility (perhaps likelihood) that, given the fact that the therapist does not live outside the culture and that patient and therapist are likely to share many social values, the therapist may, indeed, harbor some disapproving attitudes toward the patient with regard to the incident and may emit cues that reflect such attitudes in subtle ways. As Gill (1982, 1994) has argued in his cogent critique of the "blank screen" analyst, it is virtually impossible to interact with anyone without emitting cues that reflect underlying feelings and attitudes, even if not overtly expressed.

I would argue that if the therapist is aware, even if dimly, that he or she does have critical attitudes toward the patient's behavior and given the likelihood that the patient will pick up cues that express these attitudes, it would make therapeutic sense for the therapist to acknowledge and communicate these attitudes in a way that encourages mutual examination of the interaction. Such communication, I suggest, would be something like the following:

> I find myself reacting somewhat critically to your decision, in some ways similar to the way you feel and perhaps similar to the way you expected and feared that I would react. I think that to some extent, we both share the idea that you're not supposed to break a commitment for the sake of one's convenience and feel that it is equivalent to shirking one's duty. Let us examine all this.

If the therapist does harbor critical feelings, it is more honest and perhaps less potentially confusing to the patient for them to be confronted than for them to be hidden and denied and yet perhaps contradicted by cues the therapist emits. It seems to me that an honest communication is more likely to constitute a corrective emotional experience than an inauthentic denial of one's critical reactions. Further, this honest interaction may more readily allow an examination of the ways in which the patient's appropriate self-critical feelings and attitudes are transformed into harsh and primitive superego condemnations, which are then attributed to the therapist.

At the core of Alexander and French's (1946) concept of "corrective emotional experience" is the idea that the patient's maladaptive expectations of the therapist's reactions are disconfirmed by the therapist's actual behavior. However, things may not be that simple. As discussed above, on occasion, the therapist's behavior may well include cues that reflect critical and disapproving reactions. When this so, the therapist's interpretations to the effect that the patient's attributions are transference reactions (i.e., projections on to the therapist of parental attitudes) may, ironically, be experienced by the patient as a repetition of early distressing experiences characterized by a confusing combination of explicit parental denial of critical attitudes along with cues that contradict the explicit denial. Hence, a truly emotionally corrective experience may include the therapist's willingness to examine along with the patient the possibility that the therapist has emitted cues that may reflect disapproving attitudes toward the patient. This interaction may be as different from early pathogenic experiences as conveying a nonjudgmental attitude. Perhaps most important, in this type of interaction, the therapist is not presenting himself or herself as an *Übermensch*, who is always perfectly capable of nonjudgmental acceptance, but rather is an ordinary human being who, in certain respects and to some degree, like the patient, struggles with conflicting feelings and who honestly tries to examine, with the patient, the impact of those feelings on the patient, always keeping in the forefront his or her recognition of the patient's goals and aims and the importance of contributing positively to the achievement of these aims.

Research on projection as a defense

Let me begin by turning to some representative studies of projection summarized by Baumeister et al. (1998). They define projection broadly as "perceiving others as having traits that one inaccurately believes oneself not to have" (p. 1090) and go on to note that "projection can be seen as defensive if perceiving the threatening trait in others helps the individual in some way to avoid recognizing it in himself or herself" (p. 1090).

But the means by which this is supposed to occur is not adequately addressed. Baumeister et al. (1998) raise a critical question with regard to projection as a defense: why should attributing an unacceptable mental content to another help one avoid consciously experiencing that mental content or acknowledging it in oneself? For example, they raise the question of "how seeing another person as dishonest would enable the individual to avoid recognizing his or her own dishonesty" (p. 1091) and conclude that "the notion that projection would effectively mask one's own bad traits was perhaps incoherent" (p. 1091). Although this may be an unwarranted conclusion—for example, they do not entertain the possibility that the individual harbors the unconscious fantasy that by attributing it to someone else, he or she has expelled the unacceptable content—Baumeister et al. do raise an important question and point to the need to address the specific process involved. As far as I can tell, it is simply taken for granted in the psychoanalytic literature on projection that attributing an unwanted thought to someone else is a means of ridding oneself of it.

The studies on projection described by Baumeister et al. (1998) all have in common the finding that one tends to perceive others as having traits similar to one's own traits (e.g., Ross et al., 1977). Insofar as this tendency includes both good and bad traits, one can hardly view it as a defense. However, Baumeister et al. (1998) describe some findings that suggest the defensive use of this tendency. Thus, the tendency to perceive bad traits in others is associated with higher self-esteem and lower depression (Campbell, 1986; Crocker et al., 1988). Newman et al. (1997) reported that repressors not only were more likely to deny having certain bad traits (a judgment contradicted by their acquaintances), but were also more likely to interpret the ambiguous behavior of others as reflecting these bad traits. One can infer, although it is a shaky inference, that the attribution of bad traits to others plays a role in the repressors' denial of bad traits in themselves.

Newman et al. (1997) also attempted to study projection experimentally in the following way: Participants were given bogus feedback from a personality test regarding their good and bad traits and were then asked to avoid thinking about one dimension of the bad feedback. When they rated a stimulus person on all the dimensions on which they had received feedback, they rated that person about the same on all dimensions, except for the higher rating on the trait for which they had been given bad feedback and had been asked to suppress. On those traits for which they received bad feedback but were not asked to suppress, they did not rate the stimulus person higher.

Baumeister et al. (1998) interpret these findings as showing that "projection results from trying to suppress thoughts about some bad trait in oneself" (p. 1092). Relying on the work of Wegner (1994), which shows that trying to suppress a thought makes it more accessible, Baumeister et al. (1998) argue that "people try to suppress thoughts of their undesirable traits, and these efforts make those trait categories highly accessible—so that they are then used all the more often when forming impressions of others" (p. 1091). To be noted here is that according to the logic of this formulation, whereas suppressing thoughts of one's bad traits is motivated, attributing these traits to others is not. Rather, the latter is the "automatic" outcome of the greater accessibility of these traits engendered by attempts to suppress them. That is, because the act of suppressing thoughts about bad traits lowers their availability threshold, they are more likely to be cognitively accessible and therefore more likely to be used in the description of another person—somewhat similar to the rebound effect reported by Wegner (1994) in which the effort to "try not to think of a white bear," seemingly paradoxically, results in greater intrusion of that thought into consciousness.

The key point here is that according to Baumeister et al.'s (1998) formulation, attributing one's bad traits to another does not serve to rid oneself of these traits, but rather is the *result* of trying to rid oneself of these traits. Hence, from this perspective, projection of one's bad traits on to the other per se does not appear to serve any defensive function. It is not clear, therefore, how Baumeister et al. (1998) can conclude that there is evidence for projection in the revised form that they conceptualize it. For in that form, it is no longer a defense mechanism, but rather a general cognitive tendency in which "people's conceptions of themselves shape their perceptions of other people" (p. 1092).

There is a potentially serious problem of ecological validity with the suppressing thoughts about one's bad traits paradigm. In the Newman et al. (1997) study, participants were instructed by an experimenter to suppress thoughts. This differs from the psychoanalytic formulation in at least two important ways: first, from a psychoanalytic perspective, people are *internally* motivated to rid themselves of certain thoughts rather than instructed to do so; and second, the process of trying to rid oneself of certain thoughts is viewed not as an entirely volitional and conscious one, but rather an unconscious "automatic" one.

Even if one accepts Fingarette's (1963) and Stern's (2003) alternatives to the Freudian conception of unconscious processes, which focus on not spelling out and not formulating, respectively, we are nevertheless not dealing with a fully conscious and volitional act, but rather an automatic process that is at the periphery of consciousness or only fleetingly in consciousness. From either perspective, Baumeister et al.'s (1998) account of projection (i.e., attribution of unwanted mental contents to others) as due to the greater accessibility of thoughts one is trying to suppress does not seem apt. For according to Baumeister et al.'s (1998) view, accessibility of these unwanted thoughts is due, putting it loosely, to being preoccupied with trying to suppress them. Without such a "preoccupation," there is no reason to expect a Wegner-type rebound effect of suppressed thoughts. Hence, the admittedly clever account that projection is the *consequence* of an attempt to rid oneself of unwanted thoughts rather than the means of doing so works only when these attempts are volitional and conscious and thus render suppressed thoughts more accessible. But, to reiterate, the analogue of instructing people to suppress unwanted thoughts does not really capture the psychoanalytic understanding of the processes involved in ridding oneself of unwanted thoughts and, hence, lacks ecological validity. This criticism, however, is attenuated if one maintains that there is no sharp dichotomy between repression and suppression.

Baumeister et al. (1998) identify a possible motive for attributing bad traits to others that is different from, but bears a family resemblance to, the psychoanalytic concept of projection in that it is not a means of ridding oneself of these bad traits, but of attenuating their impact. That is, seeing others as having bad traits similar to one's own "reduces the distinctiveness of one's [own] bad traits" (p. 1090). It is captured by the expression "misery loves company." Thus, although reducing the distinctiveness of one's bad traits by attributing them to another does not rid oneself of these traits, it serves, in a subtle way, to minimize their affective impact and personal importance in a sort of "everyone is that way" maneuver.

In the psychoanalytic literature, particularly the Kleinian literature, the means through which attributing one's bad traits to another is assumed to serve the aim of ridding oneself of them is *fantasy*. That is, from this perspective, essential to the conception of projection as a defense is the assumption that projection entails not only the attribution of unacceptable aspects of oneself to another, but also the fantasy that doing so entails ridding oneself of these unacceptable aspects. Merely viewing projection as the attribution of one's bad traits to another is not sufficient for understanding it as a defense.

Baumeister et al.'s (1998) critique is useful in encouraging one to rethink and clarify the concept of projection as a defense. In particular, it highlights the distinction between the process of projection, the essence of which is the attribution of unacceptable aspects of oneself onto another and its presumed function of ridding oneself of these unacceptable aspects. The latter may or may not occur. The Baumeister et al. (1998) critique also alerts us to other distress-reducing defensive functions served by projection, in particular, helping one feel that certain unacceptable aspects of oneself are not unique to oneself.

If the distinction made by Baumeister et al. (1998) is a valid one, it follows that when we see evidence of projection, we should not automatically assume that this always entails the motive to rid oneself of unacceptable aspects of oneself. It may serve other defensive functions, including the need to see others as having the same negative traits or wishes that one feels one has. One important implication of this somewhat enlarged conception of projection as a defense is that it is incumbent upon the clinician invoking this defense in any given case to specify its function and identify the clinical evidence on which the clinical inferences are made (e.g., evidence of attempts to reduce the distinctiveness of one's own bad traits; and in the psychoanalytic context, evidence of an expulsion fantasy).

If correct, Baumeister et al.'s (1998) argument would appear to raise questions regarding the commonly held idea that a central factor underlying prejudice is the attempt to rid oneself of undesirable qualities by projecting them on to, say, an ethnic group, as expressed, for example, in Allport's (1954, p. 386) widely accepted claim that a stereotyped group provides a target for the projection of one's unwanted traits. Is there evidence that attributing negative traits to a stereotyped group helps one psychologically rid oneself of them?

Govorun et al. (2006) carried out a series of four studies on the relationship between stereotypes and defensive projection. In study 1, half of the participants were asked to think of failure in college and half of success in college in the areas of leadership and intelligence. Participants who recalled failure in intelligence were more likely to attribute lack of intelligence to sorority women; and those who recalled failure in leadership were more likely to attribute lack of leadership to sorority women. These finding are compatible with Baumeister et al.'s (1998) activation or priming hypothesis and do not themselves demonstrate *defensive* projection.

In an attempt to rule out semantic priming, participants were asked to recall failure (in intelligence) of an acquaintance or of oneself. They were then asked to rate student athlete traits. Results showed that compared to participants recalling an acquaintance's failure, participants who recalled their own intellectual failure were faster to identify lack of intelligence traits as stereotypical of student athletes. Thus, because recall of one's own failure or an acquaintance's failure both activates failure networks, semantic priming as an explanation appears to be refuted. However, projection as a defense is not yet demonstrated.

Studies 3 and 4 extended the methods of studies 1 and 2 to rate and included the variable of threat induction (in the areas of intelligence and hostility). The findings showed that compared to the control condition, the black man target was rated as less intelligent when the threat of low intelligence was induced. The authors concluded first, that stereotyped derogation is linked to self-threat; and second, that projection occurred only when a stereotyped target was available. The authors also note that an important limitation of these studies is not investigating the effect of projection on self-evaluation. The effect on self is, of course, at the heart of the issue of whether the participant's projections can be seen as *defensive* projections, that is, as enabling one to feel that he or she does not possess the projected traits.

That participants in studies 3 and 4 projected traits specifically related to the threat induction suggests the possibility of a defensive function. That is, it suggests that one sees in others traits that one does not want to see in oneself (traits that are threatening to one's self-esteem). But, again, the critical question is whether seeing unwanted traits in others serves to make it more likely that one will not experience these traits in oneself.

Bornstein (2007) carried out two Rorschach studies that indirectly address this issue. In study 1, when participants who reported low dependency on an Interpersonal Dependency Inventory (IDI) were told that they were highly dependent, they showed an increase in Rorschach Oral Dependency (ROD) scores. This did not occur with participants who scored high on IDI or who received low dependency feedback. In study 2, providing low IDI participants the opportunity to attribute dependency to a fictional target person attenuated the impact of high dependency feedback on ROD scores. Thus, participants who see themselves as low in dependency and are told that they are highly dependent, if given an opportunity to project dependency on to another person, are less likely to produce oral dependency scores on the Rorschach. These findings suggest that the opportunity to employ projection as a defense helps one rid oneself of a dependency trait, as reflected in Rorschach responses. However, there is a serious question as to whether fewer oral dependency responses on the Rorschach is an ecologically valid measure of having rid oneself of an unwanted trait. (Also, why assume that the independent person is necessarily defending against being dependent—i.e., needs to get rid of it?)

Schimel et al. (2003) carried out two studies directly addressing the question of whether projection of an unwanted trait would serve to reduce accessibility of that trait and enhance denial of that trait in oneself. In study 1, participants were given feedback that they were either high or low on repressed hostility. They then read about and rated a target on hostility whose behavior was ambiguous with regard to hostility, and were asked to rate the target on hostility. They were also asked to complete word fragments. The results showed that compared to low anger feedback, participants given high hostility feedback rated the target higher in anger. There were no effects with regard to positive and negative traits unrelated to feedback.

On the word fragment task, compared to participants who were given low hostility feedback, participants who were given high hostility feedback, when given the opportunity to project anger on to a target showed the lowest anger accessibility. In a second study involving dishonesty as an unwanted trait, the results were as follows: (1) participants given high dishonesty feedback projected more (i.e., rated a target in an ambiguous situation as more dishonest) than participants given low dishonesty feedback; and (2) participants who were given high dishonesty feedback and given the opportunity to project dishonesty on to a target rated themselves as less dishonest than participants also given high dishonesty feedback, but not given the opportunity to project dishonesty on to a target. These findings seem to illustrate the use of projection as a defense in that they entail projection onto another of an unwanted trait along with the effect of reducing the belief that one has that trait.

Schimel et al. (2003) raise the question of the processes through which projection of unwanted traits reduces the threat to oneself. They offer three alternative accounts: first, by attributing a negative trait to another, the accessibility of the trait can also be attributed to the other, with the result that one can stop thinking about it and reduce its accessibility. Second, in accord with social comparison theory, by seeing others in a negative light, one can feel better about oneself. Third, which also seems to include social comparison, by judging oneself more favorably than the target of projection, the accessibility of the negative trait is reduced. Schimel et al. (2003) go on to comment that the lowered accessibility of the negative trait may be an unintended by-product of projection, which may then take on motivational properties.

The Schimel et al. (2003) studies stand out as the most directly related to the question of projection as a defense insofar as they focus on the core issue of the effect of attributing a negative trait to another on the experience of that trait in oneself. However, the ecological validity of these studies is somewhat compromised by the fact that the participants were informed by the experimenter that they were hostile or dishonest rather than intrinsically struggling with these issues on their own. Indeed, we do not know how seriously they took the false feedback or even whether they really believed it. The essence of projection as a defense is that it is put into play by the motive to rid oneself of a trait (or a wish or desire) that, at some level, one feels or believes one possesses, about which one is conflicted, and with regard to which one would experience anxiety and other dysphoric affects were the trait fully consciously experienced.

The Schimel et al. (2003) studies show that when one is told that one has a negative trait, the opportunity to attribute that trait to someone else serves to lower self-attribution of that trait. That is an interesting and important finding. And the strength of these studies is that, although an experimental analogue, they bear a meaningful family resemblance to defensive projection in a real-life context. However, the family resemblance is a modest one and leaves one still waiting for ecologically valid studies of projection as a defense.

Projective identification

I now turn to the concept of projective identification. Unlike other psychoanalytic concepts that I have discussed thus far, as far as I know, there is little or no research on projective identification (given the fact that the concept is defined and understood in so many different ways, it would be quite difficult to carry out any research). Hence, my discussion of projective identification will be limited to conceptual critique and clinical evidence.

I begin my discussion with some brief anecdotes. Some years ago, my supervisees and colleagues began using the term with increasing frequency as a means of accounting for certain events in the therapeutic situation, frequently having to do with their own emotional and cognitive reactions to the patient. Each time, I would ask, curiously and receptively I would like to believe, what they meant by the term. The responses to my question were frequently vague and confused and tended to vary with each supervisee or colleague to whom the question was posed. Furthermore, this experience was repeated in classes I taught to candidates at various psychoanalytic institutes. The frequency with which projective identification was mentioned by candidates as a presumed explanation of some therapeutic interaction was not at all matched by the degree of stability of its meaning or the clarity of the candidates' apparent understanding of what it meant.

In one supervision experience which stands out in my memory and which I have described elsewhere (Eagle, 2000), a supervisee informed me that when she presented the case on which I was supervising her to a case conference and informed the group that she had experienced headaches when she saw this patient, she was told by some participants in the case conference that her headaches were the result of projective identification. After I registered some surprise that she had not told me about the headaches earlier and indicated that this needed to be discussed further, I asked the supervisee how she understood the idea that her headaches were because of projective identification. She replied that the patient had "put the headaches into me." I asked how the patient had put the headaches into her. She replied, "through projective identification." When I asked her what she meant by projective identification, she replied that it meant that the patient had put something into her. I then suggested that her use of the term was preventing both of us from looking into and understanding just what was going on in her and in her interaction with the patient that would lead to frequent headaches with this patient and not with other patients (the headaches occurred only with this patient).

Although not quite so egregious, something like this experience was repeated a number of times in seminars I taught and in informal discussions with colleagues. It was not uncommon for the individual who used the term to be unable to provide a clear working definition, let alone a clear idea of what he or she intended by the term. I formed the impression that there were almost as many formulations and understandings of the term as the number of people employing it. (As we will see, this is not an altogether inaccurate impression.)

Freud's account of projection as the foundation for the concept of projective identification

Freud (1913[1912–1913]) understood the concept of projection as a defense as the attribution to another of unconscious mental contents that are unacceptable to oneself. For example, an unacceptable hostile wish may be projected onto another, with the result that the other is now experienced as harboring hostile wishes toward oneself. This process is an intrapsychic one that can be carried out in fantasy without direct interpersonal contact with the object of one's projection. Some theorists do not make a sharp distinction between projection and projective identification; they simply add to the concept of projection the idea that the projector then identifies with the object of his or her projection (presumably because of the unconscious fantasy that they now share the same mental content). This formulation is not convincing because, among other reasons, identification with the object of one's projection would undercut the primary motive of projection in the first place, namely, ridding oneself of an unacceptable mental content. Identification with the object of one's projections would seem to be the product of loss of boundaries and, therefore, should be seen as a failed projection.

The concept of projection has morphed into projective identification by extending the former in a number of other ways: first, it is not only wishes and desires that can be projected onto another, but also parts of the self and internal objects; second, and most important, projection, which is essentially an *intrapsychic* process, was extended and transformed into an *interpersonal* process in the following way: "In projective identification, parts of the self and internal objects are split off and projected into the external object, which then becomes possessed by, controlled and identified with the projected parts" (Segal, 1973, p. 14).[6] It is this interpersonal conception or projective identification that is most frequently invoked in the context of the patient–analyst interaction.

Klein's conception of projective identification

In her earliest formulation of the concept, Klein (1946) describes the process of projective identification as follows:

> Together with these harmful excrements, expelled in hatred, split off parts of the ego are *also projected on to the mother or, as I would rather call it, into the mother* [my emphasis]. These excrements and bad parts of the self are meant not only to injure the object but also to control it and take possession of it. Insofar as the mother comes to contain the bad parts of the self, she is not felt to be a separate individual but is felt to be the bad self.
>
> Much of the hatred against parts of the self is now directed towards the mother. This leads to a particular kind of identification which establishes the prototype of an aggressive object relation. Also, since the projection derives from the infant's impulse to harm or control the mother he feels her to be a persecutor . . .
>
> It is, however, not only the bad parts of the self which are expelled and projected, but also good parts of the self. Excrements then have the significance of gifts . . .
>
> (Klein, 1946, p. 102)

Spillius (2012a) writes that "In essence these paragraphs are a definition of projective identification" (p. 5). She then examines Klein's unpublished notes where she refers to projective identification. I will cite the following two passages, a theoretical one and one in which the concept of projective identification is invoked in relation to clinical material:

> Projective identification is the basis for many anxiety situations of a paranoid nature. Since projection and introjection operate simultaneously, paranoid anxieties focus on persecution within the self and within the object which the self has forcefully entered. The attempts

to control an external object by entering it give rise to the fear of being controlled and persecuted by this object. The subject may be unable to withdraw from this object; it is kept imprisoned and subjugated by the object. Once part of the ego, or the whole ego, might be felt to have got lost forever etc. (I have described formerly, in *The psycho-analysis of childre*n, such fears as being not only at the bottom of paranoid anxiety but also as a cause for disturbances in the male's sexuality—impotence—and as a basis for claustrophobia.) In addition, the re-introjection of this object, which now represents a combination of a persecutory object and the bad self, reinforces inner persecution. The accumulations of anxiety situations of this nature—particularly the fact that the ego is, as it were, caught between external and internal anxieties—is one of the basic features of paranoia. (Cf. chapter on "Notes on some schizoid mechanisms," also H. Rosenfeld's paper "Analysis of a schizophrenic state with depersonalization," IJPA, Vol. XXVIII, 1947, and Joan Riviere's paper. [Title? Published?])

[. . .]

Patient "M"
October 12, 1946
The influence the projective identifications have on sexual intercourse are seen quite clearly in somebody whose analysis has not been carried to any length yet. His fear of influencing or molding the women he is interested in such a way that they are greatly changed and become really like himself. He saw with dismay that a girl he likes and who likes him and changed her style of dressing in the way in which he sometimes likes women to be dressed and he called this "the thin edge of the wedge." In the same hour he told me that he does not like this influence at all and is strongly trying to prevent it in present relations. He speaks with great concern about an earlier relation in which this seemed to be one of the factors which made the girl too fond, too dependent on him and finished unsatisfactorily because he cannot bear too much dependence in the woman. Somebody said that he is apt to choose people (in working conditions) who are so receptive to his ideas that they will make a perfect staff. In referring to this influence he said: "They become really too much like myself and [I] don't want to see so much of myself about." The sexual relations too

> were obviously impeded and influenced by these fears. All relationships, but particularly with women, were affected. He does not seem to feel having such powers over men.
>
> Conclusion: The penis being used as a controlling object, as an object to be split off, and then the mechanism of splitting is very active. Not only faeces are split off, but parts of the body which are entering the body and controlling it. Now the penis is then felt to remain inside in a controlling, guiding, etc. way. That too must have a bearing on difficulties in potency, because if it is too much a sent out part of oneself it impedes the capacity.
>
> (Klein Archive, PP/KLE, B98, as cited in Spillius, 2012a, pp. 9–10; p. 14)

Since Klein formulated the concept of projective identification, there have been many other formulations of the concept, far too many to discuss in any detail. Indeed, Spillius and O'Shaughnessy (2012) have devoted an entire edited book to different formulations of the concept, some of which, one should add, are largely incomprehensible. Consider the following passage from Massi (2012):

> In Ogden's vision, the ineffable subject of the unconscious communicates to the immanent subject the individual's anonymous pains through symptoms, dreams, actings, and so on; in the opposite manner, the conflicts of daily life are transmitted to the ineffable subject of the unconscious, which processes them through unconscious dreaming. Thus, an internal process of projective identification is created, through which emotional experiences can be thought and so transmitted to oneself and others.
>
> (p. 348)

I am at a loss to make much sense of the above passages and leave it to the reader to make his or her own attempt. In making this attempt, one should keep in mind that Klein is attributing to the infant literally fantastic processes such as expelling excrements motivated by hatred and intent to injure the object, controlling and taking possession of the object, and so on—all these attributions made, remarkably, without any reference to what one may even remotely think of as the evidential basis for such wildly fantastic speculations. Instead, and quite ironically, the infant becomes a screen on to which the theorist projects his or her fantasies regarding the nature of early psychological life.

Different conceptions of projective identification

I commented above that it was my impression that there seemed to be almost as many different definitions of projective identification as there are different individuals employing the concept. My impression receives much support from the Spillius and O'Shaughnessy (2012) book in which different contributors offer their particular formulation of projective identification. In addition, the book contains chapters on the views of projective identification in seven different countries, revealing that the understandings and uses of the concept are different in each country.

Although one can perhaps understand that attitudes toward and reception of a concept may vary with country, it is more difficult to comprehend why *definitions* of a concept, that is, how it is understood, would be different in different countries. At the very least, communication regarding the concept, let alone examining the evidence in relation to it, becomes quite difficult when it is not clear that each participant is employing and understanding a concept in the same way.

The situation is even more confusing. Not only are there differences in the conceptualization of projective identification among different countries, but also within each country. Thus, in her chapter on "A brief review of projective identification in American psychoanalytic literature," Spillius (2012b) divides American contributors into "adopters," "partial adopters," and "definers and doubters" (pp. 245–263). (For reasons that I do not understand, I am identified as a "partial adopter.") There are differences even among the "adopters." For example, while Grotstein does not distinguish between projection and projective identification, Ogden and Kernberg do distinguish between the two.

Ogden's concept of projective identification

Because Ogden (1979) presents a fairly accessible description of the interpersonal conception of projective identification, I will devote a good deal of discussion to his formulation. He posits a three-aspect process: first, "the fantasy of projecting a part of oneself into another person and of that part taking over the person from within" (Ogden, 1979, p. 358); second, "pressure exerted via the interpersonal interaction such that the 'recipient' of the projection experiences pressure to think, feel, and behave in a manner congruent with the projection"; and third, "the projected feelings, after being 'psychologically processed' by the recipient, are reinternalized by the projector" (p. 360). According to Ogden (1979), the first step of projection is motivated by "wishes to rid oneself of a part of the self either because that part threatens to destroy the self from within, or because one feels that the part is in danger of attack by other aspects of the self and must be safeguarded by being held inside a protective person" (p. 358).

Implicit in Ogden's concept of projective identification are: first, the blurred boundaries between self and other; and second, the fact that, as Ogden (1979) puts it, "Projective identification does not exist when there is no interaction between projector and object" (p. 279). Thus, in Ogden's formulation, projective identification has been transformed from a solely intrapsychic fantasy to an interpersonal process that entails an actual interaction between self and other. Ogden also distinguishes between projection as an independent process and projection in the context of projective identification. In projection as an independent (defensive process), "the aspect of oneself that is expelled is disavowed and is attributed to the object of the projection. The projector does not feel kinship with the object and, on the contrary, often experiences the object as foreign, strange, and frightening" (p. 296). In projection, as part of projective identification, which Ogden (1979) refers to as a "projective mode of thought" (p. 296),[7] the individual has the "fantasy of ridding himself of a part of himself and inhabiting another person with that part. The subjective experience is one of being at one with the other person with regard to the expelled feeling, idea, self-representation, etc." (p. 296).

In the second aspect of projective identification, the "induction phase" (p. 279), "there is a pressure exerted by the projector on the recipient of the projection to experience himself and behave in a way congruent with the projective fantasy" (p. 278). Ogden's clinical example of this phase includes the description of a 12-year-old inpatient, "who as an infant had been violently intruded upon" (p. 279). She was perpetually jostling and bumping into people, especially her therapist, who "felt as if there were no space in the room for him" (p. 359).

Ogden (1979) writes that "this form of interaction represents a form of object relationship wherein the patient puts pressure on the therapist to experience himself as inescapably intruded upon. This interpersonal interaction constitutes the 'induction phase' of this patient's projective identification" (p. 359). A question that arises is whether the patient is *motivated* by the desire to have the therapist feel intruded upon.[8]

Ogden (1979) presents other clinical examples of this "induction phase" of projective identification including a patient who behaved in a way (e.g., kicking the therapist's furniture) that "invited retaliatory anger on the part of the therapist" (p. 359). Ogden writes that "the patient was fully conscious of both his attempts to get the therapist to feel angry, as well as the calming and soothing effect that that had on him" (p. 359). Ogden interprets:

> this therapeutic interaction as an enactment of the patient's fantasy that anger and tension are noxious agents within him that he attempted to get rid of by placing them in the therapist. However, as with his projectile vomiting [the patient was born with pyloric stenosis and suffered from severe projectile vomiting for the first month of his life], a solution is not simple; the noxious agents within that he wishes to rid himself of (anger/food/parents) are also essential for life. Projective identification offers a compromise solution wherein the patient could in fantasy rid himself of the noxious, but life-giving objects within himself while at the same time keeping them alive inside as a partially separate object. This solution would be merely an intrapsychic fantasy without the accompanying object relationship in which the patient exerted terrific pressure on the therapist to conform to the projective fantasy. When there was evidence of verification of the projection (i.e., when the therapist showed evidence of tension and anger), the patient experienced a sense of relief since that offered confirmation that the noxious/life-giving agents had been both extruded and preserved.
>
> (p. 359)[9]

Ogden presents a third clinical example characterized by "a profound lack of concern for a patient on the part of the therapist" that "often immediately precedes the patient's suicide." This phenomenon can be:

> understood as reflecting the patient's attempt to induce in the therapist his own state of total lack of caring for himself or for his life. This could be viewed as an attempt on the part of the patient to: (1) rid himself of this malignant absence of concern for life; and (2) make himself understood by the therapist by inducing the feeling in him. The process of this "induction" of feelings constitutes the second stage of projective identification.
>
> (p. 359)

Ogden sums up the two aspects of projective identification in the following way:

> The first involves a fantasy of ridding oneself of an aspect of the self and of the entry of that part into another person in a way that controls the other person from within. The second aspect of projective identification that has been discussed is the interpersonal interaction that supports the fantasy of inhabiting and controlling another person. Through the projector's interaction with the object, two aspects of the fantasy are verified: (1) the idea that the object has the characteristics of the projected aspects of the self; and (2) that the object is being controlled by the person projecting.
>
> (p. 359)

With regard to the first aspect of projective identification, Ogden assumes not only that one attributes an aspect of oneself (e.g., a trait) to another person, a not unusual phenomenon; he also proposes, one, that one has the fantasy that one is ridding oneself of that aspect of oneself by putting it "*into* another person" (p. 360) (my emphasis); and two, that one then "controls the other person from within" (p. 360). The problem here is that, little or no clinical evidence is presented, direct or indirect, for the inference that the patient has the fantasy that he or she is ridding himself or herself of an aspect of the self by putting into another and is then able to control the other from within.

As for the second aspect played out in the interpersonal interaction, here, too, there is a huge leap from the clinical material to the inferred processes. In the clinical material, we see that the patient behaves in a way that elicits a particular reaction in the therapist. For example, the patient kicks the therapist's furniture or repeatedly rings the waiting room buzzer and the therapist gets angry, hardly an unexpected reaction. It is certainly true that the patient's behavior triggered or "induced" the therapist's anger. This does not require any deep interpretation. Indeed, as we have seen, Ogden notes that the patient was fully conscious of his attempt to get the therapist angry. Clearly, it is important to understand why the patient wants to get the therapist angry. Ogden (1979) understands it "as an enactment of the patient's fantasy that anger and tension are noxious agents within him that he attempted to get rid of by placing them in the therapist" (p. 360). What is the clinical evidence for this interpretation? Does the patient do or say anything that would support this interpretation? Is it based solely on the fact that the patient is conscious of his attempt to get the therapist angry? If so, this would be a circular and arbitrary account.

Ogden reports that the patient is not only conscious of his attempt to get the therapist angry, but also of "the soothing and calming effect that had on him" (Ogden, 1979, p. 359). Ogden (1979) appears to take this later reaction as evidence for his interpretation regarding the motive for the patient's fantasy of expelling his tension and anger and placing them in the therapist. He writes: "When there was evidence of the verification of the pressure of the projection (i.e., when the therapist showed evidence of tension and anger), the patient experienced a sense of relief since that offered confirmation that the noxious/life-giving agents have both been extended and preserved" (p. 359). Thus, the basis for Ogden's interpretation appears to be something like the following: the patient must have had the fantasy of putting his anger into the therapist because once that fantasy appeared to be fulfilled, the patient felt soothed and calmed. But this, too, is arbitrary. Rather than imposing a formulaic projective identification account, would not the therapist want to openly explore why, from the patient's perspective, he would feel soothed and calmed when he succeeded in getting the therapist angry? One possibility is that seeing the therapist angry is reassuring because it suggests a strong affective involvement on the part of the therapist.

The third aspect of Ogden's (1979) formulation of projective identification "involves the 'psychological processing' of the projection by the recipient, and the re-internalization of the modified projection by the projector" (p. 360). The nature of the "psychological processing" by the recipient of the projection (e.g., the therapist) includes attempts at mastery through understanding and, in contrast to projective identification, "methods of dealing with feelings" that "are not basically efforts to avoid, get rid of, deny, or forget feelings and ideas" (p. 360). Through interaction with the therapist, in particular, through the patient's experience of the therapist's ability to "metabolize" or "digest" the projected feelings, the patient is able to reinternalize the projected feelings and develop the "potential for attaining new ways of handling a set of feelings that he could only wish to get rid of in the past" (p. 361).

The discourse and jargon of metabolizing, digesting, modified projections, and reinternalization make unnecessarily complex and obscure processes that can be described in a more straightforward way. The above process described by Ogden of learning to modulate and accept one's feelings and thoughts by observing how a person one endowed with a certain degree of respect and authority (i.e., the therapist) handles these thoughts and feelings is referred to as *modeling* (a form of identification) in the social and personality psychology literature (e.g., Bandura, 1974; Bandura & Kupers, 1964). It is not clear what explanatory value, if any, is added by the language of metabolizing, digesting, reinternalizing, and modifying projections.

Further, the learning process that is entailed in modeling can occur without any projection at all. For example, say that in contrast to the inadequate and maladaptive way that one deals with one's angry feelings, one observes one's therapist, despite provocations and inducements dealing with such feelings in a modulated way that does not entail disavowal, counterattack, and so on. Such interactions themselves, whether or not they include projection, can serve as a basis for the patient's modeling and consequent increasing ability to handle uncomfortable thoughts and feelings in a different way. One way to put this, using Ogden's term, is to say that the patient can internalize the other's behavior. That is, independent of projection and inducement, an ingredient of the therapeutic process may entail identification with and internalization of aspects of the therapist's mode of functioning, certainly a familiar idea.

Projective identification and early development

Let me turn now to what Ogden (1979) refers to as "the early developmental setting" of projective identification. According to Ogden, as a means of dealing with "an extremely complicating, confusing, and frightening barrage of stimuli, . . . the infant utilizes fantasies of ridding himself of aspects of himself (projective fantasies) and fantasies of taking into himself aspects of others (introjective fantasies). These modes of thought help the infant to keep what is valued psychologically separate from, and in fantasy safe from, what is felt to be dangerous and destructive" (p. 363). Ogden goes on to say that "It is in this developmental setting that the infant develops the process of projective identification" (p. 363).

He describes a hypothetical example in which "a child [who] is frightened by his wish to destroy and annihilate anyone who frustrates or opposes him" (p. 363), handles these feelings by projecting "unconsciously his destructive wishes and fantasy into his mother, and through the real interaction with her, engenders feelings in her that she is a ruthless, selfish person who wishes to demolish anything standing in the way of satisfaction of her aims and wishes" (p. 363). Ogden goes on to say that the child can engender these feelings in mother "through persistently stubborn behavior in many areas of daily activity" (p. 363).

There are a number of major difficulties with the above formulation. An especially serious problem with the concept of projective identification emerges when it is applied to infants. As we have seen earlier, based on the theoretical concept of the death instinct, Klein (1946) assumes that the infant experiences hatred against parts of the self that are split off and projected into the mother and which "are meant not only to injure the object but also to control it and take possession of it" (Klein, 1946, p. 8). And similarly, Ogden assumes that infants and young children experience wishes to destroy and annihilate which, because they are so frightening, need to be projected into mother. What is remarkable about these formulations is their arbitrariness and the absence of any evidence. Assumptions and assertions about the infant's presumed experience and fantasies are made without any reference to observations of infants, available research findings on infants' cognitive and affective capacities, and research and clinical findings on infant–mother interactions. Attributions regarding the infant's experiences and fantasies are based on abstract theoretical assumptions such as the death instinct and introjective and projective processes. It is as if the infant were a blank screen on to which the theorist can project his or her fantasies, unrestricted by available findings, regarding the mind of the infant. The great irony here is that in a discussion of projection in infancy, it appears to be the theorist rather than the infant who is engaging in projection.

I noted above that quite apart from the patient's projections, interpersonal pressure, and the supposed metabolizing of projections, an important ingredient of the therapeutic process may consist simply in the patient's internalization (modeling) of the therapist's mode of functioning. A similar point can be made with regard to infant–mother interaction. Ogden writes that through the mother's mastery and integration of the feelings projected on to her by her infant, "the processed projection . . . would be available to the child for re-internalization" (p. 364). Thus, the mother's behavior would reflect, for example, "healthy self-interest, her acceptance of her right to anger" (p. 364) rather than, say, retaliatory or overprotective behavior. But, paralleling the patient–therapist situation, quite independently of any projection and interactional pressure on the part of the infant, and mother's "metabolizing" of projected feelings, the former set of maternal behaviors (healthy self-interest, acceptance of anger, etc.) constitute a far more constructive basis for identification and modeling than the latter set of behaviors (retaliation, overprotectiveness, etc.). This is even more likely to be the case than in the therapeutic situation given the child's greater plasticity and openness to learning. It is not clear that any explanatory power is added by assuming that the mother's behavior toward her child is mainly the product of how successfully (or unsuccessfully) she has "metabolized" the child's projections. Also, as noted, no evidence is presented indicating that the child is projecting anything.

It is, of course, the case that maternal (and paternal) behaviors and feelings toward their child are likely to be influenced by the child's behavior, which may trigger a whole host of mother's feelings, fantasies, and representations with regard to her own childhood and her own interactions with her mother (Fraiberg, Adelson, & Shapiro, 1975). However, all this can and does take place without the child's projections of his or her feelings, motivation to induce similar feelings in mother, and therefore without the mother's need to "metabolize" the affective consequences of the child's projections. One needs independent clinical evidence, not simply theoretical assertions, to warrant the inference that the child (as well as the adult patient) has engaged in projection and interpersonal pressure.

A mother being retaliatory in her reaction to her child's anger and stubbornness or overprotective in reaction to her guilt about her hostile feelings can take place without the child's projections and interactional pressure. And contrastingly, one can say that a mother who is able to express healthy self-interest and appropriate anger is likely to be a good model for the child without any talk of the child's projections and interactional pressure and the mother's "metabolizing" of the child's projected feelings.

In addition to the above major problems, there are logical inconsistencies even within the context of Ogden's own formulation. For example, Ogden suggests both that the primary motive for projection is the child's wish to be rid of hostile and destructive feelings and, at the same time, that it is the child's hostile and destructive behavior that induces these feelings in the mother. If the child's fear of his or her hostile and destructive wishes motivates the projection of these wishes into the mother as a means of getting rid of them, why do they persist as reflected in the infant's hostile and destructive behavior that presumably induces mother to feel hostile and destructive?

This is a general problem with Ogden's formulation of projective identification. That is, if one's motive for projection is to rid oneself of unwanted feelings by putting them into another person, why are those feelings so readily available in the phase in which one's behavior induces similar feelings in the other person? For example, if I rid myself of hostile feelings by projecting them onto you, why do these feelings remain sufficiently available to "fuel" behaviors that are sufficiently hostile to induce hostile feelings in the recipient of my projection? As Ogden acknowledges in one of his clinical examples of projective identification, the patient can be aware of his hostile behavior during the time he is indulging them, which certainly does not suggest that the patient is expelling feelings through projection.

The fact is that an "average expectable" reaction to someone (including to a child) who is being attacking, angry, stubborn, demeaning, etc., in relation to you is to get angry and perhaps want to counterattack. This kind of interaction is not an uncommon one and does not require the assumption that your anger is the product of something projected into or onto you. The latter assumption requires clinical evidence, independent of your simply being angry, that warrants the inference that projection as well as motivated interpersonal pressure are linked to your anger. Without such evidence, the assumption of projection and interpersonal pressure appears to be arbitrary, dictated mainly by a theoretical construct rather than by clinical phenomena.

Patients putting feelings into the therapist

There are reports in the literature of therapists being seemingly overcome by strange and unusual feelings, including feelings of being controlled, that are presumably the product of the patient's projective identification. Further, these strange and unusual feelings are accounted for not simply by the ordinary process of interpersonal pressure discussed above, but rather by the claim that somehow the patient put these feelings directly *into* the therapist. The process or processes through which this strange event is supposed to occur is most often left hanging and not discussed. Instead, we find in much of the literature the not insignificant shift from a formulation of projective identification in terms of the patient's *fantasy* that he or she has put aspects of himself or herself into the therapist and can now control the latter, to a formulation in which the therapist's strange and unusual feelings, including feeling controlled by the patient, are held to be the product of the patient *actually* putting feelings into the therapist. Further, this is no longer a matter of the patient inducing the therapist's reactions by behaving in a certain way, a familiar enough interactional process. Rather, it is a matter of the therapist having strange feelings, including the feeling of being controlled through some mysterious unnamed processes, which, at least some commentators have suggested, may include mental telepathy or, to use Freud's term, "thought-transference." (Freud, 1933[1932], wrote that "the scales weigh in favor of thought-transference" [p. 54].)

Clinical phenomena and projective identification

Are there clinical phenomena to which the concept of projective identification seems to apply, that is, where there is the occurrence of either projection or attribution to another of unwanted aspects of oneself as well as identification with the object on to whom the unwanted aspects have been projected? There is evidence that areas in one's brain that are activated when one carries out an action or experiences an emotion are also activated when one observes another's action or emotional expression (see Gallese, Eagle, & Migone, 2007; Iacoboni, 2009; Iacoboni & Depretto, 2006). This implicit simulation may bear a distant family resemblance to some aspect of what is referred to as projective identification. However, this simulation model has little to do with one projecting anything onto or into another.

When I examine my own clinical experiences and think of clinical phenomena that entail both projection and identification with the person onto whom one has projected one's feelings and thoughts, the following clinical example seems to fit: A patient, Mr. X, was struggling with the decision as to whether or not to leave his wife. He reported that he was very worried that his wife would fall apart if he left her. He also reported that when he discussed separation with his wife, he would sob uncontrollably and did not know whether he was crying for himself or for her, the latter in reaction to the thought of what separation would do to his wife.

Mr. X never reported any evidence that leaving his wife would in fact emotionally destroy her. Indeed, from his descriptions of her, she appeared quite resilient. Rather, there was much clinical evidence that, at some level, he feared that *he* would fall apart should he leave his wife, suggesting that he *projected* his feelings of dependency and weakness onto his wife. Added to this was an unconscious *identification* with his wife with regard to projected feelings of dependency and weakness so that, as he reported, he did not know whether he was crying for her or for himself. In other words, we have here evidence of both projection onto another and identification with that other with regard to the contents projected.

Note that there is a relative loss of boundaries on Mr. X's part between him and his wife. He experiences a presumably empathic identification with his wife that is not truly empathic, but is based on projection rather than on an ability to truly take her perspective. An important difference between the process operating in Mr. X's case and the classical conception of projection as a defense is that rather than, as would be the case in the latter, creating a distance between himself and the object of his projection (e.g., I am different from you; I am not weak and dependent, you are), Mr. X *identifies* with the object. Thus, while classical projection does not necessarily entail loss of boundaries, projection in projective identification does entail such loss, as suggested by Mr. X not knowing whether he was crying for himself or his wife.

This loss of boundaries suggests that, insofar as the projection in projective identification does not succeed in keeping one separate from the object of projection, it can be described as a *failed projection* (see Migone, 1995). One can also say that the "identification" in projective identification is not a true identification in the sense that it is based not on modeling or identifying with the other's actual behavior or feelings, but rather on identifying with one's projected image of the other. In this sense, the identification is a solipsistic phenomenon characterized by the identification with one's own projection, that is, with a part of oneself (see Fairbairn's discussion of the internal object and primary identification).

As Ogden and others have noted, what renders projective identification an interactional phenomenon is the interpersonal pressure component in which one person induces certain feelings and reactions in another person. In the case of Mr. X, he would behave toward his wife in ways that seemed unconsciously intended to induce feelings of dependency and weakness in her in relation to the issue of separation. One can think of this aspect of Mr. X's behavior (the phase of interpersonal pressure) as intended to support his projection. That is, if Mr. X gets his wife to feel or behave in a certain way in accord with his projection, he can convince himself that she really is who he perceives her to be and therefore, his attributions are accurate and valid. Thus, the presence of interpersonal pressure can be seen as an indication of an unsuccessful projection, one that needs to be propped up. In the case of Mr. X, if he succeeds in getting his wife to feel dependent and weak, he can convince himself that his attributions are accurate, that is, that she really will fall apart if he leaves. And this, in turn, will help him avoid awareness of and confrontation with his own fears of falling apart. Thus, Mr. X continues on a path of uncertainty and ambivalence, without adequate awareness of an essential source of that ambivalence and uncertainty.

I have worked with a patient, Ms. Y, who was also highly ambivalent about leaving her (abusive) spouse. However, in contrast to Mr. X, she was fully consciously and intensely fearful that she would fall apart if she left him. Even harboring serious thoughts about leaving led to severe depression and suicidal feelings. Unlike Mr. X, she did not show much evidence of projecting these feelings onto her spouse. Indeed, she frequently experienced him, in painful contrast to herself, as independent and not needy, and therefore, strong. The result was that she felt more helpless and suffered much more intensely than Mr. X. appeared to suffer consciously. It appears that Mr. X's ability to employ projection (and thereby not fully experience his own sense of weakness and neediness), however defective it may have been and however much it sustained his uncertainty and indecision, nonetheless protected him from the kind of intensely painful sense of impotent weakness and neediness (and the accompanying self-derogation and self-contempt) experienced by Ms. Y.

Why the current popularity of projective identification?

What are the reasons for the increasing popularity and references to the concept of projective identification? Migone (1995) has suggested that an interest in projective identification began when:

> many analysts . . . working with extremely difficult or regressed psychotic patients . . . felt very uncomfortable with them, overly "controlled" or under pressure, or experienced a new set of feelings that were difficult to index as "countertransference." For them, it was more clinically useful (and possibly reassuring) to believe that in those moments they were not experiencing an old (and not well analyzed) aspect of themselves, but a new and disturbing feeling that was simply "put into them" by these very sick patients.
>
> (p. 627)

Migone (1995) also notes that a focus on the concept of projective identification "ran in parallel to [a concern] with a new 'enlarged' view of countertransference that started in the fifties" (p. 628). He goes on to observe that this "enlarged" view of countertransference "produced many interesting clinical intuitions, such as the use of the analyst's own feelings to know and understand the unconscious" (p. 628). I think Migone is quite right in noting the parallel between references to projective identification and the "enlarged" view of countertransference. In both the cases, because the analyst's feelings have been presumably "put into" him or her by the patient (whatever that may mean), they presumably serve as an invaluable source of what is going on in the patient's (unconscious) mind.

What is not entirely clear is the nature of the clinical usefulness that Migone sees in the assumption that the analyst's disturbed feelings were "put into" him or her by the patient. As discussed earlier, in any interpersonal interaction, including the one between patient and analyst, one's feelings and thoughts (as well as one's mood) may, indeed, serve as a useful source of what is going on in the mind of the one with whom one is interacting. This is often due to subtle cues emitted by the other and nuances of the other's verbal and nonverbal behavior (of which one may be unaware or dimly aware).

However, there is nothing mysterious about this phenomenon and there is certainly nothing useful, but only obfuscating, in the discourse of one person "putting something into" another. Further, it is extremely important to note that one's feelings and thoughts in any given interaction may serve not only as an aid, but also as a *misleading* source of what is going on in the other's mind. One may not register the cues emitted by the other or one may misconstrue them. Further, misconstruals and failure to register cues may be related to one's conflicts and blind spots, a consideration that attests to the value of the classical concept of countertransference. Thus, just as the patient may misconstrue the meaning of aspects of the analyst's cues and communications, so similarly, may the analyst misconstrue the meanings of the patient's cues and communications. The "enlargement" of the concept of countertransference, however useful it has been, does not come with the guarantee of accurate construals (see Eagle, 2000).

Concluding comments

One of the more troubling features of some current discussions of projective identification are the implications, first, that the phenomena it points to defy explanation by ordinary processes; and second, that we must therefore invoke mysterious and arcane processes. For example, in characterizing how the term projective identification is used in the literature, Migone (1995) refers to the "therapist who receives" a projective identification from a patient and may then develop a new set of feelings, and only during later self-scrutiny come to understand that they, so to speak, "belonged" to the patient. Furthermore, since this process is unconscious and can be very subtle, sometimes the therapist, in a way, "becomes" someone else (p. 627). The need for quotation marks around the words "belonged" to the patient and "becomes" someone else seem to me indications that a careful investigation of the processes involved in the phenomena described is being bypassed; instead, one is left with the impression that something very mysterious, beyond ordinary explanation, is at work.

Toward the end of their book on projective identification, Spillius and O'Shaughnessy (2012) approvingly cite the following passage from Freud (1933[1932]): "There is, for example, the phenomenon of thought-transference. . . . It claims that mental processes in one person—ideas, emotional states, conative impulses—can be transferred to another person through empty space without employing the familiar methods of communication by means of words and signs" (p. 39). Of course, Freud does not spell out further on what these "unfamiliar" methods of communication might be. The last sentence of the Spillius and O'Shaughnessy book, following the above-cited passage from Freud, reads as follows: "We think that the concept of projective identification gives a name to, and a clarification of, the dynamics of direct communication and the phenomena of transference and countertransference that are universal among humankind" (p. 366). Nothing further is said about the nature of this "direct communication" or how the concept of projective identification has contributed to the "clarification" of the "dynamics of direct communication." It is these sorts of mystifications and obfuscations that have bedeviled the concept of projective identification and that can serve as a useful example of the pitfalls and serious problems with too much of psychoanalytic theorizing.

Notes

1. One can see a direct line from Freud's (1900) discussion of perception in chapter 7 to Hartmann's (1939) discussion of an adaptive perspective and his positing of ego autonomy and conflict-free spheres of ego functioning (see also Rapaport's, 1951, discussion of ego autonomy).
2. The ability to see an object in different ways, that is, as having different uses, as measured by the Alternative Uses Test (Guilford, 1967) has been found to correlate with creativity, as, for example, in the uses of an object. Thus, the ability to think of a golf club as a weapon as well as a golf club is not, in itself, pathognomonic. However, whereas the individual in a fit of rage may be able to think of the golf club only as a weapon, creativity is characterized by flexibility, that is, by the ability to think of many different uses of a golf club.
3. This also holds, in certain respects, with regard to the differences between the infant's and the adult's experiential worlds. Although there are several continuities between the infant and adult worlds, there are also discontinuities. For example, Spelke (1990) has shown that for the very young infant, objects that move together tend to be perceived as the same object. This is quite different from the adult perception of sameness in objects.
4. It is interesting to observe that even in both the extreme conditions of de-animated and excessively animated experience, the object percepts formed by Renee match the external reality in some reasonable way. Thus, although experienced as robot-like, the category of children and teacher remains. The seams of nature continue to be cut along the lines of the familiar and socially shared objects of children and teachers. Figure–ground organization is retained.

Similarly, in the case of the howling winds. Although Renee experiences them as bearing a message to her and attributes to them the intention to crush and destroy the world, she accurately forms the percept of howling winds. This is not always the case when, for example, ingestion of LSD may lead to fragmentation in which a delineated and bounded object is not subjectively experienced.

5. We have always been fascinated with the link between madness and creativity. And, indeed, one can see a connection between Renee's animistic and physiognomic mode of perception and thought and the creation of poetry.
6. Although I understand that Segal wants to point to the interpersonal nature of projective identification, she sheds little light on how one becomes possessed by, controlled, and identified with the projected parts. Little or nothing is said about the specific processes that might be involved.
7. Ogden is using the term "projective mode of thought" quite differently from my use of the term in this chapter. As I (and others) use the term, in contrast to projection as a defense, a projective mode of thought does not include the component of expelling one's mental contents on to an object. For example, in giving a Rorschach response, one does not expel unwanted contents on to the ink blots.
8. Ogden suggests that the patient's behavior of jostling and bumping into the therapist is motivated by her desire to induce the therapist to feel "inescapably intruded upon." The suggestion is that through this behavior the patient wants the therapist to experience just what she, the patient, did as an infant when she felt "violently intruded upon." However, it is not clear what the patient is projecting.
9. The patient could have felt relieved in response to the therapist's anger because of the therapist's affective presence (Stechler, 2003).

Chapter 4

Psychoanalytic styles of writing, thinking, and habits of mind

In Chapter 3, we have seen some serious problems in the conceptualization of projective identification. In this penultimate chapter, I examine certain problematic styles of thinking, writing, and habits of mind all too frequently found in the psychoanalytic literature. I am not suggesting that the entire psychoanalytic literature is afflicted with these problems. It is not. However, much of it is. And further, these problems seem to have become more rather than less prominent. This is a serious problem which influences how psychoanalysis is viewed in the larger culture and which needs to be confronted.

The problem of jargon and obfuscation

One of the afflictions of a significant portion of the psychoanalytic literature is the presence of jargon and obfuscation, which often go together insofar as jargon tends to direct the reader's attention away from substantive issues with a necessary degree of clarity. This problem is seen not only in published articles and books, but also in other contexts. Along with my colleagues, I frequently receive announcements from various psychoanalytic institutes of papers to be given by speakers and psychoanalytic candidates along with abstracts of these papers. Not infrequently, I am struck by the extraordinary degree of jargon that characterizes the titles and abstracts of many of these papers. Below are few examples. The first paper entitled "Narcissistic identification: Phenomenology and technical problems (the claustrum revisited)" is by an invited speaker at a psychoanalytic institute and is followed by the following abstract:

> "The Claustrum" is a psychopathological entity that is present in narcissistic and borderline states and consists of a withdrawal from the world of object relations through intrusive identification into internal objects represented in unconscious phantasy by the internal mother's body. Dr. [X] will give an overview of the main concepts that may allow us to think further about this constellation in its clinical and theoretical implications.

The next two "prizewinning papers" were given by psychoanalytic candidates for full membership and are entitled: (1) "Autistic syntax as an inverse use of the psychic organ point;" and (2) "Hoodwinked: The use of the analyst as autistic shape." Both the papers deal with the work of Frances Tustin.[1] And as a final example, the following is the abstract of a paper on the work of Bion and Meltzer:

> In the afternoon, Professor [X] will present his paper, "Orientability and Non-orientability: The Models of Psychic Spaces in Bion's and Meltzer's Work." Bion's book, *Transformations* (1965), is devoted to the study of the transformations of the psychic space all along the psychoanalytic process. Bion defines psychic spaces as the places where partial objects used to be, that is, as a psychic transformation of a libidinal object or a "nonrealization." The main reference used by Bion here is a *topological* one. Meltzer (1975), on the other hand, uses a *geometrical* reference when he defines the dimensionality of psychic space in his study of child autism. Professor X suggests that the topological concept of orientability can be applied to what Meltzer has described as a bi-dimensional space, which can be understood as resulting from a kind of boomerang effect twisting the psychic space on itself and confusing the internal and external spaces. He will illustrate this hypothesis with clinical material.

As a final example, I, along with other members of the listserv of Division of Psychoanalysis (Division 39) of the American Psychological Association received an email announcing the presentation of a paper. The paper is entitled: "Mother is the whole world: On mass murder-suicide, malignant phallic narcissism and child trauma." The abstract of the paper includes the following description: "This inquiry looks at the possibility that suicide-mass homicide is motivated in part by matricidal and reunion wishes animated by familial, cultural, and societal impingements and excitements and resting within the irrevocably bonded libido-aggressive core. The event becomes the actualization of an omnipotent fantasy in assuming the role of the phallic mother . . . to have all and to be all. As well, the construal of the self-image as an unbearably over-stimulated phallus with an obligatory desire for the ultimate orgasm fulfillment leads to the explosive incident."

I have read the titles and abstract of these papers over and over again and I have only the foggiest idea of what they are about; and I doubt that I am alone in this reaction. Were the nature of these titles and abstracts rare and exceptional they would not merit much discussion. However, they are not. And perhaps most troubling, my impression is that for many their very obscurity and jargon-saturated quality appear to endow them with a privileged status that is accorded to presumed profound matters. I also worry that they may serve as a model for psychoanalytic candidates to mirror.

Melanie Klein's writings

There are prominent models and precedents in our discipline that have paved the way for this state of affairs. Consider the following passages from Melanie Klein's writings:

> I have found these anxiety-situations of the early phases of mental development to be the most profound and overwhelming. It is my experience that in the phantasied attack on the mother's body a considerable part is played by the urethral and anal sadism which is very soon added to the oral and muscular sadism. In phantasy the excreta are transformed into dangerous weapons: wetting is regarded as cutting, stabbing, burning, drowning, while the faecal mass is equated with weapons and missiles. At a later stage of the phase which I have descried, these violent modes of attack give place to hidden assaults by the most refined methods which sadism can devise, and the excreta are equated with poisonous substances.
>
> (Klein, 1930/1964, p. 23)

> I shall first describe the ramifications of the infant's relation to the bad breast. If we consider the picture which exists in the infant's mind—as

we can see it retrospectively in the analyses of children and adults—we find that the hated breast has acquired the oral-destructive qualities of the infant's own impulses when he is in states of frustration and hatred. In his destructive phantasies he bites and tears up the breast, devours it, annihilates it; and he feels that the breast will attack him in the same way. As urethral- and anal-sadistic impulses gain in strength, the infant in his mind attacks the breast with poisonous urine and explosive faeces, and therefore expects it to be poisonous towards him. The details of his sadistic phantasies determine the content of his fear of internal and external persecutors, primarily of the retaliating bad breast.

(Klein, 1952a/1975, p. 63)

Powerful oral desires, increased by the frustration experienced in relation to the mother, are transferred from the mother's breast to the father's penis. Genital desires in the infant of either sex coalesce with oral desires and therefore an oral, as well as genital, relation to the father's penis ensues. Genital desires are also directed toward the mother. The infant's desires for the father's penis are bound up with jealousy of the mother because he feels she receives this desired object. These manifold emotions and wishes in either sex underlie both the inverted and the direct Oedipus complex.

(Klein, 1952a/1975, p. 78)

We know that the ejection of faeces symbolizes a forcible ejection of the incorporated object and is accompanied by feelings of hostility and cruelty, and by destructive desires of various kinds, the buttocks receiving importance as an object of these activities. In my opinion, however, the anal-sadistic tendencies contain more profound and deeply repressed aims and objects still. The data I have been able to collect from early analyses reveal that between the oral-sadistic and the anal-sadistic stages there exists another stage in which urethral-sadistic tendencies make themselves felt, and that the anal and urethral tendencies are a direct communication of the oral-sadistic ones as regards the specific aim and object of attack. In its oral-sadistic phantasies the child attacks its mother's breast, and the means it employs are its teeth and jaws. In its urethral anal phantasies it seeks to destroy the inside of the mother's body, and uses its urine and faeces for this

> purpose. In this second group of phantasies the excrements are regarded as burning and corroding substances, wild animals, weapons of all kinds, etc.; and the child enters a phase in which it directs every instrument of its sadism to the one purpose of destroying its mother's body and what is contained in it.
>
> (Klein, 1975, p. 253)

The above truly extraordinary passages are not isolated anomalies, but are representative of much of Klein's writings on presumed infant fantasies. What is one to make of this sort of thing? And why would one expect a discipline that takes passages of this kind seriously to itself be taken seriously? Keep in mind that the above passages are representative of material that is often included in the curriculum of psychoanalytic training institutes, particularly those whose orientation is primarily Kleinian, and who believe that this sort of material sheds light on infant development and infant as well as adult psychological functioning.

Assertions and appeal to authority

In a 1957 paper, Klein writes: "Abraham's work and my own brought out more fully and more deeply the significance of destructive impulses" (p. 176). What this means, of course, is that Freud and Abraham have made similar claims. What we do not know and are not told is how Klein and Abraham came to know the significance of destructive impulses more deeply and more fully.

Klein (1952b/1975) writes: "I have referred in the previous paper to my hypothesis that difficulties in sucking occurring at the beginning of life are bound up with persecutory anxiety. The infant's aggressive impulses towards the breast tend to turn it in his mind into a vampire-like or devouring object, and this anxiety could inhibit greed and in consequence the desire to suck" (p. 97). The reader is given no information as to how Klein arrived at this hypothesis.

Appeal to clinical experience

Klein attempts to provide some basis for her speculations through appeal to her clinical experience. Consider the following material from the analysis of a young boy: “The child was indifferent to most of the objects and playthings around him, and did not even grasp their purpose or meanings. But he was interested in trains and stations and also in door handles, doors, and the opening and shutting of them. The interest in these things and actions had a single source: it really had to do with the penetration of the penis into the mother’s body. Doors and locks stood for the ways in and out of her body, while the door-handles represented the father’s penis and his own. Thus what had brought symbol-formation to a standstill was the dread of what would be done to him (particularly by the father’s penis) after he had penetrated into the mother’s body” (Klein, 1930/1964, pp. 28–29). The interpretation of the boy’s behavior is asserted with great authority, but with little clinical evidence supporting that particular interpretation.

Retrospective inferences regarding childhood from analysis of adult patients

Klein attempts to support her formulations through appeal not only to the analyses of children, but also to the productions of adult analytic patients. Remarkably, Klein assumes that adult analyses reliably reveal early infant states of development. As we have seen, this position has been defended by Green (2000) who distinguishes between the “real” child of developmental psychology, which is based on actual observations of infants and children, and the “true” child of psychoanalysis, which is based on inferences from adult analyses. Equally remarkable is the assumption that pathological states (e.g., paranoid-schizoid position, depressive position) characterize normal stages of infant development.

Universalization from limited cases

Beginning with Freud, psychoanalytic theorizing has been characterized by a tendency to postulate universal theories based on a limited number of instances. This is also characteristic of Klein’s writings. For example, she writes: *As the analysis of every grown-up person demonstrates* (my emphasis), in the oral-sadistic stage which follows upon the oral-sucking one, the small child goes through a cannabilistic phase with which are associated a wealth of cannabilistic phantasies” (Klein, 1975, p. 253).[2]

Although the content of psychoanalytic theories has varied over the years, unfortunately, the jargon and kind of thinking reflected in the above passages and formulations are still very much with us. Jargon and vague concepts with little or no reference to identifiable behaviors or psychological processes continue to characterize too much of the psychoanalytic literature. Also, strong claims are made without supportive evidence beyond a general appeal to clinical experience and/or selected clinical vignettes. There are virtually no careful and comprehensive case studies published (see Eagle & Wolitzky, 2011; Edelson, 1985).

Lacan's writings: the problem of jargon

Just as in the case with Klein, a significant number of analysts have found Lacan's writings and formulations very meaningful and insightful. Over the years, I have made a number of attempts to read Lacan's writings and the writings of Lacanian scholars. And, indeed, I have found some interesting and useful formulations and observations in this material. For example, Lacan's comments on the insatiability of desire are insightful and compelling—although they were anticipated by Freud's (1912c) observation that "something in the nature of the sexual instinct itself is unfavorable to the realization of complete satisfaction" (pp. 188–189). What distinguishes these observations, however, from other of Lacan's concepts and formulations are the related facts that (1) one can understand them without the need for extraordinary exegesis and deciphering; and (2) one can link them to actual experiences and identifiable psychological processes. This is certainly not the case, however, with regard to such central Lacanian concepts as the Real, Symbolic, and the Imaginary described as "Registers," "The Third," and the "Name-of-the-Father" (Lacan, 1966/2002). If one naively thinks that words such as "real," "symbolic," and "imaginary" can be understood in their usual quotidian meaning, one would be sadly mistaken. The convention (affectation?) of using capital letters for these terms attests to the special meaning they are given. Similarly, for the "Name-of-the-Father." Recently, I received an email announcing the publication of a new book tracing Lacan's ideas. The email describing the book included the following sentence: "It is argued that in these years the Name-of-the-Father is redefined as the symptom of neurosis." Unless one is privy to the special meaning given to the "Name-of-the-Father," the sentence is virtually incomprehensible.

I have found many scholarly exegeses of Lacan's writings not much more clarifying than the writings themselves. For example, in the course of working on this chapter, I came across a review of a book written by Zafiropoulos (2010) on the intellectual relationship between Lacan and Levi-Strauss in the winter 2011 issue of the Division 39 (Division of Psychoanalysis of the American Psychological Association) *Division/Review* (Winn, 2011). Following is a representative passage from that review:

> Lacan, however, is articulating a position that is a radical extension of that of Levi-Strauss, who posited the totem as a kind of zero point that inaugurates culture through an identification of the group with the signifier of the dead father. Lacan on the other hand says that the Name-of-the-Father is no such thing, but functions as the "signifier of the lack of this zero symbol." This is an important distinction, and has significant implications that are quite different from those that Levi-Strauss draws. What Lacan indicates is that the unconscious subject does not find a stable identity in relation to the Other. The primary trauma that founds the unconscious is the discovery precisely that the Other is castrated, that the Other is lacking. The Name-of-the-Father, while founding the subject, founds him in relation to the very signifier of the lack of the zero point.
>
> (Winn, 2011, p. 8)

According to the reviewer, the author of the book, Zafiropoulos, showed the manuscript of his book to Levi-Strauss, who stated that he and his compatriot Merleau-Ponty (who was also a compatriot of Lacan's) "confided to each other that they had never bothered to read Lacan, they considered the effort too great" (p. 9). And after reading the Zafiropoulos manuscript, he remarked that "Lacan remained hermetic for him" (p. 9)—not an insignificant comment from someone whose own writings are a challenge.

In a recent discussion on the relationship between relational and Lacanian psychoanalytic schools, David Lichtenstein (Harris, Lichtenstein, & Christian, 2015), who in my view, is one of the more understandable and interesting commentators on a Lacanian perspective, describes a clinical vignette in which the patient states "I detest the taste of camembert." Lichtenstein interprets this comment as an expression of the patient's distaste not only for the cheese, but also for the Camembert region where he and his family would vacation, as well as the analyst functioning like a parental figure. He then states that "what I did was end the session" (p. 15). When asked by a member of the audience why, Lichtenstein responded by saying that the patient "heard the sense in which he was taking about Camembert the region, and also about feeling fed up in the analysis. It was my recognition that he heard all of that, that led me to say that the best interpretation at that point is the cut. So that I leave open all of the meanings that can then come out of that" (p. 16).

Lichtenstein's vignette is an interesting one and perhaps it was useful to the patient to have the session end at that point. However, there are certainly other possibilities, including the possibility that abruptly ending the session just at the moment when, according to Lichtenstein, "what [the patient] did is named [sic] his desire" (p. 16), would be experienced by the patient as punishment for "naming his desire" as a kind of negative reinforcement. What is troubling to me is the failure to bring up alternative possibilities or consider the question of how one might assess the therapeutic usefulness of a particular therapeutic intervention. Rather, the abrupt ending of the session appears to be dictated by adherence to a theoretical rationale for which there is little or no evidence. Furthermore, there seems to be little or no interest in entertaining the question of whether the theoretical rationale is warranted by the evidence.

Bion's writings: the problem of jargon and obfuscation

The writings of Bion (e.g., 1962, 1965, 1970) are so filled with jargon, obscurity, and pseudomathematical formulations and notions as to make the work of Lacan and the above-cited passages of Klein seem like models of clarity. Nevertheless, the work of Bion is "in," not only in the United States but also in Europe (in particular, Italy) and Latin America. Because one can select virtually any page in Bion's work and find specific illustrations of my general characterizations, I believe that the passages I cite below are representative of Bion's writings:

I begin with a copy of Bion's "Grid"

	Definitory hypothesis 1	Ψ 2	Notation 3	Attention 4	Inquiry 5	Action 6	... n
A β-elements	A1	A2				A6	
B α-elements	B1	B2	B3	B4	B5	B6	... Bn
C Dream thoughts dreams, myths	C1	C2	C3	C4	C5	C6	... Cn
D Preconception	D1	D2	D3	D4	D5	D6	... Dn
E Conception	E1	E2	E3	E4	E5	E6	... En
F Concept	F1	F2	F3	F4	F5	F6	... Fn
G Scientific deductive system		G2					
H Algebraic calculus							

The medium in which the psycho-analyst works is verbalized thoughts. Using the grid to categorize the verbalized thoughts more precisely, they should be true and fall within the categories of rows E, F, and possibly D and G, and columns 1, 3, 4 and 5. Row G and H apply to phenomena endowed with a greater degree of sophistication and precision than any to which psycho-analysis attains at present. If the statements made in the course of interpretation are expressions of feeling they should fall in the same categories. The patient's contribution is not restricted and may fall in any grid category; the grid categories are intended to be adequate for all the elements and psychoanalytic objects met with in the practice of psycho-analysis. They should therefore be adequate for the requirements of a theory of transformations.

(Bion, 1965, p. 38)

A mathematical illustration is afforded by the use of numbers for enumeration and record. An increase in sophistication marks the manipulation of numbers to solve a problem *in the absence of the objects giving rise to the problem.* Applying this analogy to the elements of psycho-analysis, as I have categorized them in the grid, it is evident that an advance in sophistication separates the categories of columns 1 and 3 from the categories in all other columns. A distinction must be made between categories in column 2 and those of columns 4 to n-1, n, but in this case the distinction is one of kind, not sophistication.

(Bion, 1965, p. 39)

Columns 1 and 3 represent uses of a relatively simple kind; if a word, hypothesis, theoretical system, myth, or transformation were limited to uses represented by those columns, it would not be suitable for working with. An analyst's notes on his cases are useless for the statement of problems and adumbration of solutions if their form prevents extension beyond definition and record. The theory of transformations must serve to illuminate and solve the problems that lie unsolved at the heart of certain forms of mental disturbance; and to do the same for problems inherent in the psycho-analysis of such disturbances.

(Bion, 1965, p. 39)

A theory of transformations must be composed of elements and constitute a system capable of the greatest number of uses (represented by the horizontal axis of the grid) if it is to extend the analyst's capacity for working on a problem with or without the material components of the problem present.

(Bion, 1965, p. 39)

The term alpha-function is, intentionally, devoid of meaning. Before I indicate the area of investigation in which I propose to employ it, I must discuss one of the problems incidental to this investigation.

> Since the object of this meaningless term is to provide psycho-analytic investigation with a counterpart of the mathematician's variable, an unknown that can be invested with a value when its use has helped to determine what that value is, it is important that it should not be prematurely used to convey meanings, for the premature meanings may be precisely those that it is essential to exclude. Yet the mere fact that the term alpha function is to be employed in a particular investigation inevitably leads to its reinvestment with meanings derived from the investigations that have already been carried out in that field. Constant vigilance must therefore be exerted to prevent this development or the value of the instrument is impaired at the outset. The area of investigation is approximately that covered by the writings described in my next chapter.
>
> (Bion, 1965, pp. 2–3)

Let me turn now to an exegesis of Bion's writings. In a recent paper contrasting Freud with Bion and Jung, Rosegrant (2012), who is sympathetic toward Bion's work, refers to the notorious difficulty of Bion's writing style and cites Meltzer's (1978) reaction to Bion's (1965) transformations: "In the present work no such hope sustains us in the face of the proliferation of mathematics-like notations, pseudo-equations, followed by dots, lines, arrows over (or should it be under?) words, and not just Greek letters, but Greek words. How are we to bear such an assault on our mentality?" (p. 341).

Rosegrant comments that "a style that so dominates the message is better taken seriously in itself, not as incidental, but as an integral part of Bion's message" (p. 724). He then goes on to describe "the psychotic mechanisms in Bion's writing" (p. 724). These include "attacks on linking" and denudation of meaning" (p. 725), a major "massive" example of which is Bion's notorious grid. Rosegrant writes with regard to the grid: "he may or may not be describing psychologically and clinically useful ideas, but displaying these ideas in a grid is an attack on the usually linked ideas that a grid will simplify and help with understanding" (p. 727).

Rosegrant's most telling comment is: "Bion's writing, which on first glance appears to be *about* psychosis, is on a more fundamental level *an inducement to* psychosis. Without providing the grounding that would come from alerting the reader that this is about to happen, Bion immerses the reader in the experience he is ostensibly describing: to read Bion is to be psychotic" (p. 727). He then goes on to state: "to recognize that Bion's writing is mad does not mean that it is without value or meaning, but clarifies that its value and meaning are romantic" (pp. 227–228). Rosegrant makes clear that what he means by romantic in the present context is essentially a search for the "mystical one, god, the god head" (p. 729) that Bion refers to as O. Further according to Rosegrant, for Bion, "the experience of O is the proper goal of analysis" (p. 730).

According to Rosegrant, "there is a Bionian project that differs from the Freudian project in the choices it makes about the fundamental ways of being in the world" (p. 721). At the center of the Freudian project, Rosegrant maintains, is the reflection on personal experience, whereas at the center of the Bionian (and Jungian) project is the striving toward a "higher truth outside of personal experience" (p. 721), presumably a mystical striving toward the "experience of O," the godhead.

If one adopts Rosegrant's perspective on Bion, one would need to read Bion not as one would read any discursive material, namely, for the meaning it conveys, but rather for the psychological states it induces in the reader, in particular, the "inducement to psychosis." Although the function of inducing a mood or state can perhaps be defended in the case of poetry, it can hardly be defended in reaction to writings that claim to possess clinical, theoretical, and even scientific significance. In any case, Bion's obscure and turgid writing is as far removed from poetry as one can imagine.

One can also ask whether one can justify as a goal of psychoanalytic treatment, or for that matter, any psychotherapeutic treatment, achievement of a mystical experience of O? One needs to remember that psychotherapy is embedded in a social context that includes such features as professional training and standards, insurance payments, tax deductions, expectation of some form of accountability, and so on. It is not clear how the goal of a mystical experience of O fits into that context.[3]

Given the undeniable and acknowledged obscurity of Bion's writings, why are they so highly valued by many analysts? And why is so much effort devoted to their exegesis and to searching for meaning in what is so obscure and incomprehensible? I do not know the answer to this question and can only speculate. Perhaps one reason is the all too frequent tendency in our field to read profundity into that which is obscure and difficult to understand. Another reason may be the need to be part of the cognoscenti, a member of a special in-group that understands difficult and obscure material that others do not understand.

However, whatever the reasons for the enchantment with this murky and largely incomprehensible material, the fact of this enchantment, in my view, cannot help but have a damaging effect on the standing of our discipline in the larger culture, not in the sense of public relations, but because of serious substantive concerns. It is quite understandable and legitimate for the culture at large to be skeptical about a discipline in which the kind of discourse I have cited is taken as profound and insightful by many members of that discipline.

It may well be the case that there are nuggets of real clinical value in Bion's more clinical papers. However, an examination of Bion's more clinically oriented papers does not support that supposition. Consider the following exchange between Bion (1954) and a schizophrenic patient who had a habit of picking his blackheads:

> *Patient:* I picked a tiny piece of skin from my face and feel quite empty
> *Analyst:* The tiny piece of skin is your penis, which you have torn out, and all your insides have come with it.

Bion writes that

> the patient started the next day's session with disjointed associations and complained that he could not think. I reminded him of the session I described, whereupon he resumed correct speech, thus:
>
> *Patient:* I cannot find any interesting food.
> *Analyst:* You feel it has all been eaten up.
> *Patient:* I do not feel able to buy any new clothes and my socks are a mass of holes.
> *Analyst:* By picking out the tiny piece of skin yesterday you injured yourself so badly you cannot even buy clothes; you are empty and have nothing to buy them with.
> *Patient:* Although they are full of holes they constrict my foot.
> *Analyst:* Not only did you tear out your own penis but also mine. So, today there is no interesting food—only a hole, a sock.

> But even the sock is made of holes, all of which you made and which have joined together to constrict, or swallow and injure your foot.
>
> (pp. 114–115)

Nothing is said in the paper regarding the basis for this interpretation. The only comment regarding clinical evidence that Bion makes is: "This and subsequent sessions confirmed that he felt he had eaten the penis and that therefore there was no interesting food left, only a hole. But this hole was now so persecutory that he had to split it up. As a result of the splitting the hole became a mass of holes which all came together in a persecutory way to constrict his foot" (p. 115). Just how this and subsequent sessions confirmed Bion's interpretations is not made clear.

Let me describe at some length a recent paper published in the flagship journal of the American Psychoanalytic Association in which the author uses Bionian concepts as a guide to working with PTSD patients. According to Potik (2016), "Bion's ideas can help analysts trained in PTSD-focused treatment better understand this disorder and the patient's subjective experience" (pp. 730–731). According to Potik, the following Bionian ideas can contribute to better understand PTSD: (1) "catastrophe and catastrophic" change (p. 732); (2) "beta screen as dissociation" (p. 734); (3) "restoration of the alpha function" (p. 741); and (4) "processing the traumatic experience: movement from –K toward K" (p. 745).

Let us examine each of these ideas and the ways in which they further enhance one's understanding of PTSD.

Catastrophe and catastrophic change

According to Potik, after explaining to patients that "the treatment will include encounters with traumatic experience . . . the patient is terrified at the thought of having to re-experience the catastrophe" (p. 733). The author distinguishes between "catastrophe" and "catastrophic change" and cites Bion's (1965) description of the latter in terms of "overturn[ing] the old order," "evok[ing] feelings of disaster," and being "sudden and violent." What is not at all clear is what Bion's account of "catastrophic change" adds to the straightforward description of the PTSD patient's terror at the prospect of re-experiencing the trauma. Adding Bion's comment to the straightforward and understandable description of the patient's fears gives it an illusory patina of depth. As we will see, this same pattern is present throughout Potik's paper.

Beta screen as dissociation

Similar to the above account, Potik describes a relatively clear and straightforward way the experiences, including dissociative ones, of veterans suffering from PTSD. In one case, a veteran "who witnessed his comrades being burned alive . . . now becomes numb whenever he smells something burning" (p. 735). In another case, the veteran who "helped carry dead and wounded soldiers into ambulances . . . freezes every time he hears a siren" (p. 735). In still another case, a veteran who after experiencing the detonation of a bomb and ensuing "horrific sights of dismembered bodies, and crying children looking frantically for their parents" (p. 736), became dysfunctional, suffering from hyperarousal, avoidance, hypervigilance, and aggression bordering on physical violence. Encountering a man carrying a sack on his back, during a walk with the therapist, the patient grabbed the man, shouted "what do you have in the sack?," examined the sack, shouted "what are you doing here?," and appeared about to attack the man, which was prevented by the therapist who literally stood between the patient and the man and who suggested that they leave together. The author's description is straightforward, poignant, and chilling.

Presumably adding an explanatory account to the above descriptions by invoking Bionian concepts, the author writes:

> During these tense minutes, the therapist had to experience the beta elements of this aggressive experience and process them to understand Joe's internal world. In other words, in the treatment of PTSD patients, the use of alpha function lets the therapist walk in the patient's shoes and experience his subjective reality. Only then can the process of projective identification take place, as the therapist uses his alpha function to process the raw material of the session.
>
> This short vignette illustrates also how the therapist can use his alpha function to help PTSD patients transform unprocessed fragments of the traumatic experience into digestible material. When Joe and his therapist encountered the peddler, Joe, lacking the ability to verbalize

> his sense of impending danger, became dissociated for a few seconds. The therapist tried to identify each fragment of Joe's fear of impending death, to name it, and to return it to him as a processed element that can be used for thinking. Bion (1963), in his writing on projective identification, notes that "the infant, filled with painful lumps of faeces, guilt, fears of impending death, chunks of greed, meanness and urine, evacuates these bad objects into the breast that is not there" (p. 31). This process helps the patient understand that the inner fear of impending catastrophe is enhanced when he encounters certain objects, and leads to a freeze reaction. However, when the threatening fragments he perceives are given a name and put in context, they may lose their intimidating quality.
>
> Joe became dissociated because a causal encounter in external reality threatened to create a link with his frightening internal reality. Had his alpha function been able to function, Joe might have told himself he was encountering a man who reminded him of a threatening situation from his time in the military, or he could have shared his impression with the therapist. However, since his alpha function was reversed and the fragments (beta elements) of the explosion were dissociated behind his beta screen and could not be metabolized, they were experienced as the traumatic event itself. In such a situation, the beta elements move toward the beta screen and touch it, attempting to enter consciousness and create a link of knowledge (K) between external and internal reality. As a result, a feeling of impending catastrophe arises and the psyche, if it is to survive the threatening vortex, must aggressively evacuate the beta elements.
>
> (p. 737)

The questions and considerations to be raised here include the following: first, what of an explanatory nature do the references to "beta elements" and "alpha functions" add to the author's descriptive account?; and second, what is the relevance of the reference to the infant's evacuation of bad objects? What the author appears to be doing is to take an event, which has already been clearly described in the narrative language of ordinary discourse and now redescribe it in the language of jargon, which presumably adds depth, but in fact obfuscates and adds nothing of explanatory value to the account.

Narrative exposure therapy and the restoration of alpha function

The author describes "narrative exposure therapy," which largely consists in, with the help of the therapist, the patient becoming increasingly able to develop a coherent narrative while reliving the traumatic experience. This is direct and straightforward. The author then adds the following:

> In this phase, both patient and therapist enter into the trauma vortex and face the core of the unspoken horror, as they try to pass through the beta screen and reach dissociated memories. In their journey, physical, visual, or emotional fragments of the traumatic memory attack both the patient and therapist, and fasten on the joint effort to process the nameless dread and restore the patient's alpha function.
>
> (p. 741)

A clinical illustration is provided in which the patient describes being hit by a missile while on patrol: "A missile was fired at us, I remember a big hit, fire, smell of something burning, and then I found myself on the floor" (p. 743). This is followed by the author's comment: "As I understand him, the missile hit created a caesura in Ron's experience. In Bion's (1977) words, 'he was challenged to move from one state of mind to another' (p. 48)" (p. 743). Here, the issue is not simply whether the passage from Bion adds anything of descriptive or explanatory value—it clearly does not. Rather it seems to have little to do with Ron's experience.

The author writes that:

> The presence of another mind enables psychic survival, and the presence of an analytic mind helps the patient process the elements of an unbearable reality. Those elements are memory fragments that dwell in remote areas of the patient's mind that cannot be explored and processed without the analyst's help. The analyst lends or imparts his alpha function to the patient and helps him relive and process threatening memory fragments. The sharing of the analyst's alpha function during NET enables the patient to process and link sensory, emotional, and physical elements of the traumatic experience.
>
> (p. 742)

This passage can be translated into ordinary English as: "In a condition of safety represented by the therapist, and with the help of the therapist, the patient can attempt not only to re-live the traumatic experience, but also put words to various elements of the experience."

Processing the traumatic experience: movement from –K toward K

The author informs the reader that in Bion's system, K refers to knowledge, and –K to its negation, and that:

> PTSD patients suffering from combat-related trauma constantly encounter reminders of their traumatic experience, starting a movement from –K toward K. . . . This inner movement toward K elicits fears . . . [and] avoidance [which] protects them from feeling the mental pain arising from the linking.
>
> (p. 746)

We know that PTSD patients suffer from intrusions of the traumatic experience, which elicit fear and avoidance. Once again, one has to ask: Beyond this simple description, what of any descriptive or explanatory value is added by reference to –K and movement toward K?

A final comment: The author refers to the importance of "psychoanalytic skills" (p. 747) in treating PTSD patients. It is not clear which specific psychoanalytic skills he is referring to and the specific ways in which they enhance the treatment.

Consider as another example of the use of Bionian ideas in clinical work a paper by Ferro (2006) entitled "Clinical implications of Bion's thought." The paper includes such passages as:

> I believe that the "*waking dream thought*" (Bion, 1962) is the most significant and important of his concepts. Aside from the night dream, our mind, through its α-function, constantly creates a continuous operation of alphabetization of all the sensory stimuli and proto-emotions which we receive. The end point of this operation is the formation of α-elements, which, when we put them into sequence, produce the waking dream thought.
>
> (p. 989)

> This continuous interplay [between projective identifications and reverie] is what will lead to the formation of the container and the development of the contained as well as the constant oscillation between the schizoparanoid position and depressive position (PS↔D). That is between nonaggregated and raw emotion states (the artist's palette with all his colors) and elaborated and well-defined states of mind (the canvas to which the artist gives life with his colors).
>
> (pp. 989–990)

The particular clinical implications of Bion's thought are never made clear.

Jargon, lack of evidence, and universalization: contrast between two papers

Recently, I received the latest issue of *American Psychoanalyst* and downloaded a paper from internationalpsychoanalysis.net on the same day. The former contained an article by Stone (2012) entitled "Establishing empathy by analyzing psychosis" and the latter a paper by Kogan (2012) entitled "From psychic holes to psychic representations." The two papers could not have been more different from each other, and the differences between these two papers are, in my view, illustrative of what is right and wrong about much of the psychoanalytic literature.

Stone introduces his paper with the modest statement that:

> Today, we are more inclined to use psychoanalysis not as a treatment method but as a way to understand the conflictual forces—the psychodynamics—that underlie both the outburst of the psychotic episode and the continual roiling within the patient's unconscious that keeps the psychosis "alive"—for brief periods if the patient is fortunate; for many months or years in less fortunate situations. The ameliorative steps may vary.
>
> (Stone, 2012, p. 18)

He then discusses the case of a paranoid schizophrenic man who first broke down in graduate school, partly recovered, and then became psychotic again when his fiancée told him she was pregnant. After mysterious "powerful forces" commanded him to kill her, he did so. Stone writes that, after a year of treatment:

> I felt more and more convinced that the "mysterious forces" were nothing more exotic than the prospect of husbandhood and father hood, along with the necessity to function well professionally so as to provide adequate monetary and emotional support for his family. Sensing (correctly, in my view) that he was not up to this demanding task, he was left only with the options of abortion (which the fiancée had adamantly opposed), abandonment (too shameful a choice for him), or murder (under the guise of bowing to the implacable "force"). His reaction, in the form a persecutory delusion, allowed him to save face.
>
> (Stone, 2012, p. 19)

Stone also briefly describes the case of a woman with a delusional fear of germs, and who felt afraid of fat people and becoming pregnant (without sexual intercourse). In addition, he relates these symptoms to the dynamics generated by the quality of her upbringing. "Her mother used to beat her severely if she caught her daughter masturbating or even appearing to have done so. If, when she was six or seven, she played with another girl behind closed doors, her mother understood this as a prelude to some unmentionable sexual play—and again, the beatings. She grew up as a result with an oppressively heavy sense of sinfulness and dirtiness" (Stone, 2012, p. 19).

Of course, I am not suggesting—and neither is Stone—that the above brief accounts fully explain the outbreak of the psychosis in the schizophrenic man or the woman's delusional fear of germs and of becoming pregnant. And unquestionably, there is a great deal more that can be added to Stone's brief account. I cite Stone's remarks as illustrative of lack of jargon, clarity of thought, and modesty of clinical formulations.

Now let me briefly describe the paper by Kogan (2012). The paper was stimulated by the author's visit to the Jewish Museum in Berlin and deals with the "psychic hole" in cases of Holocaust survivors' offspring (p. 6). What Kogan appears to mean by "psychic hole" concerns the "transgenerational impact of the memory hole resulting from negation of survivor parents on the lives of their offspring, up to the third generation" (p. 6). The description of children of Holocaust survivors continues:

> Children who become burdened with memories that are not their own . . . often echo the dramas existing in their parents' inner worlds by

> enacting them in their own lives. . . . These often violent enactments intermingle death wishes with potentially dangerous situations. . . . In many cases, they are caused by persecutory anxieties which develop in delusional fantasies of paranoid proportions, anxieties that demonstrate a lack of differentiation between self and others, past and present, inner and outer reality. At the core of the compulsion to enact the parents' traumatic experiences in the offsprings' own lives is a kind of identification with the damaged parent, termed "primitive identification". . . . This identification leads to a loss of the child's separate sense of self and to an inability to differentiate between the self and the damaged parent. . . . The coexistence of the offspring's global identification on the one hand, and the "negation" (which is defined by Freud as the "cognizance of the repressed") . . . on an intellectual level, while the feelings connected to it remain repressed), of the parents' trauma on the other—a coexistence present in many cases of Holocaust survivors' offspring—creates a gap in the offspring's emotional understanding, which I conceive as a "psychic hole." The "psychic hole" can be regarded as a two-sided coin, one side of which is conscious ignorance of the parents' trauma, and the other side, unconscious knowledge of it.
>
> (p. 7)

The concept of "psychic hole" is then elaborated as follows:

> I wish to compare the "psychic hole" with a metaphor borrowed from the world of astrophysics—the phenomenon of the "black hole." . . . In the world of astrophysics, the "black hole" is defined as a body that sucks all the forces of gravitation into it. It is described as a "region of space-time where infinitely strong gravitational forces literally squeeze matter and photons out of existence. . . .
>
> (p. 7)

I cite the above passages to give the reader an adequate sample of the kind of writing that is not uncommon in the psychoanalytic literature. Such writing, because it is strongly evocative, is appealing to many and can override other considerations such as clarity, consistency, and accuracy. For example, the relevance of the discussion of premature and/or traumatic separation from mother or troubled symbiosis or premature psychological birth to the topic at hand is not at all clear. One can also ask what evidence there is for asserting that generally characteristic of Holocaust survivors are "violent enactments [that] intermingle death wishes with potentially dangerous situations" which "are caused by persecutory anxieties which develop into delusional fantasies of paranoid proportions, anxieties that demonstrate a lack of differentiation between self and others, past and present, inner and outer reality?"

Kogan may have seen a number of patients who were children of Holocaust survivors and then generalized to all or most children with a similar history. Of course, children of Holocaust survivors who are leading relatively unproblematic lives are not likely to be seen by mental health professionals, with the result that generalizations made on the basis of necessarily limited clinical experiences are virtually certain to be unrepresentative.

I also suspect that even for those children of Holocaust survivors who are seen in treatment, the above description is likely to be unrepresentative and contain more than a bit of hyperbole. Delusional fantasies of paranoid proportions, and lack of differentiation between self and others, past and present, and inner and outer reality are often indicative of severe psychotic pathology and are not likely to characterize most children of Holocaust survivors, even those who are experiencing much distress, and are in need of treatment. As for talk of "psychic holes," and its comparison to "black holes" of astrophysics, I am not at all clear as to what such locutions and such comparisons contribute to our understanding. Indeed, however evocative they may be, to the extent that they substitute jargon for clear phenomenological description of the patient's experience as well as an attempt to identify underlying psychological processes, they are likely to mislead rather than clarify.

Kogan notes that "the concept of a 'black hole' was first applied clinically by Bion (1970) in a reference to the infantile catastrophe of the psychotic . . . [and] was further developed by Tustin . . . who applied it to psychogenic autism of children" (p. 8). The reader is not informed any further regarding the "infantile catastrophe of the psychotic." As for Tustin's use of the term, from everything we know about autism, it is highly unlikely that there is any such phenomenon as "psychogenic autism."

The point here is that the use of terms such as "psychic hole" and "black hole"—without a clear delineation of what they mean—allows one to pile one obscurity upon another and to maintain the illusion that one is providing an adequate explanatory account of great depth (see Wachtel, 2003, on the metaphors of surface and depth).

Some personal experiences: fuzzy thinking, thematic affinity as explanation, and imposition of theory on clinical data

In addition to the published literature, styles of thinking are also revealed in other ways. I want to describe some examples from varying sources, including my personal experiences. The first example is taken from a class I taught to candidates at a psychoanalytic institute. During a discussion of infant attachment, two of the candidates informed the class of an amazing phenomenon: the mere presence of their infant observation instructor increased the level of a premature infant's oxygenation level. (They did not indicate how this was determined.) I commented that I suppose that this might be possible if the baby perceived the presence of someone, and asked for more information. "Oh, no," I was told, "the baby was asleep." I was also told that had I been present and aware of the "energy" emanating from this instructor, I would not be surprised that the baby's oxygenation level could rise. Most disturbing, there seemed to be little or no interest in questioning how this could be possible or what processes could possibly be involved. It seemed sufficient to report this presumably amazing phenomenon. How and why did this sort of thinking find its way to a psychoanalytic training institute? I think we need to ask this question.

My second anecdote concerns a case conference in which the cutting behavior of a patient diagnosed with a borderline personality disorder was being discussed. The patient's history included the information that her mother had a mastectomy when the patient was about seven years of age. One of the training analysts at the case conference immediately linked the patient's cutting to the fact that her mother's breasts had been "cut off," as if this "clever" interpretation of a thematic link somehow shed light on the patient's cutting behavior. We know that cutting, quite independent of whether or not a patient's mother had a mastectomy, is a frequent symptom in borderline personality disorder. But that information played no role in the interpretation offered. Its superficial cleverness apparently was sufficient. I am reminded of Meehl's (1973) wonderful paper entitled "Why I do not attend case conferences." Of course, this individual's cutting *could* be connected in some way to her mother's mastectomy. But one would want clinical evidence beyond thematic affinity and at least some careful thought given to the hypothesized process that would link the two.

Both of the last two incidents are characterized by the patent imposition of theoretical notions on the phenomena. In the former incident, the implicit assumption seems to be that the patient's cutting is linked to in some way to an earlier event in the patient's life that also has to do with cutting. Even if such a link could be established, it is not clear what it would explain. Would one expect to find similar thematic links in a significant number of borderline patients for whom cutting is a common symptom? (see Spence, 1994).

The third incident took place at a meeting in which Dr. Elyn Saks' comments on her extraordinary book, *The Center Cannot Hold* (2009), were followed by a well-known and senior analyst interlocutor presenting questions to her. One of the questions put to Dr. Saks was whether she recalled any trauma that may have played a role in her schizophrenic break. Dr. Saks' response was that there were no specific traumas she could identify. Upon further questioning regarding her family make-up, Dr. Saks reported that she had a younger sibling. "Ah, there's the trauma," the interlocutor pronounced. I recall Dr. Saks' characteristically good-natured response: a kind of I suppose anything is possible gentle shrug.

The imposition of theory on the phenomenon is striking here. The interlocutor obviously has a theory (for which there is little or no evidence) that a trauma is always or frequently present in the onset of a schizophrenic breakdown. Given this theoretical expectation, he "finds" the trauma in the birth of a sibling despite the fact that there is no evidence that this event was experienced as traumatic by Dr. Saks or played any role in her schizophrenic break. In this style of thinking, one's theoretical expectation guides one to search for and eventually "finds" confirmatory evidence. Unfortunately, such thinking, characterized by Schafer (1992) as "narrative strain" (p. 275), provides support for the Popperian criticism that whatever the hypothesis or formulation, psychoanalytic accounts find only confirmatory, never contrary, evidence.

As troubling as these incidents themselves are, equally disturbing is the fact that in both of the above incidents, no comments were made by anyone in the audience (which included the author of this book) regarding the arbitrary nature of the theoretical impositions on the material presented. One wonders whether the inhibition against making a critical comment was at least partly motivated by politeness and fear of appearing too critical. Both factors certainly played a role in my silence. However, it is difficult for me to imagine a conference or meeting in another discipline (e.g., psychology, neuroscience, philosophy) in which such patently arbitrary thinking would pass without critical comment. There appears to be something about our training and how we approach such issues as critical thinking and the nature of evidence, including clinical evidence, that permits and perhaps, in some ways, even encourages what Meehl (1997) referred to as "muddle-headed" thinking.

Attitudes toward training in psychoanalytic institutes

In a recent rather courageous paper on psychoanalytic training and education, Kernberg (2012) briefly discusses some issues raised by site visitors on a routine visit to the Columbia University Center for Psychoanalytic Training. One of the site visitors' concerns was "about the influence of empirical research on the training of candidates" (p. 98). Kernberg cites the following comment made by the site visitors: "The fact that the Columbia Center is located in a Department of Psychiatry with strong research interest has raised questions in the past, both in prior site visitors and in the center itself, about the degree to which the candidates' training experiences are overly influenced by a descriptive perspective, resulting in more superficial analytical processes" (pp. 98–99). As Kernberg observes, "We feel that this comment reflects an [equally] unsubstantiated bias that empirical research will somehow preclude learning and practicing 'deeper' treatments. Again, this is an assumption that not only is untested but, if representative of the organization (and field) at large, is potentially stultifying for the progress of psychoanalytic education and research, and for the reputation of our field" (p. 99).

It seems quite remarkable that in this period in our history, a group of site visitors evaluating a psychoanalytic institute can express concern that a "strong research interest" may result in "more superficial analytic processes." Such attitudes reflect thinly disguised biases against research, biases that, as Kernberg (2012) notes, "are damaging to the progress of psychoanalytic education and the field at large" and "that at best are untested and that at worst impede the progress of psychoanalysis and psychoanalytic research" (p. 99).

Attitudes and values of psychoanalysts

Quite a number of years ago, Cioffi (1970, 1998), a distinguished philosopher, argued that psychoanalysis was a pseudoscience, not primarily on the basis of its hypotheses and theoretical formulations, but on the basis of the dominant attitudes and values of its followers and practitioners. I believed at the time that Cioffi's position constituted an overly sociological perspective on the nature of science and took the position that psychoanalytic propositions should be evaluated independently of the attitudes and values of psychoanalysts. I continue to believe that my position has some merit; after all, figures such as Gallese, and two Nobel prize laureates, Kandel and Lord Adrian, were drawn to psychoanalysis by its propositions, not by the practices of psychoanalytic institutes or the values and attitudes of many psychoanalysts. However, I have come to believe that Cioffi pointed to some very significant issues that have important implications for the future of psychoanalysis. For, as I have tried to show, the content of many psychoanalytic propositions themselves, in particular, their lack of clarity, their degree of jargon, and their lack of links to empirical evidence, including clinical evidence, have been strongly influenced by the nature of our education and training and by the attitudes, values, and the habits of mind that we encourage in our training.

Perhaps this should not be surprising. For the fact is that, as Kernberg (2012) notes, the site visitors' attitude is shared by some faculty at the institute being evaluated. Further, it appears to be also shared by a large number of analysts, as evidenced by the standing ovation given to Hoffman's (2007) plenary address entitled "Doublethinking our way to 'scientific' legitimacy: The dessication of human experience" (see Hoffman, 2009, for a published version of the address). The very title of the address so widely cheered, which includes such rhetorically charged terms as "doublethinking" and "dessication of human experience," and places scientific in quotation marks certainly does not promise a reasoned discussion of the role of research in psychoanalysis. Rather, it conveys a sense of danger and threat and reflects a marked hostility to the presumed source of that danger and threat.

So, perhaps Cioffi is at least partly right, after all, in insisting that any assessment of the scientific status of psychoanalysis (or any other discipline) should take into account the practices, attitudes, and values of at least many of its practitioners. Unfortunately, these attitudes and values often include enchantment with obscurantism and jargon, which is equated with profundity.

Problems with psychoanalytic theories of development and of psychopathology

Among the most egregious conceptual errors that characterize the habits of mind of too many psychoanalytic theorists is the conceptualization of adult psychopathology in terms of normal and presumably universal stages of early development. Or to put it another way, normal stages of infant development are described in pathological terms, which implies an equivalence between these normal early stages and pathological adult states. Familiar examples include the paranoid-schizoid and depressive positions (Klein, 1952/1975), normal autism (Mahler, 1968), splitting (Kernberg, 2000), primary narcissism (Freud, 1915[1914]), and archaic narcissism (Kohut, 1984). These are not simply harmless locutions. For common to all these concepts is the assumption that every infant goes through stages of development that are essentially equivalent to pathological adult states. The very terms, paranoid-schizoid and depressive positions, normal autism, splitting, primary narcissism, and archaic narcissism reek of psychopathology.

The assumption underlying these terms is that various forms of adult psychopathology can be meaningfully understood as an arrest at a particular stage of development or a regression to these early stages of development. For example, Kernberg (2000) proposes, first, that at a particular stage of development all infants employ splitting; and second, that the splitting characteristic of borderline personality disorder is because of an arrest at the developmental stage at which presumably splitting normally occurs or to a regression to that earlier developmental stage. One should note that quite apart from other problems with this formulation, no evidence is presented that splitting predictably occurs at a particular stage of development. Indeed, there appears to be no awareness that developmental evidence is necessary. One can, of course, find some surface similarities between certain infant characteristics and adult characteristics that are present in certain forms of psychopathology. For example, both the infant and narcissistic adult may be egocentric. However, the assumption that the infant's and child's egocentricity is the same, not just superficially, but essentially and functionally the same as the egocentricity of an adult with narcissistic personality disorder, is where the fundamental error lies.

There have been a number of cogent critiques of this kind of thinking. For example, as early as 1978, Peterfreund described "The tendency to view early states of normal development in terms of hypotheses used for later states of psychopathology" (p. 426)—a combination of "adultomorphization" (p. 426) and "pathomorphization" (Milton Klein, 1981) of infancy. Especially significant in the present context, these compelling and decisive critiques have had little or no impact on the use of such concepts as paranoid-schizoid or depressive positions to describe both adult pathology and purported stages of normal development. Nor have they had an impact, for example, on the theory that splitting in the borderline individual is the result of a developmental arrest at a stage at which splitting universally occurs or at regression to that universal developmental stage. There seems to be a refractoriness to cogent conceptual critiques and evidence.

This is not simply an historical or sociological observation, but is relevant to the assessment of any empirical discipline. For the hallmark of such a discipline is openness to reformulation of ideas in the light of both cogent critiques and challenging empirical findings. This has simply not happened in the case of psychoanalytic theorizing (see Eagle, 1993). Nor, as Cioffi (1970, 1998) has pointed out, has psychoanalysis as a discipline developed attitudes and procedures that serve to constrain theorizing and to link theory to empirical evidence, including contrary evidence. Rather, as Gedo (1989) has observed, "experienced clinicians would refuse to alter their convictions on the basis of . . . [research] results. Instead, they would continue to form their psychoanalytic views in direct response to their personal experiences. . . . The belief that psychoanalytic theory will make progress by validating the best hypotheses through refined scientific method is implausible" (p. 514). That Gedo intends his comments to be not only descriptive, but also prescriptive is made clear when he goes on to say that "what we need are innovative ideas powerful enough to compel acceptance by significant portions of the analytic community" (p. 514). Of course, as reflected in the proliferation of psychoanalytic "schools," the latter is precisely the current state of affairs.

The problem is not simply that, for the most part, cogent critiques and findings from other disciplines have been largely ignored. It is also the case that arguments have been made by influential figures against integrating these kinds of critiques as well as research findings from developmental psychology into psychoanalytic theorizing. For example, Andre Green (2000), highly respected and influential psychoanalytic theorist, argues that infant research is irrelevant to psychoanalysis and distinguishes between the "real" infant of developmental psychology and the "true" child of psychoanalysis, the latter essentially referring to the presumed residues of infantile experience inferred from the analysis of adult patients. It is, indeed, mind-boggling to think that one can develop an adequate theory of child development based on the productions of adult patients.

Another serious problem with much of psychoanalytic theorizing, particularly developmental theorizing, is that every psychoanalytic theory of development based solely or largely on clinical data is almost certainly inadequate and simplistic and also likely be misleading. This is so for a number of reasons. First, the authors of these theories do not study infant and child development and make no reference to the many rich findings in that area. For example, Kohut (1984) proposes that early lack of parental empathic mirroring is causally linked to adult self-defects and the development of narcissistic personality disorder. However, there is no reference to any empirical research or to the need for longitudinal studies to evaluate this kind of hypothesis. Kohut, along with most other psychoanalytic theorists, simply does not think that way. This may not be a serious problem in the context of clinical work. But it is an enormous barrier to the formulation of an adequate developmental theory.

Follow-back versus follow-up data

Virtually, all psychoanalytic theories of personality development, particularly etiological theories of psychopathology, are based on follow-back or retrospective clinical data which simply cannot serve as adequate evidence for these theories (Kohlberg, La Crosse, & Ricks, 1972). Let me provide both an actual and a hypothetical example illustrating why this is the case.

In a follow-back study, Robins (1966) found that 75 percent of adult alcoholics were truants as juveniles (as compared to 26 percent of the control group). However, employing follow-up data, he found that 11 percent of children who were truants as juveniles were diagnosed as alcoholics as adults (compared to 8 percent of the control group) (Eagle, 1984, pp. 155–156).

As for the hypothetical example, let us say that 100 young adult patients who have suffered sexual abuse as children all receive a diagnosis of borderline personality disorder (BPD). Based on these data, the clinicians seeing these patients in treatment formulate an etiological theory positing a strong relationship between early sexual abuse and later BPD. As we will see, this formulation is likely to be misleading.

Now by contrast, imagine a follow-up or prospective longitudinal study in which 1000 individuals are followed from childhood to young adulthood. Let us say that 10 percent of children subject to sexual abuse are diagnosed with BPD as young adults, whereas 90 percent do not receive that diagnosis. These longitudinal data point to a very different assessment of the role of early sexual abuse in the development of BPD. From these data, one can conclude that although early sexual abuse is a risk factor for BPD, it interacts with other factors in determining the strength of that association. Further, one is then encouraged to carry out additional research devoted to identification of the various factors that play a role in the development of BPD.

The fact is that most formulations based on clinical material rely on follow-back or retrospective data rather than follow-up prospective data and therefore cannot generate adequate developmental theories. This may not be a problem in clinical work, but it is a serious limitation inherent in all psychoanalytic developmental theories based solely on clinical data, whatever the particular psychoanalytic "school." A recognition of this limitation and of the importance of including other methods and findings from other disciplines is necessary if one is to develop an adequate psychoanalytic theory of development.

The jargon, the mystification and obscurantism, the uncritical thinking, combined with the hostility to research that I have described are especially unfortunate because they obscure the important contributions psychoanalysis does and can make to understanding human nature, the human condition, and the functioning of mind. Were the former all there is to psychoanalysis, it would hardly be worthwhile to write a book evaluating core concepts and formulations of psychoanalysis. Given the valuable contribution and insights psychoanalysis has provided and can continue to provide, it is important, so to speak, to separate the wheat from the chaff.

In my view, the main ways of doing this are: (1) to render psychoanalytic formulations and concepts in the language of ordinary psychological processes; (2) to the extent possible, link these formulations and concepts to empirical data from clinical and nonclinical sources; (3) to evaluate and modify these formulations and concepts in the light of such evidence; and (4) to change the nature of psychoanalytic training and education.

Notes

1. Francis Tustin's work, which deals with autism from a psychoanalytic perspective, is itself characterized by much jargon and could serve as a prime example of profound problems that have characterized etiological theories of autism in psychoanalysis. The following account of Tustin's views appears on the website devoted to her work on autism:

    > "Tustin came to feel that autism was a self-protective reaction that shielded the child from experiences that could otherwise have been overwhelming. She described the use for this purpose of what she called autistic objects and autistic shapes. Autistic objects are typically hard, like a toy car that the child may clutch in his hand: the hard sensations they engender allow the child to feel strong. Autistic shapes, on the other hand, are soft sensations the child can provide for himself, with his breath and saliva for example, and can be used for purposes of self-soothing. Tustin stressed the vital need, from the child's point of view, for these means of self-regulation, but also the fact that they were self-engendered and therefore took him away from human relationships."

    There is no reference to any research on autism.
2. Unfortunately, the tendency to universalize from limited cases remains very much with us. In scanning the daily schedule of the 2012 mid-winter meeting of the American Psychoanalytic Association, I came across a paper presented at a discussion group on the psychoanalytic treatment of eating disorders. The description of the paper begins with the following sentence: "The case of an adult patient in psychoanalysis will be presented to demonstrate common

defensive patterns of eating disorder patients and the relationship to food that *all persons* especially these with eating problems, have in unconscious mental life" (my emphasis). Note the easy transition from a single case to defensive patterns in all persons.

3. There are, of course, other contexts and traditions, such as master student, guru disciple, and charismatic leader follower relationships to which the search for the mystical experience of O would perhaps belong.

Chapter 5

Some concluding comments

Based on the material presented in the preceding chapters, the following conclusions seem warranted:

1. Research evidence supports the psychoanalytic claim that transference is ubiquitous, but does not support the canonical assumption that transference interpretations are necessary for positive therapeutic outcome.
2. There is little evidence in support of the claim that the therapist's countertransference reactions regularly serve as a reliable guide to the unconscious mental states.
3. There is evidence that individual differences in therapist behaviors and countertransference reactions are related to therapeutic outcome.
4. The concept of projective identification is understood in a variety of different ways and is in much need of clarification. It is frequently employed in a way that is quite distant from clinical material and from identifiable processes.
5. Too much of psychoanalytic writing is obtuse and distant from clinical data as well as any other observable phenomena.

I have focused on concepts that, although represented in classical theory (transference and countertransference), have been given special attention and/or significantly reconceptualized in contemporary psychoanalytic theories. I have also devoted a chapter to the concept of projective identification, which has gained prominence among a wide range of contemporary psychoanalysts, particularly followers of Klein and Bion. In addition,

I have included a chapter on styles of writing, thinking, and habits of mind reflected in much of the psychoanalytic literature, particularly in the writings of Klein and Bion and their followers. In this chapter, I sum up some salient points regarding each of the concepts.

Transference

As we have seen, the centrality of transference (along with countertransference) has been referred to as the "common ground" that cuts across different psychoanalytic theories, despite other theoretical differences. The psychoanalytic theory of transference consists of the following fundamental assumptions: first, the assumption that transference is ubiquitous; second, the assumption that the patient experiences the analyst as a stand-in for early parental figures; third, as a corollary of two, the assumption that the patient attributes to the analyst attitudes, expectations, and characteristics of early parental figures; fourth, as a further corollary, the assumption that the patient looks to the analyst for gratification of unconscious conflictual infantile wishes experienced in relation to early parental figures; fifth, the assumption that in view of the analyst's anonymity and opaqueness (constituting a "blank screen"), the patient's experience of and attributions to the analyst are primarily, if not entirely, distortions, that is, products of the patient's projections; sixth, the assumption that along with analysis of defense, analysis of the transference is an essential and defining aspect of psychoanalytic treatment; indeed, for some interpretations of the transference are the only significant activity of psychoanalytic work; and seventh, the assumption that resolution of the transference is the expected outcome of successful treatment.

What conclusions can one draw regarding the above assumptions in light of the foregoing discussion of transference in Chapter 1? The following conclusions are warranted based on the current evidence and the current state of knowledge:

1. There is a good deal of research evidence suggesting that transference is ubiquitous, when transference is understood as the tendency to attribute qualities and characteristics of significant others (which presumably includes parental figures) to a new person.

2. There is little or no evidence for the proposition that as a regular and inherent aspect of treatment, the patient attempts to have the analyst gratify unconscious infantile conflictual wishes and desires. Although there is some overlap between conflictual wishes expressed toward the therapist and toward significant figures in the patient's life, it is only a modest one. Further, there is little or no evidence that the patient's wishes expressed in relation to the therapist are primarily unconscious infantile sexual and aggressive wishes. Indeed, there is evidence that many patients seek gratification of not only infantile wishes, but also age-appropriate wishes (e.g., to be understood), which they may view as infantile.
3. There is no such thing as a "blank screen" therapist who emits no cues. All therapists emit cues, often inadvertently. Further, the factors that influence patient's experience of the therapist are not only limited to representations of parental figures, but also include the therapist's cues and characteristics. However, the fact that the patient's transference reactions are influenced by therapist cues does not rule out the possibility of patient distortions regarding how they construe these cues as well as patient's selective attention to particular sets of cues.
4. Despite its canonical status, there is little or no evidence that analysis of the transference is a necessary ingredient in positive therapeutic outcome. Indeed, as a main effect, presence or absence of transference interpretations is unrelated to therapeutic outcome. Rather, transference interpretations are related to positive therapeutic outcome only for those patients who show a relatively low level of object relational functioning.
5. The above findings are only the beginning of necessary investigations of the effects of transference interpretations on therapeutic process and outcome. To enhance ecological validity of research, we would need to know a great deal more about the role of such factors as the particular content, timing, tone, tactfulness, and context of transference interpretations. This work that may require mixed methods (e.g., disciplined case studies along with qualitative and quantitative methods) has yet to be done.
6. There is little evidence that resolution of the transference is a predictable accompaniment of psychoanalytic treatment or positive outcome.

Indeed, a variety of transference reactions, including idealization and invoking a representation of the therapist during distress, persist long after the termination of treatment.

7. There are a number of findings from research on self, other, and relational schemas that add to our knowledge of transference. One such finding is that one's representations of significant others influence not only how one experiences a new person—the standard conception of transference—but also how one experiences oneself, including one's level of self-esteem, one's moods and affects, and the value of the activity in which one is engaged. For example, activation of the representation of a critical figure tends to make one more critical of one's performance, and activating an important rejecting other results in depressed mood and self descriptions characterized by a sense of rejection in individuals who are prone to depression. These findings are congruent with the emphasis in the contemporary psychoanalytic literature on the interactional nature of transference, including the complex dynamic relationship among self-representations, representations of others, and relational or interactional schemas.
8. Although there is a chronic tendency to attribute characteristics representative of significant others to a new person, the perceived similarity between the significant figure and the new persons additively contribute to the degree of such attributions. This latter finding suggests that however much the therapist attempts to be an anonymous and opaque "blank screen," the patient will not only pick up cues (including both focal cues, such as the age, gender, and physical characteristics of the therapist, and background cues, such as the location of the setting, the office furniture and decorations, and so on), but, on the basis of these cues, will also make implicit judgments about the therapist, including his or her similarity to significant figures in the patient's life. Indeed, for at least some patients, the very anonymity and opaqueness of the therapist may activate representations of early unresponsive parental figures. In short, a good deal of research not only specifically on transference, but also on the social psychology of interpersonal interactions, is entirely congruent with a complex and nuanced conception of transference in which it is understood not simply as an intrapsychic phenomenon, but also as a profoundly interactional one, characterized by circular interactional processes (Wachtel, 2014).

There are many unanswered questions and much more research that needs to be carried out in this area. However, I think it is fair to say that based on the information we have and on a number of cogent conceptual critiques, a good deal of skepticism is warranted regarding much that is canonical and presented as received wisdom in the psychoanalytic literature and psychoanalytic training. Indeed, I think there is a good deal of merit in the suggestion by Schachter (2000) and Gill (1984, 1994) that perhaps the term "transference" should be replaced by more neutral and descriptive concepts such as "habitual relationship patterns" and patient–therapist interactional patterns.

Countertransference

I pose the same question regarding the concepts of countertransference addressed to the concept of transference, namely, based on the material presented and discussed in Chapter 1, what conclusions are warranted?

As noted in Chapter 2, there are two literatures on the concept of countertransference, a psychoanalytic literature and a research literature. Further, there is virtually no overlap between these two literatures, partly because of their different conceptualizations of countertransference. The contemporary psychoanalytic literature defines countertransference "totalistically," that is, encompassing all the therapist's thoughts and feelings in relation to the patient and the therapeutic situation, and views it as an indispensable tool in the treatment. In sharp contrast, the research literature retains the classical conception and defines countertransference as "the therapist's idiosyncratic reactions . . . to clients that are based primarily in the therapist's own personal conflicts, biases, or difficulties (e.g., cognitive biases, personal narratives, or maladaptive interpersonal patterns) . . . these reactions can be conscious or unconscious and triggered by transference, client characteristics, or other aspects of the therapeutic situation (e.g., termination), but not by extratherapy factors" (Fauth, 2006, p. 17). Thus, in the contemporary psychoanalytic literature, countertransference is viewed as an indispensable aid to treatment, whereas in the research literature, following Freud, it is viewed as a barrier to the treatment.

There is little doubt that, notwithstanding Freud's (1912b) surgeon metaphor, analysts and other therapists experience a wide range of feelings and thoughts in relation to their patients. Furthermore, rather than necessarily constituting barriers, therapist feelings (e.g., the therapist's affective presence [Stechler, 2003]) may further the treatment (e.g., through enhancing the therapist's affective presence [Stechler, 2003]). This was already recognized by Fenichel (1945) and Ferenczi and Rank (1923). It is not entirely clear how this plausible and modest idea morphed into the claim that the analyst's feelings serve as a reliable guide to the patient's unconscious mental states. Be that as it may, it is important to distinguish between this claim and the commonly observed phenomenon that the patient's behavior and cues elicit affective reactions and, in Strupp and Binder's (1984) term, "pull for" certain responses in the therapist. This latter observation has only an indirect link to the idea that the thoughts and feelings that emerge in the therapist somehow mirror the patient's unconscious wishes and intentions.

How the therapist's feelings and thoughts serve as a reliable guide to the patient's unconscious mental states is often accounted for by reference to mysterious processes. Ironically, this begins with Freud's (1912a) metaphor of the analyst's unconscious as a telephone receiver that picks up the patient's unconscious and his judgment that "there remains a strong balance of probability in favor of thought-transference as a fact" (Freud, 1933, p. 43). As we have seen in the discussion of projective identification, something like thought-transference is suggested by reference to patients putting mental contents *into* the analyst.

Rather than viewing the idea of one person putting mental contents into another as a *fantasy*, much of the contemporary literature on countertransference (and projective identification) suggests that it is an actual process that occurs in reality. Furthermore, gaining access to the mental contents that are put into the analyst by the patient is presumably made possible by the analyst's "reverie," intuition, and becoming at one with the patient. Unless one believes in mental telepathy or thought-transference, there is no identifiable process through which one person can put mental contents into another. Further, no systematic evidence is presented for the claim that one's "reverie" and intuitions will reliably lead one to gain access to "the nature of the patient's unconscious impulses and defenses" (Heimann, 1950, p. 84). For one thing, although intuition may be quite useful in many situations, there is little evidence that it is an unerring guide to understanding another's unconscious inner life, let alone the other's unconscious impulses and defenses. Indeed, in a recent study, participants whose propensity to solve problems through rational thinking versus intuition were better able to accurately infer the emotions of another person (Ma-Kellems & Lerner, 2016). I am not suggesting that intuition cannot be a useful tool in understanding another. It often is. What I am arguing against is its mystification and what I am arguing for is the recognition that it may or may not be accurate depending on a variety of factors. I am also arguing that it is not necessarily superior to rational inference based on observation.

The claim that countertransference, totalistically defined, serves a reliable guide to understanding the patient's unconscious mental states is authoritatively asserted, with no systematic evidence, including systematic clinical evidence, presented in support of this claim. Instead, presumably illustrative self-selected clinical vignettes are presented. Little or no attention is given to the question of how and whether the presumed understanding of the patient's unconscious mental states achieved through examining one's countertransference reactions influences therapeutic outcome. Let us say, for the sake of the argument, that current claims regarding the value of countertransference in understanding the patient's mental states are warranted. What is done with this understanding? How is it communicated to the patient? What role does it play in the treatment? Is it systematically related to therapeutic outcome? As far as I can tell, these sorts of questions are not systematically addressed in the contemporary literature on countertransference.[1]

This state of affairs can be contrasted with the work on countertransference in the research literature, which is characterized by a relatively clear definition of countertransference, namely, therapist's idiosyncratic reactions based on their conflicts, biases, and difficulties. This conception of countertransference enables one to investigate variations in therapist effectiveness as a function of different therapist reactions and behaviors. For example, Dahl et al. (2016) reported that therapists' disengaged feelings (which one can understand as a countertransference reaction) have a negative influence on treatment process and outcome, particularly with patients who have a history of poor object relations. Complementing this finding, Zuroff (2010) reported that therapist effectiveness (as measured by therapeutic outcome) varies with the patient's perception of the extent to which the therapist provides "positive regard, empathy, unconditional regard, and congruence" (p. 687). Contrast this relatively straightforward finding and description with references to "reverie," being at one with the patient, and the assertion, nay, conviction that the thoughts and feelings that emerge in oneself are a reliable guide to the patient's unconscious mental contents.

What is striking in all this is that all the talk about being at one with the patient and expressing "analytic love," understanding his or her mental contents, takes place with virtually no reference to the patient's conscious experience of the therapist's behavior, let alone unconscious experiences. For example, little attention is addressed to the question of what the patient experiences when, following Bion and Ogden, the analyst feels at one with the patient. Does the patient feel that someone is at one with him or her? Is the feeling helpful? Similarly, when the analyst feels that he or she understands the patient through accessing and examining the thoughts and feelings that emerge in him or her, does the patient feel understood? Although analysts may describe their work as an expression of analytic love, it is not clear what patients experience. Do they feel loved? And when analysts describe one of their functions as serving as a "container," does the patient feel "contained"?

Related striking features of the contemporary psychoanalytic literature on transference, countertransference (and projective identification) are, first, its near exclusive focus on the analyst's perspective and relative neglect of the patient's experiences; and second, the great distance of its concepts from the patient's subjective experience. Perhaps one might expect distance from subjective experience in abstract theoretical formulations (although such formulations should bear some explanatory relationship to subjective experience). The concepts discussed—transference, countertransference, and projective identification—are more directly relevant to the therapeutic situation, the problem of distance from the patient's experience is especially noteworthy.

I want to share some admittedly speculative thoughts regarding how the "totalistic" conception of countertransference may have come about. In the speculative narrative I am proposing, the story begins with a reaction against the conception of the analyst as an emotionally cold and opaque surgeon. As noted earlier, this reaction begins with Ferenczi and resurfaces with a series of publications by Heimann, Little, and Racker in the 1950s and 1960s, all of which have in common the central ideas: first, that rather than assuming a stance similar to that of a surgeon, analysts should acknowledge that they react emotionally to their patients; second, they should recognize that rather than constituting an impediment to treatment, these emotional reactions represent an indispensable tool for treatment; and third, the main way in which the analyst's emotional reactions constitute an indispensable tool is their usefulness in serving as a reliable guide to understanding the patient's "unconscious impulses and defenses." All this is simply descriptive and not yet speculative. My speculation is that to say that the analyst's behavior per se, including his or her emotional reactions, plays a separate and distinctive role in treatment gets dangerously close to taking the heretical position that the therapeutic relationship, in particular the "corrective emotional experience" it provides, is itself a primary curative ingredient of treatment. If, however, one can claim that the analyst's emotional reactions constitute an indispensable route to uncovering and understanding the patient's unconscious mental contents and therefore point to the primacy of interpretation, we are back in the acceptable framework of the primacy of understanding, interpretation, and insight. One can now recognize the importance of the analyst's emotional reactions and remain in the fold, without risking heresy.

I think a similar dynamic is at work with regard to the new acceptability of "analytic love." From a classical point of view, it would appear that loving the patient would be seen as a quintessential instance of the classical conception of countertransference understood as a barrier to the treatment, but not to worry. For insofar as analytic love is rendered essentially equivalent to understanding the patient, it need not be viewed as a countertransference transgression. Thus, once again, so long as something that smacks of the analyst's strong emotions—as love certainly does—is wedded to the primacy of understanding (and its presumed link to interpretation), all is well.

It takes someone outside the psychoanalytic community to raise the critical questions, which when addressed, appear to puncture the discourse of analytic love. As we have seen, by posing some probing questions, Nussbaum (2005) makes it clear that what is referred to as "analytic love" has virtually none of the attributes that we normally think of as constituting love. Rather, she notes, what is described as analytic love is much closer to Adam Smith's (1776/2009) concept of a "judicious spectator" (p. 378). This was already apparent in Loewald's 1960 description of the analytic stance as one of "objectivity and neutrality the essence of which is love and respect for the individual and individual development" (p. 229).

Surely, love in its ordinary meaning is anything but objective and neutral. It seems to me that, as is the case with the concepts of transference, given the many definitions it has been given and the confusion brought by these multiple definitions, it might perhaps be wise to drop the term "countertransference" altogether and limit our vocabulary to a description of the specific nature of the therapist's feelings, thoughts, and behaviors in relation to the patient and the therapeutic situation. One can then establish a typology of these different feelings, thoughts, and behaviors, which can be related to therapeutic process and outcome.

Projective identification

There is a close conceptual relationship between the claim that the therapist's countertransference reactions serve as a reliable guide to the patient's unconscious mental contents and the concept of projective identification. That is, the idea that patients project their unconscious mental contents *into* the therapist renders plausible the claim that to gain access to the patient's unconscious mental contents, the therapist need only consult his or her countertransference feelings and thoughts.

One problem with this view is that it is not at all clear what it means for one person to put his or her mental contents, including unconscious mental contents, into another. For many who appeal to the concept of projective identification as somehow explanatory, there appears to be either little interest in identifying the psychological processes that would account for this sort of phenomenon; or, if such interest is expressed, it is shrouded in mysterious processes. As for another aspect of projective identification, namely, one person inducing certain feelings and thoughts in another, when one does not rely on mysterious processes such as mind reading or telepathy, it turns out that ordinary social interaction processes (e.g., in the interaction of two people, cues from one person influence the reactions of another person) are quite adequate to account for the phenomenon.

The confusion regarding the concept of projective identification is increased when one learns that it is understood in different ways in different countries; and that there are "adopters," "partial adopters," and "deniers." Perhaps most important, there appears to be little or no interest in the reasons for one being an "adopter" or a "denier."

Psychoanalytic styles of writing, thinking, and habits of mind

The above comments on the concept of projective identification lead one quite naturally to an examination of psychoanalytic styles of writing, thinking, and habits of mind. The formulation of the concept of projective identification is but one instance of a psychoanalytic mode of thinking and writing that is characterized by obtuseness, lack of reference to ordinary psychological processes, and invocation of arcane and mysterious processes. These characteristics are especially evident in the writings of Klein and Bion and their followers. Mystical references to O, Absolute Truth, the transcendent position, God and the Godhead, and so on are appealing to and hold great significance for many contemporary psychoanalysts.

Similarly, the complex fantasies arbitrarily attributed to young infants by Klein and her followers, without any reference to infant observation and research, resonate with a significant number of psychoanalysts. Relatedly, there are many psychoanalysts who agree with Green's (2000) argument that the productions of adult patients constitute sufficient data—nay, the only psychoanalytically legitimate data—for a theory of development, including infant development.

If one combines the number of psychoanalysts for whom this kind of thinking is appealing with the number who are either indifferent or hostile to research, one is forced to conclude, along with Meehl (1995), that "a philosopher or historian of science, however sympathetic to analysis, would be forced to say that psychoanalysis at this time shows the major symptoms of a Lakatosian degenerating program (p. 1016). Meehl made these comments in 1995. Things have not improved since then. The historical trajectory of psychoanalytic theorizing is not encouraging to anyone who looks for cumulative progress. Rather than cumulative progress, we have splintering "schools," although often hailed as desirable pluralism, tend to operate as local orthodoxies, each with its own loyal followers and training institutes. We also have a trajectory of increasing obscurity in writing and thinking and, with the exception of the cadre of researchers of psychodynamic treatment, an increasing hostility toward research.

Whatever the problems and difficulties of Freudian theory—and there are many—many of its propositions are formulated with sufficient clarity that they are susceptible to empirical test, as evidenced by the fact that virtually all the empirical research on psychoanalytic propositions having to do with the nature of mind are linked to Freudian theory. Contrastingly, Kleinian, neo-Kleinian, and Bionian theories, the most influential current psychoanalytic theories, are formulated in a language that is so obtuse and, at times, incomprehensible that the question of empirical evaluation does not even arise. Further, as Kernberg (2012) has argued, the nature of psychoanalytic training and education, along with resistance to change at many psychoanalytic institutes, do not provide grounds for optimism. All these factors taken together do not suggest an encouraging future.

It is clear that psychoanalytic theory has had much to offer to those interested in how the mind works. It has attracted the interest of Nobel laureates such as Adrian (1946) and Kandel (2007) and gifted scientists such as Gallese, the codiscoverer of mirror neurons. Indeed, both Kandel and Gallese (personal communication) have reported that at one time in their life, they seriously thought of becoming a psychoanalyst. It is important to note, however, that the inspiration for these scientists was the corpus of Freud's work on the nature of the mind rather than post-Freudian theorizing. Indeed, many of Freud's insights and formulations having to do with such topics as inner conflict, defense, unconscious mentation, and ego functions have been incorporated into other psychological theories, frequently without acknowledgement.

A psychoanalytic mode of thought can be of great value. At its best, it provides potential insights that are not readily available through other modes of thought. Let me provide an example from my own clinical experience. I was working with a patient, A. G., many years ago whose presenting symptom was his obsessive fear that he might be homosexual, which, if true, would represent for him an abominable sin. He was tormented by these thoughts. During one session, he reported that after dinner with his mother and father (at the time, he was still living at home) when his mother asked him to put a baking dish back on a high shelf (he was quite tall)—something his father used to do, he noted in passing—his obsessive thoughts about being homosexual got worse. I asked him whether he could think of other occasions when this happened. He responded that when his mother asked him to mow the lawn—again, something his father used to do—the same thing occurred. He then volunteered that after he received a job promotion, his obsessive thoughts reached their peak in frequency and intensity. Although other interpretations are certainly possible, given other information about A. G.'s experiences and difficulties, a plausible hypothesis is that a central theme common to all three events that were associated with an exacerbation of A. G.'s symptoms is that they all involved his being placed in an adult role—a role in which he does things his father used to do. And, indeed, A. G.'s severe anxiety about leaving home, both figuratively and literally, and taking on an adult role became the central issue in treatment. The point I want to make with this clinical anecdote is the following: I know of no theory other than psychoanalytic theory, particularly its formulation of primary process thinking, that enables one to identify the common symbolic meaning among activities as disparate as placing a baking dish on a high shelf, mowing the lawn, and receiving a job promotion.

Ironically, this very strength of psychoanalytic theory in finding hidden common motives and meanings in disparate activities is also a potential problem. This is so because the meanings identified in the patient's productions are often arbitrary, far removed from the patient's experience, and vary with the analyst's theoretical orientation (see Peterfreund, 1978). Therefore, it becomes very difficult to distinguish between theoretical impositions and interpretations warranted by the clinical evidence.

At their worst, psychoanalytic interpretations and formulations are often arbitrary and obfuscatory, far removed from observation and unsusceptible to empirical test by any means. Further, given the nature of psychoanalytic training and education, there appears to be no reliable self-correcting mechanism that enables psychoanalysts to distinguish between the plausible and testable, on one hand, and the arbitrary and obscure, on the other. Unfortunately, it appears that psychoanalytic formulations are increasingly arbitrary, obfuscatory, and distant from observation and evidence. Equally unfortunate is the odd appeal this kind of theorizing seems to have to a large number of psychoanalysts.

Note

1. Although undoubtedly not easy to do, one could, in principle, conduct research on the relationship between the therapist's countertransference reactions and the patient's unconscious mental contents, as inferred by independent clinical judgments based on the patient's productions. Not surprisingly, there appears to be no interest in such research by those who assert that countertransference reactions are an indispensable guide to the patient's unconscious.

References

Ackerman, S. J., & Hilsenroth, M. J. (2003). A review of therapist characteristics and techniques positively impacting the therapeutic alliance. *Clinical Psychology Review, 23,* 1–33.

Adrian, E. D. (1946). The mental and physical origins of behavior. *International Journal of Psychoanalysis, 27*, 1–6.

Alexander, F. G., & French, T. M. (1946). *Psychoanalytic therapy: Principles and applications*. New York: Ronald.

Alloy, L. B., & Abramson, L. Y. (1988). Depressive realism: Four theoretical perspectives. In L. B. Alloy (Ed.), *Cognitive processes in depression* (pp. 223–265). New York, NY: Guilford Press.

Allport, G. W. (1954). *The nature of prejudice*. Reading, MA: Addison-Wesley.

Andersen, S. M., & Baum, A. (1994). Transference in interpersonal relations: Inferences and affect based on significant-other representations. *Journal of Personality, 62*(4), 459–497.

Andersen, S. M., & Chen, S. (2002). The relational self: An interpersonal social-cognitive theory. *Psychological Review, 109*, 619–645.

Andersen, S. M., & Cole, S. (1990). Do I know you?: The role of significant others in general social perception. *Journal of Personality and Social Psychology, 59*, 384–399.

Andersen, S. M., Glassman, N. S., Chen, S., & Cole, S. W. (1995). Transference in social perception: The role of the chronic accessibility of significant-other representations. *Journal of Personality and Social Psychology, 69*, 41–57.

Anderson, J. R. (1983). A spreading activation theory of memory. *Journal of Verbal Learning and Verbal Behavior, 22*(3), 261–295.

Anderson, J. R., & Bower, G. H. (1973/2104). *Human associative memory.* New York: Routledge.

Anderson, J. W. (2014). How D. W. Winnicott conducted psychoanalysis. *Psychoanalytic Psychology, 31*, 375–395.

Bacal, H. A. (1998). Optimal responsiveness and the therapeutic process. In H. A. Bacal (Ed.), *Optimal responsiveness: How therapists heal their patients. Self psychology and intersubjectivity* (pp. 3–34). Lanham, MD: Jason Aronson.

Bach, S. (2006). *Getting from here to there: Analytic love, analytic process.* Hillsdale, NJ: Analytic Press.
Baldwin, M. W. (1992). Relational schemas and the processing of information. *Psychological Bulletin, 112*, 461–484.
Baldwin, M. W. (1997). Relational schemas as a source of if–then self-inference procedures. *Review of General Psychology, 1*, 326–335.
Baldwin, M. W., Carrell, S. E., & Lopez, D. F. (1990). Priming relationship schemas: My advisor and the Pope are watching me from the back of my mind. *Journal of Experimental Social Psychology, 26*, 435–454.
Baldwin, M. W., Fehr, B., Keedian, E., Seidel, M., & Thomson, D. W. (1993). An exploration of the relational schemata underlying attachment styles: Self-report and lexical decision approaches. *Personality and Social Psychology Bulletin, 19*, 746–754.
Baldwin, M. W., & Keelan, J. R. (1999). Interpersonal expectations as a function of self-esteem and sex. *Journal of Social and Personal Relationships, 16*(6), 822–833.
Baldwin, M. W., & Main, K. J. (2001). Social anxiety and the cued activation of relational knowledge. *Personality and Social Psychology Bulletin, 27*, 1637–1647.
Baldwin, M. W., & and Meunier, J. (1999). The cued activation of attachment relational schemas. *Social Cognition, 17*, 209–227.
Baldwin, S. A., Wampold, B. E., & Imel, Z. E. (2007). Untangling the alliance–outcome correlation: Exploring the relative importance of therapist and patient variability in the alliance. *Journal of Consulting & Clinical Psychology, 75*(6), 842–852.
Bandura, A. (1974). The process and practice of participant modeling treatment. In J. H. Cullen (Ed.), *Experimental behaviour: A basis for the study of mental disturbance*. Dublin, Ireland: Irish University Press.
Bandura, A., & Kupers, C. J. (1964). Transmission of patterns of self-reinforcement through modeling. *Journal of Abnormal and Social Psychology, 69*, 1–9.
Bandura, A., Lipsher, D. H., & Miller, P. E. (1960). Psychotherapists' approach-avoidance reactions to patients' expression of hostility. *Journal of Consulting Psychology, 24*(1), 1–8.
Basch, M. (1980). *Doing psychotherapy*. New York: Basic Books.
Basch, M. (1986). "How does analysis cure?" An appreciation. *Psychoanalytic Inquiry, 6*, 403–428.
Bateman, A. & Fonagy, P. (2006). *Mentalization-based treatment of borderline personality disorder.* New York: Oxford University Press.
Baum, A., & Andersen, S. M. (1999). Interpersonal roles in transference: Transient mood states under the condition of significant-other activation. *Social Cognition,* 17, 161–185.
Baumeister, R. F., Dale, K., & Sommer, K. L. (1998). Freudian defense mechanisms and empirical findings in modern social psychology: Reaction formation, projection, displacement, undoing, isolation, sublimation, and denial. *Journal of Personality, 66*(6), 1081–1124.

Beebe, B., Jaffe, J., Markese, S., Buck, K., Chen, H., Cohen, P., . . . Feldstein, S. (2010). The origins of 12-month attachment: A microanalysis of 4-month mother–infant interaction. *Attachment & Human Development, 12*(1–2), 3–14.

Beebe, B., & Lachmann, F. (2002). *Infant research and adult treatment: Co-constructing interactions*. Hillsdale, NJ: Analytic Press.

Berk, M. S., & Andersen, S. M. (2008). The sting of lack of affection: Chronic goal dissatisfaction in transference. *Self and Identity, 7*, 393–412.

Betan, E., Heim, A. K., Conklin, C. Z., & Westen, D. (2005). Countertransference phenomena and personality pathology in clinical practice: An empirical investigation. *American Journal of Psychiatry, 162*(5), 890–898.

Bion, W. R. (1954). Notes on theory of schizophrenia. *International Journal of Psychoanalysis, 35*, 113–118.

Bion. W. R. (1962). *Learning from experience*. London: Maresfield Reprints/Karnac.

Bion, W. R. (1965). *Transformations*. New York: Basic Books.

Bion, W. R. (1967). Notes on memory and desire. *Psychoanalytic Forum, 2*, 179–280.

Bion, W. R. (1970). *Attention and interpretation*. London: Tavistock.

Bleasdale, F.A. (1987). Concreteness-dependent associative priming: Separate lexical organization for concrete and abstract words. *Journal of Experimental Psychology: Learning, Memory, and Cognition, 13*(4), 582–594.

Bornstein, R. F. (2007). Might the Rorschach be a projective test after all? Social projection of an undesired trait alters Rorschach Oral Dependency scores. *Journal of Personality Assessment, 88*, 354–367.

Bower, G. H. (1981). Mood and memory. *American Psychologist, 36*, 129–148.

Bower, G. H. (1987). Comment on "Mood and memory." *Behavior Research and Therapy, 25*(6), 443–455.

Bowlby, J. (1980). *Attachment and loss: Vol. 3. Loss: Sadness and depression*. New York: Basic Books.

Brenner, C. (1979). Working alliance, therapeutic alliance, and transference. *Journal of the American Psychoanalytic Association, 27*, 137–157.

Brenner, C. (1982). *The mind in conflict*. New York: International Universities Press.

Bush, M. (2005). The role of unconscious guilt in psychopathology and in psychotherapy. In G. Silberschatz (Ed.), *Transformative relationships: The Control–Mastery theory of psychotherapy* (pp. 43–66). New York: Routledge.

Campbell, J. D. (1986). Similarity and uniqueness: The effects of attribute type, relevance, and individual differences in self-esteem and depression. *Journal of Personality and Social Psychology, 50*, 281–294.

Campbell, D. T. (1990). Levels of organization, downward causation, and the selection theory approach to evolutionary epistemology. In G. Greenberg & E. Tobach (Eds.), *Theories of the evolution of knowing* (pp. 1–17). Hillsdale, NJ: Lawrence Erlbaum Associates.

Castonguay, L. G., Goldfried, M. R., Blane, H., Chafetz, M. E., & Wolf, I. (1996). Predicting the effect of cognitive therapy for depression: A study of unique and common factors. *Journal of Consulting & Clinical Psychology, 64*, 78–84.

Cioffi, F. (1970). Freud and the idea of a pseudoscience. In F. Cioffi & R. Borger (Eds.), *Explanation in the behavioral sciences*. Cambridge, MA: Cambridge University Press.

Cioffi, F. (1998). *Freud and the question of pseudoscience.* Chicago: Open Court.

Clarkin, J. F., Yeomans, F., & Kernberg, O. (1999). *Psychotherapy of borderline personality.* New York: Wiley.

Connolly, M. B., Crits-Christoph, P., Barber, J. P., & Luborsky, L. (2000). Transference patterns in the therapeutic relationship in supportive-expressive psychotherapy for depression. *Psychotherapy Research, 10*, 356–372.

Connolly, M. B., Crits-Christoph, P., Shappell, S., Barber, J. P., Luborsky, L., & Shaffer, C. (1999). Relation of transference interpretations of outcome in the early sessions of brief supportive-expressive psychotherapy. *Psychotherapy Research, 9*, 485–495.

Crits-Christoph, P., Barber, J. P., & Kurcias, J. S. (1993). The accuracy of therapists' interpretation and the development of the therapeutic alliance. *Psychotherapy Research, 3*, 25–35.

Crits-Christoph, P., Cooper, A., & Luborsky, L. (1988). The accuracy of therapists' interpretations and the outcome of dynamic psychotherapy. *Journal of Consulting and Clinical Psychology, 56*, 490–495.

Crits-Christoph, P., Gibbons, M. B., Temes, C., Elkin, I., & Gallop, R. (2010). Interpersonal accuracy of interventions and the outcome of cognitive and interpersonal therapies for depression. *Journal of Consulting and Clinical Psychology, 78*, 420–428.

Crocker, J., Alloy, L. B., Kayne, N. T. (1988). Attributional style, depression, and perceptions of consensus for events. *Journal of Personality and Social Psychology, 54*, 840–846.

Cronbach, L. J. (1957). The two disciplines of scientific psychology. *American Psychologist, 12*(11), 671–684.

Cushway, R. L., & Tyler, D. P. (1996). Stress in clinical psychologists. *International Journal of Social Psychiatry, 42*(2), 141–149.

Cutler, R. L. (1958). Countertransference effects in psychotherapy. *Journal of Counseling Psychology, 22*, 349–356.

Dahl, H. J., Hoglend, P., Ulberg, R., Amlo, S., Gabbard, G. O., Perry, J. C., & Crits-Christoph, P. (2016). Does therapists' disengaged feelings influence the effects of transference work? A study on countertransference. *Clinical Psychology and Psychotherapy.* Published online in Wiley Online library (wileyonlinelibrary.com). DOI: 10.1002/cpp.2015

De Urtubey, L. (1995). Countertransference effects of absence. *International Journal of Psychoanalysis, 76*, 683–694.

Dodge, K. A., Pettit, G. S., & Bates, J. E. (1994). Socialization mediators of the relation between socioeconomic status and child conduct problems. *Child Development, 65*, 649–665.

Eagle, M. N. (1984). *Recent developments in psychoanalysis: A critical examination.* New York: McGraw-Hill. (1987 – Harvard University Press).

Eagle, M. N. (1990). The concepts of need and wish in self psychology. *Psychoanalytic Psychology, 7*(supplement), 71–88.

Eagle, M. N. (1993). Enactments, transference, and symptomatic cure: A case history. *Psychoanalytic Dialogues, 3*(1), 93–110.

Eagle, M. N. (1994, May 6). *Tension between inner and outer worlds: Perception, psychoanalysis, and philosophy*. Erickson Scholar Lecture. Austen Riggs Center, Stockbridge, MA.

Eagle, M. N. (2000). A critical evaluation of current conceptions of transference and countertransference. *Psychoanalytic Psychology, 17*(1), 24–37.

Eagle, M. N. (2006). Transference. In R. Skelton (Ed.), *Edinburgh International Encyclopedia of Psychoanalysis*. Edinburgh: University of Edinburgh Press.

Eagle, M. N. (2007). Psychoanalysis and its critics. *Psychoanalytic Psychology, 24*(1), 10–24.

Eagle, M. N. (2009). Some taboo implications of current fashions in psychoanalysis. In B. Willock, R. C. Curtis, & L. C. Bohm (Eds.), *Taboo or not taboo? Forbidden thoughts, forbidden acts in psychoanalysis and psychotherapy.*. London: Karnac.

Eagle, M. N. (2011). *From classical to contemporary psychoanalysis: A critique and integration.* New York: Routledge (Also published in Italian, 2012, by Raffallo Cortina, Milan)

Eagle, M. N. (2013). *Attachment and psychoanalysis: Theory, research, and clinical implications*. New York, NY: Guilford Press.

Eagle, M. N., & Ortof, E. (1967). The effect of levels of attention upon "phonetic" recognition errors. *Journal of Verbal Learning and Verbal Behavior, 6*, 226–231.

Eagle, M. N., & Wolitzky, D. L. (2011). Systematic empirical research versus clinical case studies: A valid antagonism? *Journal of the American Psychoanalytic Association, 59*(4), 791–818.

Edelson, M. (1985). *Hypothesis and evidence in psychoanalysis*. Chicago, IL: University of Chicago Press.

Ehrenberg, D. B. (1995). Self-disclosure: Therapeutic tool or indulgence? *Contemporary Psychoanalysis, 31*, 213–228.

Elkin, I., Shea, M. T., Watkins, J. T., Imber, S. D., Sotsky, S. M., Collins, J. F., . . . Parloff, M. B. (1989). NIMH Treatment of Depression Collaborative Research Program: I. General effectiveness of treatments. *Archives of General Psychiatry, 46*, 971–982.

Endler, N. S., & Magnusson, D. (1976). Toward an interactional psychology of personality. *Psychological Bulletin, 83*, 956–974.

Erdelyi, M. H. (1974). A new look at the New Look: Perceptual defense and vigilance. *Psychological Review, 81*(1), 1–25.

Eriksen, C. W. (1951). Perceptual defense as a function of unacceptable needs. *Journal of Abnormal and Social Psychology, 46*, 557–564.

Fairbairn, W. R. D. (1952). *Psychological studies of the personality*. London: Tavistock, Routledge & Kegan Paul.

Farber, B., & Geller, J. (1993). Factors influencing the process of internalization in psychotherapy. *Psychotherapy Research, 3*(3), 166–180.

Fauth, J. (2006). Toward more (and better) countertransference research. *Psychotherapy, 43*(1), 16–31.

Fauth, J., & Williams, E. N. (2005). The in-session self-awareness of therapist-trainees: Hindering or helpful? *Journal of Counseling, 52*, 443–447.

Fenichel, O. (1945). *The psychoanalytic theory of neurosis*. New York: W. W. Norton
Ferenczi, S., & Rank, O. (1923). *The development of psychoanalysis*. New York: Nervous and Mental Disease Publishing Co., 1925.
Ferro, A. (2006). Clinical implications of Bion's thought. *International Journal of Psychoanalysis, 87*(4), 989–1003.
Fingarette, H. (1963). *The self in transformation: Psychoanalysis, philosophy and the life of the spirit*. New York: Harper & Row.
Forguson, L., & Gopnik, A. (1988). The ontogeny of common sense. In J. W. Astington, P. L. Harris, & D. R. Olson (Eds.), *Developing theories of mind* (pp. 226–243). Cambridge, MA: Cambridge University Press.
Fraiberg, S., Adelson, E., & Shapiro, V. (1975). Ghosts in the nursery: A psychoanalytic approach to the problems of impaired infant–mother relationships. *Child and Adolescent Psychiatry, 14*(3), 387–421.
French, T. (1933). Interrelations between psychoanalysis and the experimental work of Pavlov. *American Journal of Psychiatry, 89*, 1165–1203.
Freud, A. (1968). Acting out. *The writings of Anna Freud, Vol. 7* (pp. 94–109). New York: International Universities Press, 1971.
Freud, S. (1900). The interpretation of dreams. *Standard Edition,* Vols. 4, 5. London: Hogarth Press, 1953.
Freud, S. (1905 [1901]). Fragment of an analysis of a case of hysteria. *Standard Edition*, Vol 7 (pp. 3–122). London: Hogarth Press.
Freud, S. (1912a). The dynamics of transference. *Standard Edition*, Vol. 12 (pp. 97–108). London: Hogarth Press.
Freud, S. (1912b). Recommendations to physicians practising psychoanalysis. *Standard Edition*, Vol. 12 (pp. 109–120). London: Hogarth Press.
Freud, S. (1913 [1912–1913]). Totem and taboo. *Standard Edition*, Vol. 13 (pp. 1–161). London: Hogarth Press.
Freud, S. (1915 [1914]). Observations on transference love. *Standard Edition*, Vol. 12 (pp. 159–171). London: Hogarth Press.
Freud, S. (1916/1917). Introductory lectures on psycho-analysis. *Standard Edition*, Vol. 16 (pp. 243–483). London: Hogarth Press.
Freud, S. [1917 (1915)]. Mourning and melancholia. *Standard Edition,* Vol. 14 (pp. 204–258). London: Hogarth Press.
Freud, S. (1922). Neurotic mechanisms in jealousy, paranoia and homosexuality. *Standard Edition,* Vol. 18 (pp. 223–232). London: Hogarth Press.
Freud, S. (1925). Some physical consequences of the anatomical distinction between the sexes. *Standard Edition,* Vol. 19 (pp. 241–258). London: Hogarth Press, 1961.
Freud, S. (1933). New introductory lectures on psycho-analysis. *Standard Edition,* Vol. 22 (pp. 1–182). London: Hogarth Press.
Freud, S. (1940 [1938]). An outline of psycho-analysis. *Standard Edition*, Vol. 23 (pp. 144–207). London: Hogarth Press.
Fried, D., Crits-Christoph, P., & Luborsky, L. (1992). The first empirical demonstration of transference in psychotherapy. *Journal of Nervous and Mental Disease, 180*, 326–331.

Friedman, L. (1998). Overview. In O. Renik (Ed.), *Knowledge and authority in the psychoanalytic relationship* (pp. viii–xxii). Northvale, NJ: Jason Aronson.
Friedman, L. (2005). Is there a special psychoanalytic love? *Journal of the American Psychoanalytic Association, 53*, 349–375.
Friedman, L. (2007). The delicate balance of work and illusion and psychoanalysis. *Psychoanalytic Quarterly, 76*(3), 817–833.
Friedman, S., & Gelso, C. J. (2000). The development of the Inventory of Countertransference Behavior. *Journal of Clinical Psychology, 56*, 1221–1235.
Gabbard, G. O. (1995). Countertransference: The emerging common ground. *International Journal of Psychoanalysis, 76*, 745–485.
Gabbard, G., & Horowitz, M. J. (2009). Insight, transference interpretation, and therapeutic change in the dynamic psychotherapy of borderline personality disorder. *American Journal of Psychiatry, 166,*(5), 517–521.
Gallese, V., Eagle, M. N., & Migone, P. (2007). Intentional attunement: Mirror neurons and the neural underpinnings of interpersonal relations. *Journal of the American Psychoanalytic Association, 55*(1), 131–175.
Gedo, J. (1989). Letter to the Editor. *Review of Psychoanalytic Books, 41*(4), 511–515.
Gill, M. M. (1982). *Analysis of transference: Volume 1: Theory and technique*. New York: International Universities Press.
Gill, M. M. (1984). Transference: A change in conception or only in emphasis? *Psychoanalytic Inquiry, 4*(3), 489–523.
Gill, M. M. (1993). Interaction and interpretation: Commentary on Morris Eagle's "Enactments, transference, and symptomatic cure." *Psychoanalytic Dialogues, 3*, 111.
Gill, M. M. (1994). *Psychoanalysis in transition*. Hillsdale, NJ: Analytic Press.
Goldfried, M. R., & Wolfe, B. E. (1998). Toward a more clinically valid approach to therapy research. *Journal of Consulting & Clinical Psychology, 66*(1), 143–150.
Goodman, N. (1960). The way the world is. *Review of Metaphysics, 14*(1), 48–56.
Govorun, O., Fuegen, K., & Payne, B. K. (2006). Stereotypes focus defensive projection. *Personality and Social Psychology Bulletin, 32*(6), 781–793.
Green, A. (2000). Science and science fiction in infant research. In J. Sandler, A. M. Sandler, & R. Davies (Eds.), *Clinical and observational psychoanalytic research* (pp. 41–73). London: Karnac Books.
Greenson, R. R. (1967). *The technique and practice of psychoanalysis*. New York: International Universities Press.
Grotstein, J. S. (1981). *Splitting and projective identification*. New York: Aronson.
Guilford, J. (1967). *The nature of human intelligence*. New York: McGraw-Hill.
Guntrip, H. (1975). My experience of analysis with Fairbairn and Winnicott—(how complete a result does psycho-analytic therapy achieve?). *International Review of Psychoanalysis, 2*, 145–156.
Harris, A., Lichtenstein, D., & Christian, C. (2015). To whom does the subject speak? Between the relational and the Lacanian schools of psychoanalysis: A conversation with Adrienne Harris and David Lichtenstein, moderated by Chris Christian. *Studies in Gender & Sexuality,16*(4), 229–246.

Hartmann, H. (1939). *Ego psychology and the problem of adaptation*. (D. Rapaport, Trans.). New York: International Universities Press, 1958.

Hayes, J. A. (1995). Countertransference in group psychotherapy: Waking up a sleeping dog. *International Journal of Group Psychotherapy, 45*, 521–535.

Hayes, J. A. (2002). Playing with fire: Countertransference and clinical epistemology. *Journal of Contemporary Psychotherapy, 32*, 93–100.

Hayes, J. A. (2004). The inner world of the psychotherapist: A program of research on countertransference. *Psychotherapy Research, 14*(1), 21–36.

Hayes, J. A. & Gelso, C. J. (1991). Effects of therapist-trainees' anxiety and empathy on countertransference behavior. *Journal of Clinical Psychology, 47*(2), 284–290.

Hayes, J. A., & Gelso, C. J. (1993). Counselors' discomfort with gay and HIV-infected clients. *Journal of Counseling Psychology, 40*(1), 86–93.

Hayes, J. A., Gelso, C. G., & Hummel, A. M. (2011). Managing countertransference. *Psychotherapy, 48*(1), 88–97.

Hayes, J. A., McCracken, J. E., McClanahan, M. K., Hill, C. E., Harp, J. S., & Carozzoni, P. (1998). Therapist perspectives on countertransference: Qualitative data in search of a theory. *Journal of Counseling Psychology, 45*, 465–482.

Hayes, J. A., Yun-Jy, Y., & Eisenberg, A. (2007). Good grief and not so good grief. *Journal of Clinical Psychology, 63*(4), 345–355.

Heimann, P. (1950). On countertransference. *International Journal of Psychoanalysis, 31*, 81–84.

Heinonen, E., Lindfors, O., Harkanen, T., Virtala, E., Jaaskelainen, T., & Knekl, P. (2014). Therapists' professional and personal characteristics as predictors of working alliance in short-term and long-term psychotherapies. *Clinical Psychology & Psychotherapy, 21*(6), 475–494.

Hobson, R. P., & Kapur, R. (2005). Working in the transference: Clinical and research perspectives. *Psychology and Psychotherapy: Theory, Research and Practice, 78*(3), 275–293.

Hoffman, I. Z. (2007). Doublethinking our way to "scientific" legitimacy: The desiccation of human experience. Plenary address given to the Annual Meeting of the American Psychoanalytic Association, New York, New York.

Hoffman, I. Z. (2009). Doublethinking our way to "scientific" legitimacy: The desiccation of human experience. *Journal of the American Psychoanalytic Association, 57*, 1043–1069.

Hoffman, D. (2016). The interface theory of perception. *Current Directions in Psychological Science, 25*(3), 157–161.

Hoglend, P. (1993). Transference interpretations and long-term change after dynamic psychotherapy of brief to moderate length. *American Journal of Psychotherapy, 47*, 494–507.

Hoglend, P. (1996). Analysis of transference in patients with personality disorders. *Journal of Personality Disorder, 10*, 122–131.

Hoglend, P., Amlo, S., Marble, A., Bogwald, K. P., Sjaastad, M. C., & Heyerdahl, O. (2006). Analysis of the patient-therapist relationship in dynamic psycho–therapy: An experimental study of transference interpretations. *American Journal of Psychiatry, 163*, 1739–1746.

Hoglend, P., Hersoug, A. G., Bogwald, K-P., Amlo, S., Marble, A., Sorbye, O., . . . Crits-Christoph, P. (2011). Effects of transference work in the context of therapeutic alliance and quality of object relations. *Journal of Consulting and Clinical Psychology, 79*, 697–706.

Holmqvist, R., & Armelius, K. (1996). Sources of therapists' countertransference feelings. *Psychotherapy Research, 6*, 70–78.

Holmqvist, R., & Armelius, K. (2000). Countertransference feelings and the psychiatric staff's self-image. *Journal of Clinical Psychology, 56*(4), 475–490.

Holt, R. R. (1967). Ego autonomy: Re-evaluated. *International Journal of Psychiatry, 3*(6), 481–536.

Holt, R. (2009). *Primary process thinking*. Lanham, MD: Jason Aronson.

Horberg, E. J., & Chen, S. (2010). Significant others and contingencies of self-worth: Activation and consequences of relationship-specific contingencies of self-worth. *Journal of Personality and Social Psychology, 98*(1), 77–91.

Horvath, A. O. (2011). Alliance in individual psychotherapy. *Psychotherapy, 48*, 9–16.

Huppert, J. D., Bufka, L. F., Barlow, D. H., Gorman, J. M., Shear, M. K., & Woods, S. W. (2001). Therapists, therapist variables, and cognitive-behavioral therapy outcome in a multicenter trial for panic disorder. *Journal of Consulting & Clinical Psychology, 69*, 747–755.

Hurwitz, M. R. (1986). The analyst, his theory, and the psychoanalytic process. *Psychoanalytic Study of the Child, 41*, 439–466.

Iacoboni, M. (2009). Imitation, empathy, and mirror neurons. *Annual Review of Psychology, 60*, 653–670.

Iacoboni, M., & Depretto, M. (2006). The mirror neuron system and the consequences of its dysfunction. *Nature Reviews Neuroscience, 7*(12), 942–951.

Jacobsen, J. L., & Wille, D. E. (1984). Influence of attachment and separation experience on separation distress at 18 months. *Developmental Psychology, 20*, 477–484.

Johansson, P., Høglend, P., Ulberg, R., Amlo, S., Marble, A., Bogwald, K., . . . Heyerdahl, O. (2010). The mediating role of insight for long-term improvements in psychodynamic therapy. *Journal of Consulting and Clinical Psychology, 78*, 438–448.

Kandel, E. (2007). *In search of memory: The emergence of a new science of mind*. New York: W. W. Norton.

Kazdin, A. E. (2006). Arbitrary metrics: Implications for identifying evidence-based treatment. *American Psychologist, 61*, 42–49.

Kernberg, O. (1965). Notes on countertransference. *Journal of the American Psychoanalytic Association, 13*, 38–56.

Kernberg, O. F. (2000). *Borderline conditions and pathological narcissism*. New York: Jason Aronson Press.

Kernber, O. F. (2012). Suicide prevention for psychoanalytic institutes and societies. *Journal of the American Psychoanalytic Association, 60*, 707–719.

Kernberg, O. F., Burstein, E. D., Coyne, L., Appelbaum, A., Horwitz, L., & Voth, H. (1972). Psychotherapy and psychoanalysis: Final report of the Menninger

Foundation's Psychotherapy Research Project. *Bulletin of the Menninger Clinic, 36*, 1–277.

Kiesler, D. J. (1966). Some myths of psychotherapy research and the search for a paradigm. *Psychological Bulletin, 65*(2), 110–135.

Klein, M. (1930/1964). The importance of symbol formation in the development of the ego. *International Journal of Psychoanalysis, 11*, 24–39.

Klein, M. (1946). Notes on some schizoid mechanisms. *International Journal of Psychoanalysis, 27*, 99–110.

Klein, M. (1952a/1975). Some theoretical considerations regarding the emotional life of the infant. In M. Klein. *Envy and gratitude and other works 1946–1963* (pp. 61–93). London: Hogarth Press.

Klein, M. (1952b/1975). On observing the behavior of young infants. In M. Klein. *Envy and gratitude and other works 1946–1963* (pp. 94–121). London: Hogarth Press.

Klein, M. (1975). *Love, guilt and reparation and other works 1921–1945* (Ed. M. Masud R. Khan). London: Hogarth Press.

Klein, M. (1981). On Mahler's autistic and symbiotic phases: An exposition and evaluation. *Psychoanalytic Contemporary Thought, 4*, 69–105.

Kohlberg, L., La Crosse, G., & Ricks, D. (1972). The predictability of adult mental health from childhood behavior. In B. B. Wolman (Ed.), *Manual of child psychopathology*. New York: McGraw-Hill.

Kohut, H. (1979). The two analyses of Mr. Z. *International Journal of Psychoanalysis, 60*, 3–27.

Kohut, H. (1984). *How does analysis cure?* Chicago, IL: University of Chicago Press.

Kogan, I. (2012). From psychic holes to psychic representations. Retrieved from http://internationalpsychoanalysis.net/2012/03/19/filling-in-the-painful-spaces-by-ilany-kogan/

Kumashiro, M., & Sedikides, C. (2005). Taking on board liability-focused information: Close positive relationships as a self-bolstering resource. *Psychological Science, 16*(9), 732–739

Lacan, J. (1966/2002). Ecrits: A selection. In B. Fink (Trans.), *Ecrits*. New York: W. W. Norton.

Lafferty, P., Beutler, L., & Crego, M. (1989). Differences between more and less effective psychotherapists: A study of select therapist variables. *Journal of Consulting and Clinical Psychology, 57*, 76–80.

Langs, R. (1980). *Interactions: The realm of transference and countertransference.* New York: Jason Aronson.

Levine, H. B. (1997). The capacity for countertransference. *Psychoanalytic Inquiry, 17*, 44–68.

Levy, S. R., Hilsenroth, M., & Owen, J. (2015). Relationship between interpretation, alliance, and outcome in psychodynamic psychotherapy. *Journal of Nervous & Mental Disease, 203*(6), 418–424.

Lipton, S. D. (1977). The advantages of Freud's technique as shown in his analysis of the Rat Man. *International Journal of Psychoanalysis, 58*, 255–273.

Little, M. (1951). Countertransference and the patients' response to it. *International Journal of Psychoanalysis, 32*, 32–40.
Loewald, H. (1960). On the therapeutic action of psychoanalysis. In H. Loewald (Ed.), *Papers on psychoanalysis* (pp. 221–256). New Haven, CT: Yale University Press.
Lorenz, K. (1973). The comparative study of behavior. In K. Lorenz & P. Leyhausen (Eds.), *Motivation of human and animal behavior: An ethological view* (pp. 1–31). New York: Van Nostrand.
Lopez, F. G., & Brennan, K. A. (2000). Dynamic process underlying adult attachment organization: Toward an attachment theoretical perspective on the healthy and effective self. *Journal of Counseling Psychology, 47*(3), 283–300.
Luborsky, L., & Crits-Christoph, P. (1990). The changes in CCRT pervasiveness during psychotherapy. In L. Luborsky & P. Crits-Christoph (Eds.), *Understanding transference: The CCRT method*. New York: Basic Books.
Luborsky, L., & Crits-Cristoph, P. (1998). *Understanding transference: The core conflictual relationship theme method* (Second ed.). Washington, DC: American Psychological Association Books.
Luborsky, L., McLellan, A. T., Woody, G. E., O'Brien, C. P., & Auerbach, A. (1985). Therapists' success and its determinants. *Archives of General Psychiatry, 42*, 602–611.
Mahler, M. S. (1968). *On human symbiosis and the vicissitudes of individuation*. New York: International Universities Press.
Makari, G. (2008). *Revolution in mind: The creation of psychoanalysis*. New York: HarperCollins.
Ma-Kellems, C. & Lerner, H. (2016, July 21). Trust your gut or think carefully? Examining whether an intuitive, versus a systematic, mode of thought processes produces greater empathic accuracy. *Journal of Personality and Social Psychology*. Advance online publication. http://dx.doi.org/10.1037/pspi0000063
Mallinckrodt, B., Porter, M. J., & Kivligham, D. M., Jr. (2005). Client attachment to therapist and depth of in-session exploration and object relations in brief psychotherapy. *Psychotherapy: Therapy, Research, Practice, Training, 42*, 85–100.
Masling, J., & Cohen, I. S. (1987). Psychotherapy, clinical evidence, and the self-fulfilling prophecy. *Psychoanalytic Psychology, 4*, 65–80.
Massi, M. (2012). Projective identification: Brazilian variations of the concept. In E. Spillius, & E. O'Shaughnessy (Eds.), *Projective identification: The fate of a concept* (pp. 339–353). London: Routledge.
Masterson, J., and Rinsley, D. (1975). The borderline syndrome: The role of the mother in the genesis and psychic structure of the borderline personality. *International Journal of Psychoanalysis, 56*, 163–177.
McClure, B. A., & Hodge, D. W. (1987). Measuring countertransference and attitude and therapeutic relationships. *Psychotherapy, 4*(3), 325–335.
McCullough, L., Winston, A., Farber, B. A., Porter, F., Pollack, J., Vingiano, W., . . . Trujillo, M. (1991). The relationship of patient–therapist interaction to

outcome in brief psychotherapy. *Psychotherapy: Theory, Research, Practice, Training, 28*, 525–533.
McGinnies, E. (1949). Emotionality and perceptual response. *Psychological Review, 56*, 244–251.
McGuire, W. (Ed.) (1974). *The Freud/Jung letters*. London: Hogarth.
Meehl, P. E. (1973). Why I do not attend case conferences. In *Psychodiagnosis: Selected papers* (pp. 225–302). Minneapolis, MN: University of Minnesota Press.
Meehl, P. E. (1995). Commentaries. *Journal of the American Psychoanalytic Association, 43*, 1015–1023.
Meehl, P. E. (1997). Credentialed persons, credentialed knowledge. *Clinical Psychology: Science and Practice, 4*(2), 91–98.
Meissner, W. (1979). Internalization and object relations. *Journal of the American Psychoanalytic Association, 27*, 345–360.
Meltzer, D. (1975). *Explorations in autism: A psychoanalytic study*. London: Karnac.
Meltzer, D. (1978). *The Kleinian development*. London: Karnac.
Mendelsohn, R., Bucci, W., & Chouy, A. (1992). Transference and countertransference: A survey of attitudes. *Contemporary Psychoanalysis, 28*(2), 364–390.
Migone, P. (1995). Expressed emotion and projective identification: A bridge between psychiatric and psychoanalytic concepts? *Contemporary Psychoanalysis, 31*(4), 617–640.
Miller, W., Taylor, C., & West, J. (1980). Focused vs. broad-spectrum behavior therapy for problem drinkers. *Journal of Consulting & Clinical Psychology, 48*, 590–601.
Milmoe, S., Rosenthal, R., Blake, H., Chafetz, M. E., & Wolf, I. (1967). The doctor's voice: Postdictor of successful referral of alcoholic patients. *Journal of Abnormal Psychology, 72*, 78–84.
Miranda, R., Andersen, S. M., & Edwards, T. (2013). The relational self and pre-existing depression: Implicit activation of significant-other representations exacerbates dysphoria and evokes rejection in the working self-concept. *Self and Identity, 12*(1), 39–57.
Mitchell, S. A. (1988). *Relational concepts in psychoanalysis: An integration*. Cambridge, MA: Harvard University Press.
Mohr, J. J., Gelso, C. J., & Hill, C. E. (2005). Client and counselor trainee attachment as predictors of session evaluation and countertransference behavior in first counseling sessions. *Journal of Consulting & Clinical Psychology, 52*(3), 298–309.
Moore, B., & Fine, B. (Eds.) (1990). *Psychoanalytic terms and concepts*. London & New Haven: American Psychoanalytic Association & Yale University Press.
Muran, J. C., Safran, J. D., Gorman, B. S., Samstag, L. W., Eubanks-Carter, C., & Winston, A. (2009). The relationship of early alliance ruptures and their resolution to process and outcome in three time-limited psychotherapies for personality disorders. *Psychotherapy: Theory, Research, Practice, Training, 46*, 233–248.
Nagel, T. (1974). What is it like to be a bat? *Philosophical Review, 83*(4), 435–450.

Nagel, T. (1986). *The view from nowhere*. New York: Oxford University Press.

Najavits, L. M., & Strupp, H. H. (1994). Differences in the effectiveness of psychodynamic therapists: A process-outcome study. *Psychotherapy, 31*, 114–123.

Newman, L. S., Duff, K., & Baumeister, R. F. (1997). A new look at defensive projection: Suppression, accessibility, and biased person perception. *Journal of Personality and Social Psychology, 72*, 980–1001.

Norville, R., Sampson, H., & Weiss, J. (1996). Accurate interpretations and brief psychotherapy outcome. *Psychotherapy Research, 6*, 16–29.

Novick, J., & Novick, K. K. (2000). Love in the therapeutic alliance. *Journal of the American Psychoanalytic Association, 48*(1), 189–218.

Nussbaum, M. C. (2005) Analytic love and human vulnerability: A comment on Lawrence Friedman's "Is there a special psychoanalytic love?" *Journal of the American Psychoanalytic Association, 53*, 377–383.

Ogden, T. H. (1979). On projective identification. *International Journal of Psychoanalysis, 60*, 357–373.

Ogden, T. (1982). *Projective identification and psychotherapeutic technique*. New York: Jason Aronson.

Ogden, T. H. (2015). Intuiting the truth of what's happening: On Bion's notes on memory and desire. *Psychoanalytic Quarterly, 84*(2), 285–306.

Ogrodniczuk, J. S., & Piper, W. E. (1999). Use of transference interpretations in dynamically oriented individual psychotherapy for patients with personality disorders. *Journal of Personality Disorders, 13*, 297–311.

Ogrodniczuk, J. S., Piper, W. E., Joyce, J. S., McCallum, M. (1999). Transference interpretations in short-term dynamic psychotherapy. *Journal of Nervous and Mental Disease, 187*, 571–578.

Okiishi, I. C., Lambert, M. I., Nielsen, S. L., & Ogles, B. M. (2003). Waiting for supershrink: An empirical analysis of therapist effects. *Clinical Psychology and Psychotherapy, 10*, 361–373.

Oremland, J. (1972). Transference cure and flight into health. *International Journal of Psychoanalytic Psychotherapy, 1*, 61–75.

Owens, J., & Hilsenroth, M. J. (2014). Treatment adherence: The importance of therapist flexibility in relation to therapy outcome. *Journal of Counseling Psychology, 61*(2), 280–288.

Parish, M., & Eagle, M. N. (2003). Attachment to the therapist. *Psychoanalytic Psychology, 20*(2), 271–286.

Peterfreund, E. (1978). Some critical comments on psychoanalytic conceptions of infancy. *International Journal of Psychoanalysis, 59*, 427–437.

Pfeffer, A. Z. (1961). Follow-up study of a satisfactory analysis. *Journal of the American Psychoanalytic Association, 9*, 698–718.

Pfeffer, A. Z. (1963). The meaning of the analyst after analysis: A contribution to the theory of therapeutic results. *Journal of the American Psychoanalytic Association, 11*, 229–244.

Pfeffer, A. Z. (1993). After the analysis: Analyst as both old and new object. *Journal of the American Psychoanalytic Association, 41*, 323–327.

Piper, W. E., Azim, H. F. A., Joyce, A. S., & McCallum, M. (1991). Transference interpretations, therapeutic alliance, and outcome in short-term individual psychotherapy. *Archives of General Psychiatry, 48*, 946–953.

Pistole, M. C. (1999). Caregiving in attachment relationships: A perspective for counselors. *Journal of Counseling & Development, 77*(4), 437–446.

Pistole, M. C., & Watkins, C. E. (1995). Attachment theory, counseling process, and supervision. *The Counseling Psychologist, 23*(3), 457–478.

Ponsi, M. (1999). La partecipazionedell'analista: Un tema emergente nella psicoanalisi nordamericana [The participation of the analyst: An emerging theme in North American psychoanalysis]. *Rivista di Psicoanalisi, 45*, 153–167.

Potik, D. (2016). The relevance of Bionian thinking to the treatment of PTSD patients. *Journal of the American Psychoanalytic Association, 64*(4), 729–749.

Racker, H. (1968). *Transference and countertransference.* New York: International Universities Press.

Rapaport, D. (1951). The autonomy of the ego. *Bulletin of the Menninger Clinic, 15*, 113–123.

Rapaport, D. (1967). *The collected papers of David Rapaport.* New York: Basic Books.

Renik, O. (1996). The perils of neutrality. *Psychoanalytic Quarterly, 65*, 495–517.

Ricks, D. (1974). Supershrink: Methods of a therapist judged successful on the basis of adolescent patients. In D. Ricks, A. Thomas, & M. Roff (Eds.), *Life history research in psychopathology*, Vol. 3 (pp. 275–297). Minneapolis, MN: University of Minnesota Press.

Robins, L. N. (1966). *Deviant children grown up*. Baltimore, MD: Williams & Wilkins.

Rock, I. (1983). *The logic of perception*. Cambridge, MA: MIT Press.

Rorty, R. (1979). *Philosophy and the mirror of nature*. Princeton, NJ: Princeton University Press.

Rosegrant, J. (2012). Why Bion? Why Jung? For that matter, why Freud? *Journal of the American Psychoanalytic Association, 60*(4), 721–745

Rosenberger, E. W., & Hayes, J. A. (2002). Therapist as subject: A review of the empirical countertransference literature. *Journal of Counseling and Development, 80*, 264–270.

Rosenzweig, S. (1997). Letters by Freud on experimental psychodynamics. *American Psychologist, 52*(5), 571.

Ross, L., Greene, D., & House, P. (1977). The "false consensus effect": An egocentric bias in social perception and attribution processes. *Journal of Experimental Social Psychology, 13*, 279–301.

Rubino, G., Barker, C., Roth, T., & Fearon, P. (2000). Therapist empathy and depth of interpretation in response to potential therapeutic alliance ruptures: Therapist and patient attachment styles. *Psychotherapy Research, 10*, 408–420.

Ryum, T., Stiles, T. C., Svartberg, M., & McCullough, L. (2010). The role of transference work: The therapeutic alliance and their interaction in reducing interpersonal problems among psychotherapy patients with cluster C personality disorders. *Psychotherapy: Theory, Research, Practice, Training, 47*, 442–453.

Safran, J. D., Muran, J. C., & Eubanks-Carter, C. (2011). Repairing alliance ruptures. *Psychotherapy, 48*(1), 80–87.

Sakellarapoulo, M., & and Baldwin, M. W. (2006). Interpersonal cognition and the relational self: Paving the empirical road for dialogical science. *International Journal for Dialogical Science, 1*(1), 47–66.

Saks, E. (2009). *The center cannot hold: My journey through madness*. New York: Hyperion.

Sampson, H. (2005). Treatment by attitudes. In G. Silberschatz (Ed.), *Transformative relationships: The Control–Mastery theory of psychotherapy*. New York: Routledge.

Sauer, E. M., Lopez, F. G., & Gormley, B. (2003). Respective contributions of therapist and client adult attachment orientations to the development of the early working alliance: A preliminary growth modeling study. *Psychotherapy Research, 13*(3), 371–382.

Schachter, J. (2001). *Transference: Shibboleth or albatross?* Hillsdale, NJ: Erlbaum.

Schafer, R. (1992). *Retelling a life: Narrative and dialogue in psychoanalysis*. New York: Basic Books.

Schauenberg, H., Buchheim, A., Beckli, K., Nolte, T., Brenk-Franz, K., Leichensring, F., . . . Dinger, U. (2010). The influence of psychoanalytically oriented therapists' attachment representations on outcome and alliance in inpatient psychotherapy. *Psychotherapy Research, 20*(2), 193–202.

Schimel, J., Greenberg, J., & Martens, A. (2003). Evidence that projection of a feared trait can serve a defensive function. *Personality and Social Psychology Bulletin, 29*(8), 969–979.

Schlesinger, G., & Wolitzky, D. L (2002). The effects of a self-analytic exercise on clinical judgment. *Psychoanalytic Psychology, 19*(4), 651–685.

Schut, A. J., Casonguay, L. G., Flanagan, K. M., Yamasaki, A. S., Barber, J. P., Bedics, J. D., & Smith, T. L. (2005). Therapist interpretation, patient–therapist interpersonal process, and outcome in psychodynamic psychotherapy for avoidant personality disorder. *Psychotherapy: Theory, Research, Practice, Training, 42*(4), 494–511.

Searle, J. (1998). *Mind, language, and society: Philosophy in the new world*. New York: Basic Books.

Searles, H. F. (1979). *Countertransference and related subjects*. New York: International Universities Press.

Sechehaye, M. (1951/1994). *Autobiography of a schizophrenic girl; with analytic interpretations*. New York: Grune & Stratton.

Segal, H. (1973). *Introduction to the work of Melanie Klein*. London: Hogarth Press.

Shaw, D. (2003). On the therapeutic action of analytic love. *Contemporary Psychoanalysis, 39*, 251–278.

Silberschatz, G. (2005). The Control–Mastery theory. In G. Silberschatz (Ed.), *Transformative relationships: The Control–Mastery theory of psychotherapy* (pp. 3–30). New York: Routledge.

Silberschatz, G. (2015). Improving the yield of psychotherapy research. *Psychotherapy Research, 11*, 1–13.

Silberschatz, G., & Curtis, J. T. (1993). Measuring the therapist's impact on the patient's therapeutic progress. *Journal of Consulting and Clinical Psychology, 61*, 403–411.

Silberschatz, G., Curtis, J. T., & Nathan, S. (1989). Using the patient's plan to assess progress in psychotherapy. *Psychotherapy, 26*, 40–46.

Silberschatz, G., Fretter, P., & Curtis, J. (1986). How do interpretations influence the process of psychotherapy. *Journal of Consulting and Clinical Psychology, 54*, 646–652.

Smith, A. (1776/2009). *The theory of moral sentiments*. London: Penguin Books.

Spelke, E. S. (1990). Principles of object perception. *Cognitive Science: A Multi-disciplinary Journal, 14*(1), 29–56.

Spence, D. P. (1994). *The rhetorical voice of psychoanalysis: Displacement of evidence by theory*. Cambridge, MA: Harvard University Press.

Spillius, E. (2012a). The emergence of Klein's idea of projective identification in her published and unpublished work. In E. Spillius, & E. O'Shaughnessy (Eds.), *Projective identification: The fate of a concept* (pp. 3–18). London: Routledge.

Spillius, E. (2012b). A brief review of projective identification in American psychoanalytic literature. In E. Spillius, & E. O'Shaughnessy (Eds.), *Projective identification: The fate of a concept* (pp. 245–255). London: Routledge.

Spillius, E., & O'Shaughnessy, E. (2012). *Projective identification: The fate of a concept*. London: Routledge.

Spitz, R. A., & Wolf, K. M. (1946). Anaclitic depression: An inquiry into the genesis of psychiatric conditions in early childhood. *The Psychoanalytic Study of the Child, 2*, 313–342.

Stechler, G. (2003). Affect: the heart of the matter. *Psychoanalytic Dialogues, 13*, 711–726.

Steingart, I. (1995). *A thing apart: Love and reality in the therapeutic relationship*. Northvale, NJ: Jason Aronson.

Stern, D. N. (1985). *The interpersonal world of the infant*. New York: Basic Books.

Stern, D. B. (2003). *Unformulated experience*. Hillsdale, NJ: Analytic Press.

Stiles, W. B., Glick, M. J., Osatuke, K., Hardy, G. E., Shapiro, D. A., & Agnew-Davies, R. (2004). Patterns of alliance development and the rupture-repair hypothesis: Are productive relationships U-shaped or V-shaped? *Journal of Counseling Psychology, 51*, 81–92.

Stone, M. H. (2012). Special section: Psychosis. *American Psychoanalyst, 46*(1), 18–20.

Strachey, J. (1934). The nature of the therapeutic action of psychoanalysis. *International Journal of Psychoanalysis*, 15, 127–159.

Strauss, J. L., Hayes, A. M., Johnson, S. L., Newman, C. F., Brown, G. K., Barber, J. P., . . . Beck, A. T. (2006). Early alliance, alliance ruptures, and symptom change in a nonrandomized trial of cognitive therapy for avoidant and obsessive-compulsive personality disorders. *Journal of Consulting and Clinical Psychology, 74*, 337–345.

Strupp, H. H., & Binder, J. L. (1984). *Psychotherapy in a new key*. New York: Basic Books.

Sullivan, H. S. (1947). *Conceptions of modern psychiatry: The first William Alanson White Memorial Lectures*. Washington, DC: William Alanson White Psychiatric Foundation.

Taylor, S. E., & Brown, J. D. (1994). Positive illusions and well-being revisited: Separating fact from fiction. *Psychological Bulletin, 116*(1), 21–27.

Taylor, S. E., Kemeny, M. E., Reed, G. M., Bower, J. E., & Gruenewald, T. L. (2000). Psychological resources, positive illusions and health. *American Psychologist, 55*, 99–109.

Trusty, J., Ng, K. M., & Watts, R. E. (2005). Model of effects of adult attachment on emotional empathy in counseling students. *Journal of Counseling and Development, 83*(1), 66–87.

Tyler, A. (1985). *The accidental tourist*. New York: Random House.

Tyrrell, C. L., Dozier, M., Teague, G. B., Fallot, R. D. (1999). Effective treatment relationships for persons with serious psychiatric disorders: The importance of attachment states of mind. *Journal of Consulting & Clinical Psychology, 67*(5), 725–733.

Ulberg, R., Amlo, S., & Hoglend, P. (2014). Manual for Transference Work Scale; a micro-analytic tool for therapy process analyses. *BMC Psychiatry, 14*, 291.

Valle, S. (1981). Interpersonal functioning of alcoholism counselors and treatment outcomes. *Journal of Studies on Alcohol, 42*, 783–790.

Van Wagoner, S. L., Gelso, C. J., Hayes, J. A., & Diemer, R. A. (1991). Countertransference and the repeatedly excellent psychotherapist. *Psychotherapy, 28*(3), 411–421.

Wachtel, P. (1980). Transference, schema, and assimilation. *Annual of Psychoanalysis, 8*, 59–76.

Wachtel, P. L. (2003). The surface and the depths: The metaphor of depth in psychoanalysis and the ways in which it can mislead. *Contemporary Psychoanalysis, 39*, 5–26.

Wachtel, P. (2014). *Cyclical psychodynamics and the contextual self: The inner world, the intimate world, and the world of culture and society*. New York: Routledge.

Wallerstein, R. S. (Ed.) (1992). *The common ground of psychoanalysis*. Northvale, NJ: Jason Aronson.

Wampold, B. E. (2001). Contextualizing psychotherapy as a healing practice: Culture, history, and methods. *Applied and Preventive Psychology, 10*(2), 69–86.

Watts, R. E., Trusty, J., Canada, R., & Harvill, R. L (1995). Perceived early childhood family influence and counseling effectiveness: An exploratory study. *Counselor Education and Supervision, 35*, 104–110.

Webb, C. A., DeRubeis, R. J., & Barber, J. P. (2010). Therapist adherence/competence and treatment outcome: A meta-analytic review. *Journal of Counseling and Clinical Psychology, 78*, 200–211.

Wegner, D. M. (1994). Ironic processes of mental control. *Psychological Review, 101*, 34–52.

Weiss, J. (1993). Empirical studies of the psychoanalytic process. In T. Shapiro & R. N. Emde (Eds.), *Research in psychoanalysis: Process, development, outcome* (pp. 7–29). Madison, CT: International Universities.

Weiss, J., & Sampson, H. (1986). *The psychoanalytic process: Theory, clinical observation, and empirical research*. New York, London: Guilford Press.

Wilcoxon, S. A., Walker, M. R., & Hovestadt, A. J. (1989). Counselor effectiveness and family of origin experiences: A significant relationship? *Counseling and Values, 33*, 225–229.

Williams, E. N., & Fauth, J. (2005). A psychotherapy process study of therapist in-session self-awareness. *Psychotherapy Research, 15*, 374–381.

Williams, N. E., Judge, A. B., Hill, C. E., & Hoffman, M. A. (1997). Experiences of novice therapists in pre-practicum: Trainees', clients', and supervisors' perceptions of therapists' personal reactions and management strategies. *Journal of Counseling Psychology, 44*(4), 390–399.

Winn, M. (2011). Review of *Forgotten filiations: Lacan and Levi-Strauss or the return to Freud (1951–1957)* by Markos Zafiropolous. *Division/Review, 1*, 7–9.

Winnicott, D. W. (1945). Primitive emotional development. *International Journal of Psychoanalysis, 26*, 137–143.

Winnicott, D. W. (1953). Transitional objects and transitional phenomena. *International Journal of Psychoanalysis, 34*, 89–97.

Winnicott, D. W. (1958). *Collected papers: Through paediatrics to psychoanalysis*. London: Tavistock Publications.

Winnicott, D. W. (1960). The theory of the parent–infant relationship. *International Journal of Psychoanalysis, 41*, 585–595.

Winnicott, D. W. (1968). Playing: Its theoretical status in the clinical situation. *International Journal of Psychoanalysis, 49*, 591–599.

Wolitzky, D. L. (2000). The conception of transference. In D. K. Silverman & D. L. Wolitzky (Eds.), *Changing conceptions of psychoanalysis: The legacy of Merton M. Gill* (pp. 265–287). Hillsdale, NJ: Analytic Press.

Wolson, P. (2011). The seminal therapeutic influence of analytic love: A pluralistic perspective. In M. J. Diamond & C. Christian (Eds.), *The second century of psychoanalysis: Evolving perspectives on therapeutic action* (pp. 163–185). London: Karnac.

Yulis, S., & Kiesler, D. J. (1968). Countertransference response as a function of therapist anxiety and content of patient talk. *Journal of Consulting and Clinical Psychology, 32*(4), 413–419.

Zafiropoulos, M. (2010). *Forgotten filiations: Lacan and Levi-Strauss on the return to Freud (1951–1957)*. London: Karnac.

Zittel, C., & Westen, D. (2003). The Countertransference Questionnaire. Atlanta, GA: Emory University, Department of Psychology and Psychiatry and Behavioral Sciences.

Zuroff, D. C. (2010). Between-therapist and within-therapist differences in the quality of the therapeutic relationship: Effects on maladjustment and self-critical perfectionism. *Journal of Clinical Psychology, 66*, 681–697.

Index